BEYOND PEDAGOGY

DATE DUE

BEYOND PEDAGOGY

---

*A History
of the
University of Minnesota
College of Education*

ROBERT H. BECK

*Regents' Professor,
History and Philosophy of Education*

NORTH CENTRAL PUBLISHING COMPANY
St. Paul, Minnesota

To

Faculty, Students, and Staff
of the
College of Education

Contents

Foreword

If Robert Beck's history of the College of Education can be characterized by a single idea, it is the importance of educational research. Teaching standards, the development of an adequate curriculum, and the recognition of teachers as professionals—all these have been notable achievements of the College. So, too, have been its service to the educational community and the training of teachers and administrators. Without diminishing the value of these activities or educational goals, however, Professor Beck clearly shows that research has been a sustaining force in the College's history, one which has truly moved educational thought "beyond pedagogy."

This is not to imply, however, that Professor Beck wants us to regard "research" as a single kind of activity — a matter only of testing and measurement, statistics and algorithms, or theories and empirical data. The tradition of research in the College, he points out, has been influenced by the often imbalanced — but sometimes very well balanced — pull of two powerful tendencies. The first, initiated even before the College came into being, was directed by a "vision" of education as a social tool for achieving democratic ideals. This vision belonged in part to David Kiehle, a professor of pedagogy, who laid the groundwork for the College of Education as a professional school. With its roots in a kind of social gospel which tried to combine head and hand to bring up citizens whose lives would be useful and enriched, this tendency toward values in education has continued to appear in research devoted to social change, respect for the individuality of students, and better learning opportunities for students who are handicapped or disadvantaged. The second tendency, which matured after World War I, drew research in the direction of a sound empirical or scientific basis, one which could focus clearly on causes or effects without in any way influencing their outcome or predetermining their implications. This tension between "pure" research and social values — or between the "scientists" and "humanists" in education — has not, Professor Beck implies, frustrated the mission of the College, even if it may have frustrated colleagues on its faculty at times. On the contrary, it has made the College's contribution to educational thought and practice stronger and more lasting.

Apart from revealing the importance and character of research which has informed our institutional history, Professor Beck demonstrates how fundamental this aspect of our mission has been — and how well integrated into the methods, practices, and purposes of the schools. At a time in our history that might well be considered its most critical — with steadily decreasing enrollment in public education, severe cutbacks in federal funding, legislative review and retrenchment, and increased competition among colleges of education for research grants — it might, indeed, seem prudent for many colleges or schools of education to emphasize their research activities. Yet, as is apparent here, the College of Education already stands on a historical foundation in educational research that has been built over the past half century. At the same time, the College has regularly applied faculty research to educational questions central to the University of Minnesota as a whole, to matters of educational policy and governance in the state of Minnesota, and to educational practice throughout the nation. In each of these respects, the College's contribution has had early beginnings and a continued impact.

Although the College of Education will be seventy-five years old in 1980, Professor Beck's history is not intended to be a self-congratulatory anniversary volume but rather a study of an institution and its members as they produced change, conflict, and growth in educational thought. The College as an institution has not been a monolithic entity but a complex (and sometimes fragile) enterprise which rests on the ideas, activities, and decisions of its faculty members and administrators. Some of these people stayed with the College only a short time; others remained — and bore such an imprint on its character that they can be identified with distinct periods in its history. In some cases, the College's influence can be traced only through the achievements of faculty members who moved on; in others, its character has been enhanced by what new faculty members brought to it. This flux is visible to a certain extent in the College's day-to-day operation, but its significance is fully realized only when we can take a long view. With Professor Beck's accomplished help, we *can* take that view — and it convincingly demonstrates that the reputation of the College of Education must ultimately rest on faculty members who have been colleagues across generations in the art and science of education.

WILLIAM E. GARDNER

x

Preface

The history of the College of Education is the story of an institution whose function has become something more than the training of teachers. Similarly, in this history I have tried to do something more than write a chronology of events. Ideas do not progress linearly; they appear and reappear over time, and often the full development of an idea can resemble a watershed whose sources trail back to various points. Exploring such ideas as the growth of empirical research in the College or a democratic vision of education — or even the emergence of a modern collegiate organization — requires some freedom of movement over the historical terrain. I have felt free to do this in the confidence that tracing the origin of ideas which have influenced the College of Education will make the forward movement of its history a little clearer — and, I hope, a good deal richer.

Many people have supported this history with true generosity. My indebtedness is too great for proper acknowledgement. Deans Gardner and Lewis underwrote the project handsomely and took a personal interest in advancing it. Theodore Kellogg and John Mercer in the Education Planning and Development Office provided a very great deal of assistance, as well as carefully prepared data. The unpublished essays on the development of the College of Education written by Nancy Mosier have also been of great help. In the same way I have profited from the historical notes Emily Veblen prepared on the College in the late 1930's.

Those who assisted in researching this history cannot be thanked enough. I am grateful to each — to Rivka Eisikovits, Alice O'Donnel, Margaret Hall, Leslie Mercer, Thomas Sneed, and John Zeller. They were efficient and effective. I am indebted also to Pam Espeland, the chief editor; David Wetzel in the Education Planning and Development Office; and John Zeller, who included editing in his effort as an assistant. It is a debt of which I am especially aware in the instance of David Wetzel, who added to his editorial work a conscientious and imaginative oversight of the preparation and production of the manuscript. John Bergstrand, Heidi Engelen, Margaret Hall, Nan Moore, and Esther Wittenberg also assisted in manuscript preparation as proofreaders.

I am also most grateful for the continuous, cheerfully given help of Maxine Clapp and Clodaugh Neiderheiser and their colleagues of the University Archives. The archives were the source of much of the information that was used in writing this history. Had not archival material been so skillfully arranged and available, this record would have been gravely handicapped. Not a little of the data, however, also came by way of letters and documents provided by G. Lester Anderson, Kenneth Anderson, Theodore Brameld, Evelyn Deno, Willis Dugan, Roxanna Ford, Robert Jackson, J.R. McConnell, Warren Meyer, James L. Morrill, Josephine Rollins, James Umstattd, Edgar Wesley, Gilbert Wrenn, and Edwin Ziegfeld. I appreciate the time and interest they gave to this history.

Happily a number of those who played important parts in the development of the College of Education since as long ago as 1930 were available for interview. It was both profitable and enjoyable to talk with, and listen to, a group that included: Bruce Balow, Emma Birkmaier, Ann Boardman, Clarence Boeck, Raymond Collier, Lillian Cook, Mary Corcoran, John Darley, Evelyn Deno, Robert Dykstra, Ruth Eckert, William Edson, Marcia Edwards, William Gardner, Eugene Gennaro, Carl Goossen, Patricia Goralski, Clare Gravon, Alan Humphreys, Willard Hartup, Cyril Hoyt, Eloise Jaeger, Donovan Johnson, William Kavanaugh, Stanley Kegler, Louis Keller, Robert Keller, Ronald Lambert, Dale Lange, Darrell Lewis, Donald MacEachern, John Manning, Jack Merwin, Josef Mestenhauser, Dorothy Mitchell, Forrest Moore, Gordon Mork, Jerome Moss, Norine Odland, Clyde Parker, Milo Peterson, Samuel Popper, Maynard Reynolds, Robert Schreiner, John Stecklein, James Stochl, Helen Swalin, Dorolese Wardwell, Stanley Wenberg, Lee Wesson, Edith West, E.G. Williamson, O. Meredith Wilson, Arnold Woestehoff, and Josephine Zimmar.

The early preparation of the manuscript has been the painstaking work of Sandra Oliver, assisted by Colleen Slater. Ruth Weiler prepared the final copy with equal patience and care. There are no colleagues to whom I feel more indebted. They have been prompt, expert, and uncomplaining.

The unexamined life is not worth living
Plato, APOLOGY

One

First Fruits

"THE GREAT business of . . . education in all its varied forms," Rutgers College president Merrill Gates told delegates at an 1890 meeting of the National Education Association, "is to supply the world with teachers." This was a fair statement of mission — and vision — for 1890, and it held true for 1905 as well, when the Regents of the University of Minnesota authorized the establishment of a college of education.

In retrospect, it may seem as if the regents of the time were a bit tardy in acknowledging the importance of this combined mission and vision. Almost sixty years elapsed between the founding of the University of Minnesota in 1851 and the formal birth of the College of Education. All was not quiet in the meantime, however; the lack of recognition during this period did not mean that teacher education was being ignored. Maria Sanford, regarded by many students of that era as "the best loved woman in Minnesota,"[1] gave a series of lectures on pedagogy in 1881, and the Reverend David Kiehle initiated a systematic course on the topic in 1891. Moreover, the legal groundwork for the College had been laid well before this time. In founding the University, the territorial legislature had emphasized the necessity for a department of the theory and practice of education, and in February 1860, a law addressed to "the government and regulation of the University of Minnesota" clearly stated that: "There shall also be a department for the training of teachers for the common [public] schools of the state, in which shall be taught the theory and practice of teaching, and everything that will tend to perfect the elementary and other public schools of the state."[2]

Both territorial and state legislators had acknowledged the importance of formalizing a college of education at the new university, and there were University teachers already willing and able to pass on the principles of teaching to their students. Why, then, did it take so long for the College to become a reality? Granted, other concerns of the time seemed to merit more attention. Ratification of the Minnesota Territory as a state was only one of the weighty matters at hand. Facilities had to be found for the new university, and teachers had to be recruited. In addition, these local matters were overshadowed by a national one: Minnesota, along with the rest of the country, was swept up in the tide of the Civil War.

Although the young University of Minnesota could hardly afford to lose even a single member of its small complement of scholars, it had to part with more than one during this period, including the Reverend Edward Neill. Neill, a Presbyterian minister, had arrived in St. Paul only a few years earlier, in 1849, and had made quite an impact since that time:

> He became the first chancellor of the University, the first territorial superintendent of common schools, and the first state superintendent of public instruction; he served on the St. Paul district school board, a position described as "more properly speaking, a city superintendent of common schools;" he assisted in framing the educational laws of 1849, 1851, 1852, 1860, and 1861; he wrote the St. Paul city school law, secured articles of incorporation for Baldwin School and the College of St. Paul, and later established Macalester College.[3]

Thus, when Neill resigned in 1861 from his posts as superintendent of public education and chancellor of the University, both the state and the University incurred losses from which they would need time to recover.

Even in the midst of the Civil War, the early University was intimately associated with public education. Neill and others had demonstrated how integral the University was to the public school system. The expectation had arisen that the responsibility for preparing teachers for the public schools would be shared between the University and the normal schools; the war simply meant that education was forced to mark time. This was unfortunate, since the combined mission and vision — of education in general, and of teacher education in particular — had originally been so bright. Indeed, the survival of the University during this period attests to the strength of this vision.

The University of Minnesota was not the only bearer of this standard, however. The national normal school movement was taking place, and Minnesota was playing an active part in it. The importance of professionally preparing teachers — with special emphasis on elementary school teachers — had been recognized and was being acted upon. Just two short years before the outbreak of the Civil War, the Minnesota legislature had provided for the first state normal school and named Winona as its location. Winona State Normal School had no sooner opened its doors to its first class, though, than the war forced them shut again, and not until the war's end would the school be revived.

Minnesota's losses in the area of teacher education during this time were echoed across the nation. The normal school movement, the pride of American teacher education during the first half of the nineteenth century,[4] was virtually paralyzed by the war. However, the *roots* of this movement remained healthy, at least in Minnesota; a mere four years after Appomattox, Minnesota had three normal schools with a total enrollment of 373 students, and twenty-two towns reported that their high schools had "normal departments." Elementary school teacher preparation was thus taking vigorous strides across the state; at the same time, teacher education at the University was becoming a reality, even before the founding of the College of Education.

Neill's role in public education in Minnesota made of him an ex officio regent of the University before the war; the Reverend Kiehle performed this function in the years following. Like Neill, Kiehle had come to the regents as state superintendent of public instruction, a post he had held for more than a decade (from 1881 to 1893). Kiehle had also been principal of the normal school at St. Cloud, one of three normal schools that had begun operation after the war. He had held this principalship from 1875 to 1881, when Governor John Sargent Pillsbury — one of the primary advocates of education in the state — appointed him superintendent of public instruction, a position to which he was reappointed for six successive terms. Kiehle finally resigned this post in September 1893, two years after he had embarked on his University lectures in pedagogy.

It is doubtful whether anyone meant more to the vision of education in Minnesota than Kiehle. In the years preceding the establishment of the College of Education, he proved to be a pivotal figure. Kiehle rose to such importance, in fact, that it is tempting to praise him at the expense of other major figures of the time, such as Edward Neill. The "great man" theory of history has in this case a dramatic attraction, but it is one that in all fairness must be avoided. In order to establish a context for Kiehle's influential work, then, it is necessary to review the history of pedagogy at the University before his appointment.

In 1851, the University was little more than an idea shared by its founders. Minnesota high schools were in such pathetic condition that they could not be counted upon to produce quality students for the new institution. Such a deplorable state of affairs argued for the necessity of adequately preparing secondary school teachers for the schools themselves; it also made painfully obvious the pressing need for students who were equipped to use whatever resources the University had to offer. The University itself was struggling; not until 1869, when the regents elected William Watts Folwell to the post, did it have a full-time president. Nine faculty were elected at the same time.

More than a bit of luck was involved in the University's humble beginnings. Elijah Merrill, for example, who came to the University in 1851 to organize its "preparatory department" (actually a high school), was a man of vision who had been a leader in Minnesota public education. David Kiehle would later bear an uncanny professional and ideological resemblance to him.

Merrill had been trained as a minister but was not ordained until 1863, long after he had left the University. He was originally asked to open a high school at the University with the idea that its graduates would take their places as students there. A "division of labor" seems to have existed between the University and the public school system at the time; normal schools — and normal departments — were to be responsible for preparing elementary school teachers primarily for the rural areas, while the University was to lead the way with a preparatory department. In other words, Minnesota was to have a complete system of public education.[5] Merrill's role in this system was clear; he did as he was asked, and his preparatory school was ready for its first students on October 26, 1851. An old copy of *The Minnesota Alumni Weekly* says that the school was housed "in a small building, erected by public subscription, on or near the site of the old exposition building."[6] Merrill seems to have done a good deal more than he wɛ asked, incidentally; the entry goes on to remark that "the school was carried on by Mr. Merrill for four years, he paying all of the expenses, including his own compensation out of tuition fees received."[7] Following this period, Merrill became superintendent of public instruction (as had Neill a very few years earlier, and as would Kiehle a few years later). It is doubtful that he accepted this post

4

for financial reasons, since he was paid an annual salary of only $100. His appointment is yet another piece of evidence that the University and its personnel were looked upon as integral to public instruction. This commingling of interests for the common good was more or less taken for granted and reflected the social conscience — and vision — of the Reverends Neill, Merrill, and Kiehle.

The preparatory school Merrill established at the University was the first high school in the territory,[8] and eighty-five students were enrolled there in two years' time. Merrill believed that education was an essential rather than a luxury, and the enthusiastic enrollment echoed his sentiments. The University's success was not the only result of his vision, however; the whole of the Minnesota territory was to enjoy the fruits of his efforts. In addition to establishing the preparatory school, Merrill organized the territory's first teachers' association and later went on to serve as superintendent of public instruction.

Merrill's willingness to accept sacrifice was remarkable. He certainly deserved support and encouragement, but there is little evidence that he received any. After its first four years, the preparatory department ceased functioning and did not resume again until 1858, when it reopened in only a half-hearted way. At that time, the regents appointed a Professor Barber to conduct a school in Old Main and granted him a salary of $800; once again, the salary was to be paid from tuition revenues. That source of income unfortunately yielded no more than half of Barber's stipend, and the school was discontinued after about six months.

Following this rather speedy demise, there was no preparatory department at the University until October 7, 1867, when a special board of three regents appointed W.W. Washburn as principal and instructor in German and Latin. The 1866 legislature had been moved to underwrite the department in a way that demonstrated that the matter was once more to be taken seriously. Their generosity reflected the concerns of territorial and state legislators of the past and forecast the enthusiasm of such visionary leaders as Governor Pillsbury. The sum of $15,000 was appropriated "to be expended in repairing and furnishing the university building Old Main, and for the employment of a teacher or teachers for the purpose of commencing the grammar and normal department of the University of Minnesota."[9] Some of the funds were used to pay the salaries of three of Washburn's associates: Ira Moore (mathematics), E.H. Twining (natural science), and A.J. Richardson ("English branches").

Despite the evident popularity of the school — 146 students, including 38 women, were enrolled in the third session — it closed yet again in 1869, when the regents adopted a new formal University organization and elected a president and nine faculty members. William Folwell, the new president, and his staff seemed to feel that teacher preparation and precollegiate instruction did not merit the attention or efforts of a university, at least not one whose resources were as limited as the University of Minnesota's in the 1870's and 1880's. There is little evidence that Folwell's opinions met with any opposition. He was an advocate of applied, practical, professional study — and said so very clearly in his December 22, 1869, inaugural address: "I am prepared to admit that the aim and object of higher education should be, in the best sense of the word, *practical.*" Academics, he felt, were to be taken seriously, and he would never "compel a boy or girl to drudge and agonize over any study as a mere gymnastic."[10] Apparently, teacher education did not fall within this realm of serious pursuits. The vision which had moved Neill and Merrill was suspended for some two decades; it would take David Kiehle's efforts to bring it fully back to life again.

Not all was lost in the meantime, however. There were signs that teacher education was still the focus of a few concerned educators, even if it was not formally recognized as such by the governing body of the University. In this regard, 1881 was a landmark year, for in the spring — an appropriate and perhaps symbolic time for such an effort — Maria Sanford, professor of education and rhetoric, presented a series of ten lectures on the theory and art of teaching. Her goals were as follows: "[The] work in rhetoric will consist of exemplifications of the principles of the subject drawn from the masterpieces of English literature. The aim will be to show how our language has been actually used, and by what means a correct and elegant style can be acquired."[11] The series was not repeated, but a spark had been struck. Another modest step was taken in the summer of the following year, during which the University offered a "Summer School for Teachers." This consisted of a set of five-week courses in botany, chemistry, geology, mineralogy, and zoology. Even though the session concentrated exclusively on the sciences, there was an eager audience of forty-two persons, most of them teachers. The next summer, when new courses were offered, attendance grew to seventy-three. Except for a one dollar laboratory fee, the courses were free.

The need and desire for the professional education of teachers must have been evident from the response to these sessions; nevertheless, another decade would pass before any significant progress would be made. When David Kiehle arrived, he not only did a great deal for summer schooling but also made a substantial contribution to "practical" professional training at the University as a whole. Even at the end of his University tenure, many people failed to appreciate the vision of this minister-educator which had eclipsed all past efforts. In 1881, as Sanford was offering her lectures on pedagogy, Kiehle resigned his pastorate to accept the position of state superintendent of public instruction. He relinquished this post in 1893 to become the University's first "lecturer in pedagogy" and was renamed "professor of pedagogy" the following year.

Kiehle both understood and institutionalized the philosophy of education that came to be called the "Land Grant College" point of view. In 1869, when the new University president, Folwell, spoke of "practical" education, it is likely that he had in mind the Morrill Land Grant Act and what it meant to the University. Land grant educational philosophy was a response to this 1862 act, which was the achievement of Vermont's Justin Smith Morrill, a member of the U.S. House of Representatives and later a senator. Previous land grants also proved important. Willis West (the historian father of College faculty member Edith West) wrote of the effects of such grants in *The History of Education in Minnesota*, which was published in 1902.[12] In a chapter entitled "The University of Minnesota," West recorded the prompt and affirmative response that Congress had made to Governor Alexander Ramsey's request for a land grant of 100,000 acres as an educational endowment. Congress was less generous than Governor Ramsey had hoped, however; on February 10, 1851, it provided that two townships — or a little over 46,000 acres of public land — were to be set aside for a university in the new territory. If Kiehle read West's account, it is likely that his piety — though not his practicality — may have been offended at the following brisk observation: "The endowment of State universities from the public lands, like so much else in our history goes back, of course, to the legislation for the Ohio Company connected with the Northwest Ordinance [of 1787], and is directly due to that shrewd, energetic, statesmanlike, and not too scrupulous lobbiest [the Reverend] Manasseh Cutler."[13] At any rate, the ends such land grants achieved seem to have justified the means which were used to implement them.

The 1851 grant was certainly a boon, but an even greater windfall — or, more properly, landfall — was to result from the Morrill Act, which became law in July 1862. According to this act, each state was to be allotted 30,000 acres of land for each senator and representative to which it was then entitled. The proceeds from the sale of that land were to be controlled. Only the interest on the perpetual fund created in each state could be spent, and how it could be spent was carefully specified. In short, the interest was to be

> appropriated for the endowment, support, and maintenance of at least one college where the leading object shall be, without excluding other scientific and classical studies and including military tactics, to teach such branches of learning as are related to agriculture and the mechanic arts . . . in order to promote the liberal and practical education of the industrial classes in the several pursuits and professions of life.[14]

This emphasis on the necessity for an *agricultural* college could have proved dangerous for the new state university had it not been for Kiehle's astute and successful mediation. It could have given rise to another rival institution; instead, today's College of Agriculture at the University attests to Kiehle's grasp of the situation.

An old *Alumni Weekly* tells of the crucial role Kiehle played in this instance: "Dr. David L. Kiehle, then superintendent of public instruction, had given the problem much serious study and careful investigation, visiting many manual training schools and agricultural colleges in his search for helpful information bearing upon the question [of establishing a school of agriculture at the University]."[15] In a communication to the *Farm, Stock and Home* magazine of February 1888, he outlined a course of study which was to prove substantially similar to that later adopted by the University regents in establishing a school of agriculture. The *Alumni Weekly* sketches the essentials of Kiehle's plan: there was to be a school "conducted during the winter months, when the children of the farmers would have leisure to attend; to take those who had had a common school education, and give them a school course mainly objective, manual, practical and scientific, which should fit the student for the duties of life as a farmer."[16] The school opened in 1888, three years *before* Kiehle became a lecturer at the University; once again, public education and the University exhibited their common goals.

8

Subsequent legislation, including the new Morrill bill of 1890 (which supplemented the earlier Hatch Act of 1887), further supported the goals of an agricultural college and an agricultural experimental station. Agriculture was not to be a merely technical venture, however: "domestic economy" or "household science" was also included on the agenda. Even before either of these two later bills became law, efforts were being made to include "women's courses" in the curriculum. Juliet Corson, superintendent of the New York School of Cooking, came to the University to offer a two-week lecture course on the Principles of Domestic Economy and Cookery. And, two summers after the first summer school was conducted, Juniata Shepperd directed a four-week course in household science in the School of Agriculture. These two efforts in the direction of practical education illustrated the early University's determination to prepare women to teach what later was to become home economics. In 1897, the agricultural high school listed three courses in its household science section: cooking and laundering, home economy and home management, and sewing. Six years later, the first college course in the household arts was offered.

Practical courses like these Kiehle endorsed heartily, and they flourished. The students' enthusiasm was reflected in the fact that there was a home economics club at the University as early as 1909. In that year, the Minnesota legislature separated the agricultural extension and home economics education areas within the Department of Agriculture. Five years later, the Agricultural Education Club was formed. This and the Home Economics Club may well have been the first professional organizations at the University.

Vocational education in its many forms had enjoyed a great deal of popularity within Minnesota high schools prior to the Civil War. Following the war, enough teachers at the University were interested in vocational education to allow the University to take a commanding position in this area as well. In 1912, Ashley Van Storm succeeded Dwight Mayne as "principal" of the School of Agriculture; within fifteen years, the Minnesota Vocational Association had become a viable organization. Van Storm was its first president. Industrial education was represented by Homer J. Smith, vice president, and Wylle B. McNeal, professor of home economics education, who acted as the association's secretary-treasurer. Storm, Smith, and McNeal all held positions within the University's College of Education.

In the regents report of 1910, a statement made by President

9

Cyrus Northrop summed up the University's combined mission and vision regarding these practical areas of education:

> The University of Minnesota is in hearty sympathy with that widespread public sentiment which demands that the secondary schools, the colleges and the universities shall do what they can to prepare students for successful work in agriculture, business and the mechanic arts. While not neglecting discipline and culture, it is prepared to recognize the importance of training for life and therefore of laying a proper foundation at least for vocational training. It has already done a great deal of work in this direction in relation to agriculture and it has set before it as a special object to be aimed at an equally helpful training for the mechanic arts and for business and it specially desires to furnish educated men for all the various pursuits in industrial lines where educated men are needed. Its policy in this respect is a broad one, and to the full extent of the resources placed at its disposal, it will labor to invigorate industry by a liberal and technical training.[17]

Whether industry was indeed "invigorated" by liberally and technically trained people is difficult to ascertain; the aims of the University were noble but vague. The College of Education was less vague about its proposed goals, however. In the same year that the regents' report was published, Albert Rankin offered a course on the Principles and Practice of Industrial Training within the newly-formed College of Education. He proposed that the principles fundamental to vocational training in the public school system be studied and that their effects on the arrangement of school years, the course of study, and the methods of teaching be thoroughly examined.

The regents and Professor Rankin alike were undoubtedly aware of the Putnam Act, which had been passed by the Minnesota legislature in 1909 "to provide for the establishment and maintenance of the department of agriculture, manual training, and domestic economy in state high, graded and consolidated schools, and to authorize rural schools to become associated with such state graded or high schools and making appropriation therefore."[18] A provision in the act offered $2,500 to each of ten schools and specified that the instructors of agriculture, domestic economy, and manual training were to be college graduates. This was a new emphasis — and an important one to teacher education at the University. George B. Aiton, state inspector of high schools and a "special lecturer" in the College of Education during 1913, was keenly interested in vocational education and may have been Minnesota's most aggressive advocate of having *college-prepared* personnel teach vocational education in the state's high schools. This goal was advanced by the Benson-Lee Act of 1913, which made $1,000 available each year to any high school which maintained an agricultural department and either a manual training or a homemaking department. The special understanding between the University and the public schools meant that these various fields would not have to compete for such support and that the legislature could support agricultural education, homemaking, and manual training simultaneously.

Early University growth in these "practical" areas, however, was modest, occasionally slow, and sometimes without discernible direction. It was not until Kiehle arrived that formal teaching in education really began. Nevertheless, one other person prior to Kiehle deserves mention: Harry Judson, a professor of history between 1885 and 1891, who left for the University of Chicago (of which he later became president) after Kiehle arrived at the University of Minnesota.

During his stay, Judson lectured on the Science and Art of Teaching, a course which was offered as an elective for third-quarter seniors. His qualifications for teaching such a course were unquestionable. He had taught for fifteen years in the public schools of Troy, New York, and after earning a master's degree from Williams College had acted as principal of the Troy high schools. History and the classics were his specialties. He lectured from his own experience as a teacher, distilling that experience for the benefit of his students, who were more or less his apprentices. This sort of teaching was common at the time; a true *science* of education was not to be taught at the University until after Lotus D. Coffman became the College's second dean in 1915. After Melvin Haggerty succeeded Coffman in 1920, Minnesota's College of Education quickly became one of the leading citadels of the science, alongside Columbia University and the University of Chicago.

The University of Minnesota's reputation in the field of educational science is so formidable today that it is easy to forget the early, pre-scientific steps that were taken under men like Kiehle. He and others followed what has been termed the academic (and European) notion of pedagogy — namely, a blend of practical emphases with a philosophical perspective on life flavored by a historical grasp of humankind. Kiehle's credentials suited him for this intellectual approach. He was a graduate of the Union Theological

Seminary, had been granted an M.A. and an LL.D. from Hamilton College, and as a Presbyterian minister had organized the church of that faith in Preston, Minnesota. Deeply interested in both history and philosophy, Kiehle was wholly innocent of the science of education; this lack on his part, if it may be termed such, was barely noticeable during his time at the University of Minnesota.

The years 1891 to 1893 were crucial, for the state normal schools were well ahead of the University in teacher education. In 1891, a diploma from any state normal school was recognized as a "first grade certificate" of teaching. During the following year, the University organized its first two-year course for prospective teachers; soon, graduates of this course who had been awarded University teaching certificates were given the same first-grade status as graduates of state normal schools.[19] By 1919, in contrast, the University's prerequisite in psychology was specified as ten quarter credits, at least five of which had to be in "educational psychology."[20]

At long last, teacher preparation was being taken seriously. Luckily, pedagogical instruction was able to draw on academicians from any number of disciplines, and the famous "teachers' courses" were thus offered for many years. In addition, there was a general push in the direction of making pedagogical study a graduate subject, which meant that teachers would be college graduates and that pedagogy would be a topic worth study at the postgraduate level. Although seminars were not made available until 1900, pedagogy was listed as a subject for graduate study as early as 1893.

Two-year "special courses" for teachers, initiated in 1892, met with whole-hearted endorsement from the regents, who expressed a rather high-flown ideal in their seventh biennial report to the governor: "Many teachers in the State who are unable to take the full course in the University have felt the need of higher culture for their work."[21] In subsequent generations, courses would be made available in the late afternoons and on Saturday mornings for educational specialists of all types, but this was clearly not the original intent of the regents, concerned as they were about a "higher culture":

To enable them [the teachers] to get such culture and also to meet the needs of prospective teachers who require some special training in the art of teaching, a two-years [sic] course of study in the University has been offered to three classes of candidates: 1st Graduates of State Nor-

12

mal Schools, 2nd Graduates of High Schools who have taught one year and hold a teacher's county certificate or its equivalent, 3rd Students of the University who are candidates for bachelor's degree.[22]

The University *Catalogue* for 1891-92 offered a brief description of the "Special Two-Years Course for Teachers," stating that it had been designed to qualify persons to "teach the higher branches of science, language, history, and literature. A full course in elementary psychology, history of education, and pedagogy will form a part of the work."[23] The *Catalogue* gives no indication as to which department would be responsible for the course, and it can be assumed that it was not designated a departmental obligation as such until the next academic year, when a distinct department of pedagogy was listed as a unit within the College of Science, Literature, and the Arts (CSLA).

Organizational structure and budget were quite informal in those early days and for many years following. Even after the *Catalogue* had identified pedagogy as a separate department, the biennial regents' reports sometimes itemized its budget separately and sometimes combined it with that of history or rhetoric. It is tempting to think that lumping pedagogy with rhetoric betrayed a belief that teaching was a matter of rhetoric, in somewhat of a Ciceronian tradition; yet a more persuasive explanation is that Maria Sanford's lectures of the time had been listed under rhetoric — and, when history was the host, nothing more subtle was at work than the fact that Harry Judson, then a lecturer in pedagogy, was actually a professor of history.

The attention paid to selecting teachers to perform the pedagogical function was also informal. The history faculty seemed to do the most work in the area. While Judson had lectured on the science and art of teaching, Willis West, who for six years was a Minnesota superintendent of schools, lectured on the teaching of history. Similarly, former University president William Watts Folwell lectured on politics in the school. Actual teaching *about* teaching was done here and there, but the effort was not orchestrated. During his time, Kiehle comprised a one-member department of pedagogy.

What arguments and tactics were finally used to establish a College of Education formally at the University of Minnesota are not known today. All we do know is that in 1905 the regents authorized such a college. George James, who for three years had been a professor of pedagogy (and who had replaced Kiehle in that role) was named its dean. When the school year began, James was joined by

Albert Rankin, a down-to-earth and knowledgeable man who was intimately familiar with the Minnesota schools after having spent ten years as the state's first "graded-school" inspector.

Many of the persons who helped to shape the University in its early days — who had the vision and realized the mission of education, even when no one else seemed to possess equal foresight — have faded into obscurity or left little personal trace of their influence. Elijah Merrill returned to institutional religion after his stay at the University, as did David Kiehle. Both of them have nearly been forgotten — with two exceptions. The Kiehle Visual Arts Center at St. Cloud State University and the Kiehle Library on the University of Minnesota's Crookston campus both testify to the legacy of vision which David Kiehle left to education in the state of Minnesota.[24]

Two

David L. Kiehle
and the Department of Pedagogy

IN 1931, a publication entitled *The Changing Educational World* celebrated the first twenty-five years of the College of Education at the University of Minnesota.[1] Many of the essays contained in that text faced the future, voicing confidence at a time when the Great Depression was chilling so many hopes. A few, however, eulogized the past, reassuring the faculty of the College that its academic predecessors had been a sturdy lot. One of the latter essays, "Beginnings of Secondary Education in Minnesota," was written by George Aiton, who had been the first high school inspector in the state. Aiton paid his respects to the Reverend Edward Neill, "one of the men who did a great deal toward establishing the public school system" and "curiously enough, a Presbyterian clergyman."[2] Aiton also identified another man "who deserves the highest credit and whose name should always be spoken with honor in Minnesota . . . David L. Kiehle."[3]

Aiton recalled that Kiehle had been a practical man who "came into the superintendency of instruction at a time when the decision had not been made as to whether we were to have private academies or a system of public high schools."[4] He then praised Kiehle for his "consummate skill" in handling "the public school question" and claimed that Kiehle had done "more than any other man in Minnesota to pave the way for the extension of public school work on through the high schools and . . . logically through the university."[5] These are well-deserved accolades for a man who has been virtually ignored by most University historians.

Aiton furthered his point by recounting an incident proving Kiehle's political acumen. Kiehle had persuaded Bishop John Ireland to address a meeting of the National Education Association in Minneapolis. The bishop chose to speak on the merit of public

15

schools, and "talked about the service, the indispensable service, that the American public school had done, and was doing, and would do for the nation."[6] The bishop was obviously a showman of sorts, and Aiton captured this quality in his account: "As he warmed up to his theme, John Ireland, tall, fervid, intensely earnest . . . put forth an eloquent hand and said: 'Palsied be the hand that is raised against the American School.' "[7] While this sentiment may have been decidedly un-Christian, it nevertheless had a strong effect on its audience. According to Aiton, those present at the meeting "felt at the time that [Ireland] had written the concluding paragraph of an important chapter in the history of education in Minnesota."[8] This chapter had, of course, been written in large part by Kiehle himself, and it would be naive to assume that Kiehle had been totally ignorant beforehand of the bishop's topic for that national meeting. Kiehle was not only visionary; he was also extremely shrewd.

It is interesting to note that while Aiton considered it "curious" that Neill had been simultaneously a clergyman and an advocate of a public school system, the fact that Kiehle was also a minister did not seem to bother him at all. Neither set of circumstances poses a genuine puzzle, however. As every student of the history of education learns at some point, the early Protestants were zealous promoters of literacy; they wanted everyone to be able to read the Bible. Thus, the fact that they favored public education was hardly extraordinary. Even a cursory reading of Kiehle's *Education in Minnesota* reveals what might be termed his "double vision" — a mixture of Christian fervor and a desire to see education made widely available. Like so many others of his time, he held the conventional belief that without Christianity, civilization itself would be in a precarious position — if it existed at all.

In his book, Kiehle wrote with pride of the pioneers "who had the courage and endurance necessary to face the hardships and dangers of unsubdued nature in climate, land and flood and still held by unsubdued savage life."[9] Such so-called "savage life" was not Kiehle's only concern, however. It was also necessary for Minnesota's pioneers to establish the institutions "of a Christian civilization in opposition to the corrupting vices of greed and animalism that always attach themselves to a vigorous and exuberant life of enterprise and prosperity."[10] Kiehle may have been a little intolerant and self-righteous in this, but regardless of his motives he did a great deal of good for public education in Minnesota.

Like so many others who moved to Minnesota during its early years as a territory and later a state, Kiehle was an easterner; the son of a tanner, he came to Preston, Minnesota, just as the Civil War was ending. He spent ten years as pastor of the Presbyterian church at Preston (which he also organized), but his interests were not focused on that calling alone. Apparently, the combined plight and promise of Minnesota's schools caught his attention almost at once. During the last years of his pastorate, Kiehle's interest and involvement in public education attracted enough notice that he was made superintendent of schools in Fillmore County as well as a member of the State Normal School Board.

In 1875, at the age of thirty-eight, he made a decision which was to direct the next several years of his career into educational rather than church work. This is not to suggest that there was a parting of the ways, or that Kiehle was torn between sacred and secular enthusiasms; while the "gospel" he preached for the next quarter century became steadily more secular, the fervor with which he preached remained decidedly sacred. His move was a major one, however; he accepted a position as president of the St. Cloud Normal School, which led to his appointment as state superintendent of public instruction in 1881. During the next twelve years, Kiehle found himself in a position to translate his vision into substance and applied himself energetically to this task. Not only could he speak from his influential role as state superintendent but also as an ex-officio member of the University of Minnesota's Board of Regents, which he served as secretary.

From the start, Kiehle used his position at the University to upgrade teacher education, a goal which he knew to be crucial. One of his first achievements involved winning the regents' approval for an 1881 summer session. The authorization of a summer school made it possible, according to the *Minnesota Daily*'s predecessor, *Ariel*, for teachers to "select special subjects for thorough study."[11] The faculty roster for the summer school, which offered a postgraduate course for teachers, included such luminaries as H.P. Judson, Maria Sanford, J.A. Dodge, and F.S. Jones, in addition to teachers from the Mankato, Winona, and St. Cloud normal schools. Students were charged a fee of fifty cents for the course, since the state had not as yet set aside adequate funds for this purpose.

While acting as a mover and shaker at the University, Kiehle continued to hold the state superintendency. The Presbyterian preacher-turned-educator had a thoroughly practical vision, and the rhetoric he had learned in the pulpit stood him in good stead in his campaign to finance public education. Kiehle subsequently listed among his principal achievements the establishment of a one-mill state tax for common schools and the distribution of district loans and state monies to schools on the basis of student attendance.[12] Other accomplishments included the lengthening of the school year, the passage of a compulsory attendance law, the securing of free textbooks, the establishment of a public school library fund, and the founding of a state journal of public education to serve as a sounding board for people who had ideas about improving Minnesota's schools.

Throughout his influential career, Kiehle avoided publicity and seldom accepted personal recognition for any of his efforts. Livingston Lord, a teacher at the University during Kiehle's early years there and later president of Eastern Illinois State Teachers College, remembers Kiehle as one of the few "whose influence was greatest over the whole state."[13] Lord recognized Kiehle's modesty: "The credit for any of [Kiehle's] accomplishments might be taken by others so long as what he had tried to achieve was accomplished . . . . He was a shrewd man, and . . . a wise man, too."[14] In April 1893, Kiehle realized what may have been a long-standing dream by becoming a member of the teaching faculty.

In the meantime, he was deeply involved in crystallizing a real state high school system in Minnesota. Aiton especially appreciated the former clergyman's efforts at creating a mechanism for the state inspection of high schools. Though it is tempting to give Kiehle too much credit in this area, it cannot be denied that he played an important role. As early as 1878, he was directing the policies of the State High School Board, and it is no coincidence that the state legislature voted aid to the high schools during the same year. According to Jean Alexander, who wrote a chronology of public education in Minnesota up to 1929, the laws Kiehle helped to frame which later governed state aid to high schools "are among the most important in Minnesota history."[15] Like many others, she is convinced that "state aid has been one of the most effective means used for the development of schools and the maintenance of standards."[16]

Throughout his active career in Minnesota education — as superintendent, ex-officio regent, and teacher, among other posts— Kiehle had one goal in mind: the improvement of the quality of schooling.[17] And all of his efforts — even such seemingly trivial

David L. Kiehle

ones as securing free textbooks for public school students — either directly or indirectly benefited the University. True, many of Kiehle's predecessors and contemporaries (including the early University presidents) were concerned about the preparation of would-be students and those whose education would end after high school. But it was Kiehle himself who actually did something about these concerns by gradually focusing his attention more and more on the education of prospective teachers. His vision encompassed the relationship between the public schools and the University which he knew would have to exist in order for them both to realize their full potential.

In an address entitled "The Obligation of the University to the Profession of Teaching" given at a meeting of the Minnesota Education Association in 1900, he defined what he considered to be the responsibility of the University in furthering this relationship:

> The university should offer the same professional preparation in education that it does in medicine, law, and agriculture. It should not only send forth its graduates with the usual academic learning, but . . . with the spirit of modern educational reforms . . . and the application of modern scholarship to the problems of . . . education.[18]

Other educators around the country voiced similar concerns. James E. Russell, for example, who served for nearly thirty years as pilot of Teachers College, Columbia, once said: "How and when to act, why a certain procedure is preferable to some others, what knowledge and skill are requisite for the purpose — these are the objectives of professional education."[19] Kiehle was more eloquent, perhaps, but his message was essentially the same as Russell's. Not all educators (or citizens) agreed with this approach, however; it was not in the least impractical, but it may have been ahead of its time. Kiehle's goals apparently conflicted with those of some of his contemporaries, since he was removed from his teaching position two years later, in 1902. Nevertheless, it should be noted that what he proposed was eventually embraced by the College of Education as its mission.

Kiehle returned to his Preston pastorate the year he was dismissed by the University, and he may have simply taken up again where he had left off in 1875. Looking backward, it is puzzling that this "astute," "shrewd," "wise" man, this man of "consummate skill" in political maneuvering and persuasion, failed to hold his own in the University's Department of Pedagogy once he became its sole member. It could not have been due to the fact that he concentrated on his department to the exclusion of all others at the University, or impeded their progress; in fact, he was most instrumental in expanding the existing University, serving as the catalyst for the founding of the College of Engineering and Mechanic Arts as well as the School of Agriculture.

This latter feat deserves further comment. Kiehle's ability to interest the University administration — namely, the regents — in a summer school was one thing; his success in securing two entirely new colleges was quite another. Neither astute maneuvering on Kiehle's part nor simple persistence alone accomplished these tasks. Kiehle succeeded again because he had vision. He saw something — be it in the present or the future — which convinced him to dedicate his energies to the creation of two more units within the University. The key to his success may well have been his deep appreciation and respect for manual training and the continued education of Minnesota's farmers.

In order to realize his vision, Kiehle read and traveled widely. He was constantly adding to his own first-hand experience of education and its requirements. In 1895, the National Education Association recognized his efforts by inviting him to act as its president of superintendence, and Kiehle added to his already impressive list of credentials by becoming the first person from the University of Minnesota to serve in such a position of national leadership. Others from the state would follow, but much later; in 1946, Dean Wesley Peik would found the National Commission on Teacher Education and Professional Standards and would also prove instrumental in founding the American Association of Colleges for Teacher Education.[20] In the 1950's and 1960's, Charles Boardman and Robert Keller would represent the College of Education at the University by working with the North Central Association of Schools and Colleges to formulate its policies. (Keller would finally leave the association in 1977, but would continue to serve as a consultant examiner.)

Kiehle's involvement in national leadership may provide a clue to solving the mystery of his termination from the University. Although Peik, Boardman, and Keller would be likewise involved nationally, it may have been easier for post-World War II Minnesotans to understand their dedication than it was for late nineteenth-century citizens, who were generally more provincial and less far-sighted. In short, both rural Minnesotans and some educators objected to many of Kiehle's views during the latter years of his University service.

It is probable that Kiehle's vision was simply on a grander scale than that of his contemporaries. Again, he had read and traveled a great deal, and many of the ideas he came in contact with and accepted — and worked for at the University — may have been too radical or revolutionary for his peers. Close examination of some of these ideas is necessary in order to understand what may have led to Kiehle's return to the ministry in the midst of what appears to have been a highly successful and respected career in education.

In 1899, the best-known university president in the country, Nicholas Murray Butler of Columbia, changed the name of the New York College for the Training of Teachers to Teachers College.[21] Few people know that Teachers College had *two* guiding influences: Butler himself, of course, and New York's Industrial Education Association. This association, christened in 1884, had had an earlier life and name. Formerly known as the Kitchen Garden Association, it had begun with the goal of ameliorating slum life to some degree by promoting better household management. When this seemed to have little effect, a more realistic approach was taken, and "industrial education" was wedged into the common school course of study. Butler was involved in the association and convinced its members to underwrite the predecessor of Teachers College. Thus, a bond between the manual arts and teacher education was formed, if only in a secondary way.

What was known by that time as the Manual and Industrial Education movement had joined forces with those who favored the extension of public education to generate some of the most vital ideas in American schooling. Charles A. Bennett chronicled the history of this endeavor (especially the formative years from 1870 to 1917)[22] and named several of the persons who proved influential. While Kiehle was not mentioned in Bennett's account, it is probable that he was an enthusiastic observer of what was happening in New York and elsewhere; this, of course, led to his playing an important role in the founding of the College of Engineering and Mechanic Arts at the University of Minnesota.

Calvin Woodward was another educator who helped to shape Kiehle's thinking. A former professor of mathematics and applied mechanics as well as dean of the polytechnics faculty of Washington University in St. Louis, he did a great deal to encourage industrial education in America. He believed firmly that training in the crafts was equivalent to "training the mind" and advocated learning the use of the lathe, forge, and other tools of various trades. His eminently practical educational philosophy was very convincing to a number of educators, including Kiehle. In writing his *Education in Minnesota* in 1903, Kiehle looked back at the manual training movement of the 1880's and acknowledged Woodward as being central to it. He recognized the importance of this movement when he wrote:

> In the National Education Association, which discussed living questions, and so represented the educational trend of the times, the manual training problem was then the all-engrossing one. It was not a question of professional schools for specialists; it was rather a claim for the practical training of the eye and hand of youth in the schools, a claim for manual training as part of their education in life.[23]

Not everyone was a devotee of this movement, however, as Kiehle recorded: "For successive years the ground was fought over between those who represented pure intellectual culture, and those who claimed a cultural value for manual training, and a corresponding place in the school curriculum."[24] Naturally Woodward belonged to the latter group, and Kiehle's respect for this man helped to determine the direction he himself would take.

Kiehle's influences went back even further. Rousseau's *Emile,* published in 1762, advocated the technique of using hand work to discipline the head. The end sought through this process was not a more cunning hand but a mind trained to be precise — by the carpenter's measure, the machinist's attention to tolerances, and so on. Honesty, perseverance, exactness, and other virtues were perceived as integral to manual skills. Throughout his career, Kiehle remained convinced that manual training (although he sometimes used other terms) had special value. He said as much in a long letter to University president Cyrus Northrop in 1902. This was intended as a second report on the status of pedagogical training at the University of Minnesota; the first report, written two years earlier, had gone into detail about the evolution of a university's — that is, *any* university's — obligation to prepare teachers professionally. In this second letter, he reiterated points he had made in the first, but with more urgency — with the end result that the very existence of his department of pedagogy was questioned. The new direction Kiehle recommended was innovative, to say the least:

22

I wish now to call your attention to the pressing demand upon our high schools that they recognize the broader interests of our youth and that they enlarge the scope of their culture to meet demands of youth in every relation of life, whether in the social life of the home, the common vocations of industrial life or on the higher planes of professional and scientific life to which the university is especially devoted. I refer to the training of the eye and hand in apprehending color, form and proportion, and in expressing their ideas by the use of the pencil in drawing, in manual training, and the domestic arts. Hitherto our schools have confined their training in expression to that of ideas in oral and written forms. These added methods of training the eye and hand to discriminating observation and exact and skillful expression of their ideas is believed to be of great educational value. The habit of gaining clear ideas improves oral and written expression. Obscure language comes largely from obscure notions. Taking life as a whole, no form of expression is of more general and practical value than skill in expressing ideas in material forms, whether it be for the mechanic, farmer, seamstress or artist.[25]

Not long afterward, in his *Education in Minnesota,* he again stressed the importance of "industrial education"[26] and reminded his readers that the University was obligated to both offer and promote it due to a congressional mandate of July 2, 1862 (the Morrill land-grant legislation).[27] This congressional action had permitted the sale of a specific quantity of land and had stipulated that the monies derived from such sale were to be used in certain ways. In short,

[The monies]...shall be invested and shall constitute a perpetual fund, the capital of which shall forever be undiminished, and the interest of which shall be inviolably appropriated by each state which may take and claim the benefit of this act, to the endowment, support and maintenance of at least one college where the leading object shall be, without excluding other scientific and classical studies ... to teach such branches of learning as are related to agriculture and the mechanic arts, in such manner as the legislature of the states may respectively prescribe, in order to promote the liberal and practical education of the industrial classes in the several pursuits and professions of life.[28]

The industrial education movement was generally strong, but it was slow in gaining acceptance in Minnesota. Neither Kiehle nor anyone else in the days prior to 1910 could do much of anything to further such practical manual training in the state. Minnesota was primarily agricultural, it must be remembered, and Minnesotans were far more apt to be concerned about a school of agriculture than a school of industrial education. In the meantime, a bitter controversy had developed over where such a school of agriculture should be located; not everyone was convinced that it should be affiliated with the University. Minnesota's land grant was finally determined to be 94,000 acres, and the average sale price of $5.89 per acre would yield $563,000 by the time the last parcel of land was sold in 1913. The farmers were wondering how this land grant was going to benefit them. Would their children be educated in realistic, practical ways — or would some high-handed, fancy academicians turn their heads? In Kiehle's words, these were years

> of general social and political agitation among the agricultural classes. Farmers were inquiring how they were to better their conditions. They organized neighborhood granges, co-operative enterprises and farmers' alliances. They asserted themselves, not only in agricultural matters, but in politics and education. As a part of this movement, they turned their attention to the Agricultural Land Grant, and the service it ought to render, and was rendering to the farmers of Minnesota.[29]

It would seem as if the University should have been perceived as the farmer's friend — and so it was, later on, thanks to the agricultural extension service and research into farm-related matters; but in the early years of the century this image of the University did not prevail. At least, not all were charmed by it: "Violent attacks," he stated, "were made upon the university administration, charging the regents with deliberately robbing the farmers' fund in the interest of the university."[30]

These attacks were largely aimed at Regent Pillsbury, chairman of the board; and, although Kiehle did not defend Pillsbury by name, his spirited "Reply" to E.H. Atwood, president of the State Farmers' Alliance, was masterful.[31] In essence, what Kiehle advocated — and what was subsequently accepted — was a *secondary* school "organized on an agricultural and manual training basis."[32] It was to be in session from November until April and open to boys, especially those who intended to be farmers, who were at least fifteen years of age and graduates of the common school. The courses were to be "mostly objective, manual, practical and scientific"; the goals of the school were to be those ascribed to "general education." According to Kiehle's vision, the program would "cultivate and strengthen the taste of students and their powers of judgment and observation in the lines of agricultural pursuits."[33] Specifically, it would encompass three areas:

First — Business and literary, including English, mathematics, accounts, history, political economy, and physical geography.

Second — Scientific and mechanical. The subject will be shop work, chemistry, mineralogy, botany, animal physiology, and natural philosophy. In this the student will learn the use and care of common tools; in the laboratory he will be made familiar with the common elements that enter into foods and soils, he will learn botany by the study of plants, and learn of animals their physiology and their characteristics by direct examination with his own hands and eyes.

Third — Lecture course. This will be sustained by scientific, practical, business men and agriculturists, on farm management, stock, soils, grains and plants, veterinary, etc. This course will bring to the students in familiar talks the practical experience of men who have worked and observed intelligently in these different lines.[34]

Either a great deal was expected of these adolescents, or the actual subject matter was not as formidable as it would be today. Apparently, no one was particularly troubled by these expectations.

Kiehle went on to assure Atwood (and, through him, many others) that the school he was proposing would not signal the end of the education its students would be qualified to receive; instead, those who completed this secondary program were likely to be desired by the College of Agriculture. (In later years, a similar assertion would be made — namely, that the graduates of the two-year course of the General College at Minnesota would be ready to transfer to the College of Liberal Arts.) To review the political situation of the time, there were those who thought that the University staff was too unrealistic and too far removed from the questions farmers had to have answered; on the other hand, there was active support for the University's having a school of agriculture. The Minnesota Grange favored such a school and fielded a three-member committee which lobbied vigorously for it. The committee knew that in order to be effective it would have to formulate a persuasive statement of its goals, one which revealed a convincing educational philosophy while simultaneously proposing a very clear program of studies, and so it turned to the University regents for help.

As secretary to the Board of Regents, and as one of the foremost educators in the state, Kiehle found himself responsible for providing a rationale for the Grange committee, for President Northrop, and for the editor-owner of *Farm, Stock and Home*, S.M. Owen, a powerful ally of the University. Kiehle knew that a friendly attitude on the part of those active in the "granger movement" would be most useful. The Grange was strong in Minnesota, and little wonder that it was. Oliver Kelley, who was its founder in 1867, was originally from Minnesota, and the Patrons of Husbandry grew stronger in this state than in any other. Thirty-seven active granges were in existence only two years after Kelley began organizing farmers into groups to discuss their common problems. These groups became so powerful politically that the owners of grain elevators and railroads realized that they had to reckon with them. Kiehle himself knew that he could not afford to ignore such an influential organization.

Those who favored locating the School of Agriculture at the University won their case when it opened in 1888.[35] Yet, at what appears to have been the height of his success fourteen years later, Kiehle found his University career in jeopardy. The man who had saved the School of Agriculture for the University of Minnesota found that he was barely able to save his own one-member department of pedagogy. And though he succeeded in preserving it, he ultimately lost his post. Despite all of his efforts and victories on behalf of the University, he lacked the support of his peers. Anyone in Kiehle's position should have been able to expect the University president's backing, but there is no evidence that Northrop fought on Kiehle's behalf at all.

The lack of documentation about what precisely happened to cause Kiehle to lose his position makes it difficult to accurately surmise the reasons. Perhaps, as mentioned earlier, he was viewed as being too involved in extracurricular matters. Perhaps he was perceived as being unimaginative or out-of-date. Yet, while his enthusiastic support for manual training may seem quaint today— given the long history and evolution of vocational education — it could not have been considered so in the late nineteenth and early twentieth centuries, when it was becoming an increasingly popular cause. In fact, Edgar Wesley wrote of this era (specifically, the years between the close of the Civil War and the report of the National Education Association's Committee of Ten in 1893) as "a period of relative freedom":

> During this period, many [secondary] schools introduced business courses, science laboratories, vocal and instrumental music, art in various forms, and, most numerous of all, programs and whole schools of manual training. The high schools were becoming people's colleges to provide instruction and training in cultural, classical, literary, industrial, and artistic fields . . . .Had the movement continued, it might have provided an indigenous institution that would have faithfully reflected and aided the growth of an American Culture.[36]

The knowledge that vocational training was on the cutting edge of educational thought at the time, at least where high schools were concerned, makes it difficult to believe that Kiehle was out of date in 1902. The period of which Wesley wrote ended rather abruptly when the Committee of Ten succeeded in devoting the central mission of the American high school to preparation for college, but Kiehle's philosophy was both respectable and respected when he advanced it. Perhaps he was simply too sophisticated for those who then had the responsibility for the classrooms and schools of Minnesota. Northrop, for one, may have been unable to cope with the populist feelings of the politically turbulent 1890's. The restiveness of this period was fed by the panic of 1893, whose aftermath left farmers embittered and hardly in a mood to let their children be taught by people such as Kiehle, who held what they perceived to be lofty and unrealistic ideals. By then many of these rural people belonged to the People's Party, which had been founded in 1892. They were more interested in the free coinage of silver and in the public ownership of railroads and telegraph lines than they were in educational philosophy. Kiehle may have appeared entirely too modern when he pleaded, for example, that the University assume the responsibility for preparing teachers in the fields of music and drawing. In a letter to Northrop written in 1902, Kiehle observed sadly that "no teachers of music, drawing, manual training [or] domestic science are supplied by the state University."[37] He stressed the need for the University to refrain from passing this load — and opportunity — to others: "The schools of the state which provide for these branches in their courses look to eastern institutions for teachers; and students who wish to prepare for teaching these subjects must go to eastern institutions for their training."[38]

In the final paragraph of his letter to Northrop, Kiehle sounded a revolutionary note. In his eyes, education was an opportunity that belonged to everyone, and his valedictory statement shows his unchanging visionary outlook:

> Again, in the interest of the large number of young women who are graduated every year, it deserves to be said that so far in the development of the curriculum it has been along lines required by men, and that women have been given liberty to pursue subjects with men and with equal privileges. In addition to this, there are some vocations and corresponding lines of instruction that are especially adapted to women and in the interest of home life. Among these are music, drawing

and domestic science. In view of the abnormally strong inducements urging young women into commercial vocations of various kinds, the state could not serve itself better than to make this provision for the enlarged usefulness of its educated young women.[39]

A member of Kiehle's own family was to follow in his footsteps by espousing this cause. Louise Kiehle, who headed the University's "physical culture" department from 1892 to 1900, doubtless had helped to enlighten her father before she married and left the University. Neither father nor daughter could have foreseen that the small program Louise had led would eventually grow into the Department of Physical Education for Women, whose first director would be J. Anna Norris. In little more than a decade, what Kiehle's daughter had begun would be developed by Dr. Norris, a physician as well as an educator, into a program of health education that would equal any in the country.

Kiehle headed in many directions during his educational career, but the diversity of his interests should not be looked upon as indicative of a flighty or impractical mind. He wanted the University to be aware of several fronts along which pedagogy had an obligation to move within a democracy. Above all, he felt that there had to be a center for these efforts — namely, a strong department of pedagogy — even if the regents did not feel that the University could afford "a distinct institute or college, devoted exclusively to pedagogical instruction." This, Kiehle reminded Northrop in his letter, "is after the plan of law, medical and other professional schools. Representative of this method is the Teachers College Columbia University, and the School of Pedagogy of the University of New York."[40] However, he conceded that the "expensiveness of this method makes it practicable only in the wealthy and populous centers of the older states, and therefore excludes it from consideration in the newer communities of the west [sic]."[41]

Kiehle may have recognized that his position at the University was in jeopardy; at any rate, he was beginning to trim his sails. In an earlier "Special Report" to President Northrop in 1900, he had identified the University of Minnesota with universities in general, and had seen it as preparing educators — specifically, "teachers, principals, and superintendents who have supervisory authority over the teachers who have received professional instruction and training in the normal school."[42] Kiehle was not disparaging the normal schools; rather, he simply wanted to persuade

President Northrop and the regents that the professional study of education was the rightful responsibility of *any* state university. Other states were doing as much, and Kiehle knew the relevant history. The twentieth century was under way, and Minnesota was twenty years behind the times. He recited the data more in sorrow than in anger.

"In 1879," he wrote, "the University of Michigan established the chair known as that of Science and Art of Education."[43] Since the 1880's, every state university in the country had made provision for a department of pedagogy.[44] He continued: "The University of Leland Stanford, Junior [now Stanford University] is best known by what it offers to teachers. In the University of Chicago the department of philosophy under the leadership of Dr. Dewey is most active and its head most widely known through his pedagogical services."[45] Kiehle may have taken it for granted that Northrop was aware that Dewey began his university teaching at Minnesota, where he was "professor of mental and moral philosophy and logic" from 1887 to 1889. Kiehle went on to mention other distinguished names: "The president of Clark University, Dr. G. Stanley Hall, is best known, and that most honorably in a worldwide reputation, as a student of childhood, and his university is well known through his pedagogical department. Then too, old Harvard and Columbia have responded with well-equipped schools of pedagogy" — in contrast to his own one-member department — "and President Eliot and Dr. Nichols [Nicholas] Murray Butler are prominently identified with the cause of popular education."[46] Finally, Kiehle reminded Northrop that in France and Germany "the pedagogical requirements for teachers of secondary education are as imperative as they are for primary schools."[47] Northrop may have been less than pleased at Kiehle's intimation that while other universities were well-known because of their pedagogical departments, the University of Minnesota was building a reputation in spite of its own.

Kiehle's arguments were nothing new. In 1881, Frederick Barnard had assured Columbia's young Nicholas Murray Butler that the "educational service of the country will never be what it ought to be until education is made a profession into which no one is permitted to enter without first having passed through a course of training as is required for admission to other professions."[48] Not long after — and only one year before Kiehle began lecturing on pedagogy at the University of Minnesota — the Harvard faculty approved a program of "Courses in Instruction in Teaching." Within a year, Harvard was to expand its program by offering the History of Teaching and Educational Theories, the Theory of Teaching, and the Art of Teaching, in addition to "methods" courses. By the academic year 1892-93, these "courses for teachers" were listed in the Department of Philosophy,[49] where William James lent his prestigious name to the endeavor. (His *Talks to Teachers on Psychology*, published in 1900, was a landmark.)[50]

Kiehle's letter to Northrop could have been even more detailed. The College of the City of New York had organized a department of pedagogy as a direct result of legislative action; in 1897, the New York legislature passed a law which required all who wished to teach in the common schools of that state to complete a course in pedagogy, including logic, psychology, and the theory and practice of teaching.[51] Similarly, in the Midwest, another land-grant institution, the University of Illinois, had had a chair of psychology and pedagogy as early as 1891.[52] Kiehle could have gathered even more evidence of a national movement among first-rate universities to support the introduction of pedagogics.[53]

There is no evidence that Northrop responded to Kiehle's letter, and we are left once again with the puzzle of Kiehle's fall from favor. Did he err in referring to what was being done abroad? Did that seem too far afield, too impractical, or perhaps too insulting? We know that Kiehle visited German schools and teacher training institutions; this is not surprising, since many young American intellectuals of the time were going to Germany in pursuit of academic excellence. Kiehle might have been impressed by how seriously pedagogy was being taken in Europe, but he was not entirely in favor of German methods. He gave a public lecture in 1899 which was reported in *Ariel*: "A questioning attitude is never found among German students — it is a spirit of confidence in the instructor and credence in his sayings. Independence and investigation are almost unknown. Instructors never ask for the personal opinion of a student. We hear that the schools of Germany achieved the victory of the Franco-Prussian war. This is true, because the German soldier . . . is made in the school . . . .[The Germans] have a system of education which is doing what they want it to do, to inculcate the idea of subordination to authority, to strengthen the love for a strong central government and to create soldiers."[54]

Obviously, Kiehle's vision of the purpose of education was

much broader; he did, however, choose to call one of the courses he offered a "seminar," a term principally used in German universities. In his second letter to President Northrop, written in 1902, he explained in detail the nature of the other courses he was then teaching:

> In brief there are two general and fundamental courses; the first a History of Education; the second a Philosophy of Education. The former consists of a study of the interpretation of education by the representative nations of ancient and modern history, and also of the methods by which they have prepared their young for the civilization into which they were born. The latter consists of a consideration of the principles of school organization, instruction, and training required for life as it is to be lived.[55]

These courses, both electives, constituted a year's work for juniors and seniors.

Kiehle then went on to briefly describe the seminar: it was open "to those who have taken normal courses and have had experience in teaching." (This was probably the forerunner of graduate study in pedagogy.) "This seminar is given to the study of advanced problems in education and to special subjects, together with an inspection of schools of the Twin Cities, in such subjects as the members severally prefer."[56] Apparently, none of his courses suffered from lack of attendance; the general courses were each given in two sections, which averaged forty-five members, and there were thirteen participants in the seminar. The latter was especially well regarded; on May 21, 1902, President Northrop received a letter signed by students in the seminar which echoed many of Kiehle's own sentiments: "We merely wish to call attention to the impossibility, with a single instructor, and the time now allotted to subjects therein, to make the work of this department [of pedagogy] what it ought to be."[57]

The additional resources called for by both Kiehle's students and their instructor were not to be made available for four more years, and then only after Kiehle had left the University. One of his proposals was accepted, however, although he was not credited with the idea; for years after his dismissal, the *Bulletin* of the University of Minnesota would list "teachers' courses" in many fields — including history, English, the sciences, and languages. In 1902, Kiehle had laid the groundwork for this practice when he wrote to Northrop:

Let men be appointed or selected in the several departments concerned, to whom shall be assigned this special pedagogical service . . . .They shall be given the time necessary to instruct classes and
seminars, and to put themselves in touch with the schools of the state
— this for purposes of inspection with their students, to acquaint themselves with prevailing conditions and to foster an intelligent interest in
the subjects they represent."[58]

In retrospect, then, it is clear that Kiehle was a dedicated and
involved educator, well-liked by his students and concerned with,
among other things, upgrading the education of teachers, making
sure that the University itself grew in both scope and reputation,
and keeping abreast of new ideas in the field. He was willing to
share his expertise with his peers and had a healthy respect for the
changing times. In spite of all of his unquestionably good qualities,
however, he abruptly lost his post.

This event may have even been precipitated by his 1902 report
to President Northrop, since he was dismissed so soon afterward.
Even though this report is simply dated 1902, it was clearly filed
before the first week of April. Not long after, the Board of Regents
received a letter dated April 4 in which two regents, James T.
Wyman and Thomas Wilson — who constituted a "special committee" charged with reviewing the 1902 report — wrote:

We have duly considered the report of Prof. Kiehle proposing to increase the scope and efficiency of the department of pedagogy in the
University of Minnesota, and in view of the fact that the Board of Regents has not at its command funds to spare for the purpose named, your
committee recommends that the report of Prof. Kiehle be laid on the
table."[59]

And so it was — but the regents' actions against Kiehle did not stop
there.

At the same time, Regents Wyman, Stephen Mahoney, and J.W.
Olsen were requested to "consider the advisability of abolishing
the department of pedagogy" altogether. Wyman and Mahoney
took one stance, and Olsen another:

After consulting with prominent educators in the Twin Cities and all
over the state of Minnesota, and listening to a carefully prepared statement by Dr. Kiehle of the work done and the methods in vogue in the
department, and consulting with many of the graduates of the University who have taken work in said department, the committee is of the
opinion that the department should be retained in the University, as we
believe it is regarded as an important department of university work.[60]

This from Wyman and Mahoney; so far so good. But the final paragraph of their report sealed Kiehle's fate:

> The committee is however of the opinion that the head of the department should not be retained longer than the close of the present year and that in his place a new and up to date man should be secured. This seems to be the nearly unanimous opinion of educators all over the state who have been in close touch with the department. We should therefore recommend that Dr. Kiehle be notified that his services will not be required after the close of the present school year.[61]

Olsen's response was brief:

> I concur in the opinion of the other members of your committee, appointed to consider the advisability of abolishing the chair of pedagogy, that said chair should be retained. I also concur in the view that opinion is divided among educators through the state, as to the practical value of the work done by Professor Kiehle.[62]

There is quite a difference between the "unanimous opinion of educators" cited by Wyman and Mahoney and the "divided opinion" mentioned by Olsen. How many educators were actually consulted? How representative were they? At any rate, Olsen did not think that there were grounds for failing to reengage Kiehle at the end of the academic year: "Owing to the difficulties surrounding the department of pedagogy in this, and generally in other state universities, I am not prepared to recommend that Dr. Kiehle's services be dispensed with at the end of this year."[63]

Olsen may have been the only one who came out in favor of retaining Kiehle, since the Wyman-Mahoney recommendation carried.

In later years, when writing her "Reminiscences of Faculty," Mary Folwell, whose father had been the first president of the University, remembered being told that President Northrop had called Kiehle to his office and said, "Dr. Kiehle it is my painful duty to inform you — your successor is here."[64] According to E. Bird Johnson, the head of the Alumni Association, Kiehle said nothing, merely "bowed, went to his room, picked up his belongings, and left."[65]

Three

From Pedagogy to Education

THE THIRTEEN years which separated Kiehle's departure from the old Department of Pedagogy and Lotus D. Coffman's investiture as dean of the young College of Education were uncertain ones. At first glance, it seems as if the vision which had been such a strong force in earlier days had temporarily faded. To be sure, these years were not entirely wasted; for one thing, the aims and scope of the College became better defined. What we can now appreciate as a cosmopolitan view of the essential difference between a democratic and an aristocratic philosophy of education is clear in the writings and teaching of the three men who were so important to the first year of the College — David Kiehle, George James, and Fletcher Swift. Each had observed educational patterns and practices in Europe and had given the College its first taste of cross-cultural study. Few people, however — including both educators and administrators— were aware of the significance of that experience. The College was plagued by inadequate budgetary support and recurrent doubts about its so-far insecure leadership; there was little energy left over for its real purpose.

It may be small comfort, but Minnesota was not alone. At other universities as well, schools or colleges of education had to struggle into being,[1] and they were rarely, if ever, assisted by other faculties. By comparison with similar institutions of the time, Minnesota was a promising place at which to develop a unit devoted to the professional preparation of teachers and school administrators. At the University of Illinois, for example, the Department of Pedagogy begun in 1891 was still a one-member department in 1904, when it was directed by Edwin Dexter. Dexter had a lot to complain about regarding the neglect of pedagogy at Illinois,[2] including the opposition of his peers, who were convinced that teacher training programs would have little to offer in the way of academic quality or excellence.[3] The trustees of that university shared the same philosophy, even though they eventually agreed to authorize a school of education in 1905 (the same year in which the University of Minnesota founded its own college). Proponents of this school had to deal with sentiments like those expressed in a university senate's resolution:

> [A] school of education separate in administration from the existing colleges and with a separate study registration is not advisable because of the difficulty and friction which such a plan would introduce into our administration, and because all the educational purposes of such a school can well be accomplished without it.[4]

The Illinois school, then, consisted of little more than attempts by Dexter to coordinate "teachers' courses" offered by interested faculty members who retained their individual departmental affiliations. Minnesota was undoubtedly better off; its difficulties lay primarily in the fact that the people who were responsible for shaping the College could not get along with one another.

Just as Kiehle had had his problems with Northrop and the regents of his time, the first dean of the College of Education, George James, was not on the best of terms with George Vincent, Northrop's successor. James seems to have followed in Kiehle's footsteps in more ways than one; both were dismissed rather summarily (although Kiehle was let go with more delicacy and tact than James), and both were judged as being out of touch with reality. The latter was the fate of many who shared the Socratic-Platonic thought that "the unreflective life is not worth living." Most of the Socratic dialogues probe assumptions made about conventional values: similarly, historically-minded philosophers of educational thought and practice have analyzed educational theories and questioned their worth. Occasionally they have taken individual stands; more often, they have aligned themselves with some educational view vital during their day. The German philosopher-psychologist Johann Friedrich Herbart (1776-1841) was the founder of a major school of thought, and there were a number of conspicuous Herbartians among American educators at the turn of the century. Often, the Herbartians managed to irritate others who, faced with everyday quandaries, felt that the theorists were merely luxuriating in speculation without offering real or workable solutions to problems. Although neither Kiehle nor James was a Herbartian, each was charged with being impractical and out-of-touch — allegations which often proved fatal to an educator's career.

In their classic study, *Teachers for the Prairie: The University of Illinois and the Schools, 1868-1945*, Henry C. Johnson, Jr., and Erwin V. Johanningmeier examine the fate of one educator with Herbartian leanings. William J. Eckoff was an early pedagogics instructor at the University of Illinois, and his interest in Herbartian theory "focused on the theoretical substructure" of that type of thinking.[5] Eckoff was viewed as ineffective in dealing with state educators, and David Kinley, dean of the College of Literature and the Arts (in which pedagogics was housed) thought Eckoff "undesirable" in part because of his "irreconcilability to the existing order" at the University of Illinois. Unfortunately, Eckoff was also considered to be "abrasive in the delicate role of school visitor."[6] When Kinley asked President Draper to discharge Eckoff, Draper agreed.

Coupled with the fact that he was probably viewed as impractical, James may have also been unsuccessful in coping with his academic colleagues. He had had experience with University extension programs, however, which at first must have been a point in his favor. Vincent probably looked forward to James's expanding the influence of the University beyond the bounds of the campus — but he was disappointed. James did little in that area while at Minnesota. This, combined with a number of other factors which will be examined here, resulted in Vincent's dismissal of James under what are reported to have been less than favorable circumstances.

Ironically, Vincent and James moved toward their final unhappy encounter along similar paths. In particular, they had a mutual interest in extension — or, more specifically, in making instruction, primarily by lecture, available in off-campus settings, during evenings, and wherever or whenever interested people would come. For Vincent, extension meant duplicating the sense of the Chautauqua movement, which his father, Bishop John Heyl Vincent, had originated along with Lewis Miller in Chautauqua, New York, in 1874. With its roots in the Methodist camp meeting — and its initial goal that of educating Methodist Sunday school teachers — Chautauqua was like a state fair and a revival. It provided lay people with the opportunity to take courses in a number of areas, including the arts, sciences, and humanities. Lecturers, authors, poets, scientists, and scholars were booked for appearances. People who were unable to attend the meetings were offered courses for home study groups, and lecturers were sent out to them. The Chautauqua movement became increasingly popular during the late nineteenth century, and two or three hundred additional chapters were formed throughout the country.

Chautauqua began as a family affair, and George Vincent was involved in many aspects of his father's work. (Some say that the son's legendary impromptu eloquence stemmed from his apprenticeship in the Chautauqua movement; whenever a visiting lecturer failed to appear, Bishop Vincent would have George substitute.) It may be assumed that George Vincent saw continuing education as his life's work, a calling similar to that his father had felt when he entered the ministry. In *The University of Minnesota, 1851-1951*, James Gray writes of George Vincent's total immersion in his father's life and work (in a chapter appropriately entitled "Statewide University"): "He was as close to his father as it has ever been given a son to be. His summers were spent at Chautauqua. He sat at table with a generous sampling of the intellectuals of the world and learned to speak their language as readily as the average subadolescent learns to speak the language of sport."[7] George Vincent not only embraced his father's ideas but ideals as well, and his interest in the movement did not wane when he left home:

> At twenty-one, just after his graduation from Yale, he began to preside at Chautauqua sessions and to introduce lecturers; at twenty-two he became literary editor of its publishing enterprise, the Chautauqua Press; at twenty-three he was made vice-principal of instruction and at twenty-five principal of instruction.[8]

These steps eventually led to a university presidency.

To understand the spirit of what the Vincents, father and son, referred to as Chautauqua *extension*, it is essential to recognize that the movement stemmed from religious meetings. The "message" that was delivered during each session, then, was not purely secular. A commitment to religion inspired Chautauqua. The Vincents firmly believed that ethical standards would be raised through listening to — and reading — wise and ennobling words. Thus, it seems appropriate that Vincent followed such men as Neill, Merrill, and Kiehle to the University; all of them would have understood and applauded his Christian roots and his idealism.

Like George Vincent, George James was born the son of a minister; also like Vincent, he was deeply involved in extension and believed in its goals. Between 1891 and 1893, he served as secretary of the American Society for the Extension of University Teaching and lived in Philadelphia, where the society was based. During this time, George Vincent became a member of the sociology faculty at the University of Chicago; its recently appointed president, William R. Harper, had preceded Vincent as principal of Chautauqua. It seems uncanny that both Vincent and James came to the University of Minnesota after years of similar experience in bringing education to men and women who were unable to take advantage of formal schooling. It is even more unusual that the two had such a difficult time working together as colleagues.

A detailed examination of the history of extension at the University of Minnesota will help to set the stage for the final meeting between James and Vincent. In his account of the University, Gray comments at length on the first trials of what eventually became known as the extension program. These efforts culminated in the Center for Continuation Study. Now the Nolte Center, the new building welcomed its first "non-regular" students in 1936. Harold Benjamin, assistant dean of the College of Education since 1932, acted as its first director.[9]

The years leading to the establishment of the center were ones of experimentation, trial and error, and of trying new approaches and new ideas modified to suit the requirements of the times. It may be said that extension began in 1881, when Professor William A. Pike pioneered night classes in engineering. He was followed during the 1890's by Professor Harry Judson, who developed courses in history to which the word *extension* was applied.[10]

Judson, an enterprising believer in extending educational opportunity to those who might otherwise be passed over, was the first professor of history at Minnesota (he held that post from 1885 to 1891) and previously had been connected for fifteen years with the public schools of Troy, New York.[11] It is clear from his work that his idea of extension was closely allied with his philosophical stand on education in general — he was not one to do little more than talk about education and its importance. He willingly extended his duties beyond what was expected of him. Every Tuesday, for example, according to the March 15, 1886, issue of *Ariel*, he lectured to seniors on pedagogics.[12] His approach echoed the emphasis which both Folwell and Kiehle had placed on the *practical*: in the words of another *Ariel* article, Judson "was inclined to

favor the practical . . . claiming that the purpose of the school is
not to make authors, neither literary critics, nor to give the power
to enjoy literature and art; that it is the purpose of the school to
prepare [its] students for life."[13]

Judson met George James when the latter was serving as editor
of the 1893 *Handbook of University Extension,* which was sponsored by the American Society for the Extension of University
Teaching. Judson felt sufficiently involved with and knowledgeable about extension to submit an article to the *Handbook.* In it,
he reported that during his stay at Minnesota three to four hundred people, some of them teachers, had taken extension courses
twice a week "to extend or freshen their knowledge in such ways
as seem desirable."[14] Two years earlier, he had written another
report for the first national conference of the society.[15] Though he
was not able personally to attend this conference — which James
had organized for December 1891 in Philadelphia — his report
was read by Maria Sanford, who had given the University of Minnesota's first lectures in pedagogics in 1881.[16] Maria Sanford and
Harry Judson shared a joint commitment to both extension and
pedagogics. The two of them must have been delighted when,
during that same year, David Kiehle became a full-time lecturer
attached to the first University of Minnesota department of pedagogics in the College of Science, Literature, and the Arts (CSLA).
Locating pedagogics in liberal arts colleges was customary, even
though the liberal arts and science departments were traditionally
reluctant hosts, holding that the professional preparation of teachers was no more than the training of technicians and was thus
better accomplished by the normal schools.

In writing his report for the first national conference of the extension society, Judson did not fail to show his awareness of Chautauqua. While acknowledging the pioneering of English educators
in the area of extension, for example, he claimed that "a vast deal
that passes in England under the head of 'University Extension' is
nothing but the work of the Chautauqua Circles here."[17] At the
same conference, Bishop Vincent himself delivered an address entitled "Chautauqua and University Extension."[18] James, who had
not only organized the conference but also edited its proceedings,
was certainly aware of the elder Vincent's address, in which the
distinguished audience was told of Chautauqua's ideals. These
were, in part,

the application of the highest and most approved methods of education to the out-of-school multitudes, — all of them, at all ages, in all social conditions, — that they may come to appreciate their personal possibilities and responsibilities; that they may see the harmony between things religious and things secular; that they may learn how truly to honor and dignify manual labor; how to despise the frivolity, emptiness, and selfishness of mere wealth without culture and high moral quality.[19]

Bishop Vincent had a great deal more to say about the virtues of Chautauqua, and continued to spell out the connections between the movement and general university extension. He was also moved to add that Chautauqua was not, "as some superficial observers have supposed, an evolved camp-meeting."[20] The Chautauqua movement may have had its roots in Methodist camp meetings and Sunday schools, but it had undoubtedly progressed far beyond those humble beginnings.

While Bishop Vincent chose to speak about the revolutionary educational forum he had helped to found, his son George wrote about it. He published a paper in the third volume of *University Extension* in 1893 (it ceased publication the following year) in which he praised Chautauqua for making available to its members the printed lectures of such notables as sociologist Albion Small and economist Richard T. Ely. He intended in his paper to show that Chautauqua extension played an important role in education by helping to quicken a general interest in attending college full time — in other words, that Chautauqua extension complement rather than rival university extension:

If those lectures [printed by Chautauqua] are prepared by able men, and read with reasonable intelligence, the effect cannot fail to be at least stimulating. No community educated up to the point of arranging a regular University Extension course would accept manuscript lectures as a substitute. It is conceivable, however, that a group of persons who had become accustomed to [a] course of "read" lectures, might easily aspire to a series from a living lecturer. If Chautauqua Extension can successfully play the role of advance agent, it will gladly make this contribution to the cause of University Extension in the United States.[21]

It is certain that the movement had a positive effect on education in general. James may not have been aware of it, but by 1890 the Chautauqua circles enrolled more than 100,000 persons.[22]

Again, it is obvious that the Vincents were deeply committed to both Chautauqua and university extension. It can be assumed that these two men had some influence on their readers and their listeners; each had a reputation as an outstanding educator. Although there is no written record of any reaction on the part of either the extension conference audience or of George James to the bishop's 1892 address, it is likely that it carried a great deal of weight. James, for instance, had just published his own *Syllabus of a Course of Six Lectures on Prose Fiction in America.* [23] The reading, reflection, and lecturing involved in the preparation of this syllabus may have made James especially sympathetic to one of Bishop Vincent's points on the effects of Chautauqua on college and university life:

> The effects are to be found . . . . in the large number of readers in that most popular form of the modern Chautauqua work, the Chautauqua Literary and Scientific Circle [popularly termed the C.L.S.C.] who, covering in a four years' course of English reading the college outlook, become familiar with the college world, its topics, its charms, its practical value, and who, being parents or the elder brothers and sisters of the household (there are few members of the C.L.S.C. under twenty-five years of age), are sure to induce the younger people by hundreds and by thousands to resolve upon the high-school and college course. In fact, the C.L.S.C. is a John the Baptist to the college, preparing the way for and announcing the benefits of the college, and appealing to the multitude to patronize the high centres of culture.[24]

Although we do not know what James's reaction was to Bishop Vincent's claim that Chautauqua was good for university extension in general, we do know that James was aiming at a similar goal: making education available to many who otherwise might never know its benefits.

In his three years as secretary of the American Society for the Extension of University Teaching, James recruited some of the best known intellectuals in the American — and British — academic community. Many responded by contributing to his 1893 *Handbook.* Judson was not the only historian and scholar who wrote for it: Frederick Jackson Turner, well known for his classic studies of the American frontier, wrote on "The Extension Work of the University of Wisconsin"; James Harvey Robinson added an article entitled "The Educational Value of European History"; Sir Michael Sadler, who came from Oxford to attend the first annual meeting of the national conference, wrote "The Prospects of University Extension in England"; and William T. Harris, U.S. Commissioner of Education, contributed a paper entitled "The Essential Differences of Elementary and Higher Instruction."

Harris's paper, incidentally, was an adaptation of a talk he had given to a National Education Association meeting in St. Paul in July 1890 — and David Kiehle had been instrumental in arranging that convention.

Of course, James submitted papers of his own to the *Handbook*, among them "What Is University Extension?" and "Why Teachers Should Be Interested in University Extension." Oddly enough, at what might seem to have been a high point of his involvement in the society, James severed all ties with it and left for Europe in 1894. The society underwent a drastic reconstruction that year; some explanation for James's departure may be found in the fact that the panic of 1893 had a large effect on the society's finances.

During 1894, James was awarded his doctorate in Germany by the University of Halle, which at that time was a mecca for American educators who were attracted to the Herbartian wedding of psychology and philosophy. In his dissertation, "Thomas Hill Green und der Utilitarismus," James made mention of Friedrich Wilhelm August Froebel (1782-1852), another revolutionary theorist. Even though Commissioner Harris gave Froebel's ideas his blessing and succeeded in successfully introducing the Froebelian kindergarten to American education, the German philosophic idealist simply did not appeal to the down-to-earth teachers and administrators of the day. While James himself was not a Herbartian, his acquaintance with Herbart's ideas and enthusiastic support of Froebel's techniques would not in later years ameliorate his reputation as an impractical educator; if Herbartians were thought to be too progressive, Froebelians were seen as even more daring.

James was no stranger to the European educational milieu. After receiving his M.A. in 1887 from the University of Michigan, he returned to Europe and spent three years visiting schools and talking with educators in France, Germany, and Italy. This excursion in comparative education inspired at least one of the courses James gave in the College of Education, to which he came in 1902 after serving for one year as secretary to the Chicago Education Commission and another as professor of pedagogy at the State Normal School of Los Angeles, California. We do not know what response James received from his students or from teachers and administrators in Minnesota schools; all we can do is speculate that a good deal of what James said — and, for that matter, Kiehle before him — was remote to the needs of would-be teachers or educators who faced the pressures which shaped Minnesota schools in the early years of the 1900's.

It is easy to forget, in fact, what schooling was really like around the turn of the century. Two years before he was named dean of the College, Walter Cook recalled the American school of the time — and his account was hardly complimentary. His message was in accord with one of the themes which have threaded their way through the College's history. Much of Cook's own research emphasized the importance of individual differences, and to those who knew him or his writings there was a familiar ring to such an indictment as: "In the classroom potential muleskinners, day laborers and janitors sat beside embryo research physicists, surgeons and business executives. They looked at the same texts, pursued the same educational goals and were marked on the same standards."[25] True, equality of educational opportunity should be — and has been — an overriding ideal in the American democratic system; however, it should never be construed as implying "sameness." Cook saw educators and administrators who advocated "sameness" as being grossly unfair to their students, who had differing needs and capabilities.

The diversity of students and the incompatibility of their needs must have caused some difficulty for James, who might be described as a post-Kantian idealist. Although his philosophical approach was shared by intellectuals both nationally and internationally, it was simply not closely enough related to the practical requirements of the Midwest. That philosophical approach proved important, however, if only in light of the widespread resistance it met throughout the Midwest during the latter half of the nineteenth century.

Part of the problem may have been the fact that James, along with a number of American intellectuals, had sought an advanced degree in Europe. Perhaps some of his colleagues resented this; they may have thought that European institutions were out of touch with American goals. This may have served to lessen James's popularity, but it did not seem to significantly harm others who were similarly educated. For example, Edmund James, George James's older brother, became the president of both Northwestern University and the University of Illinois after receiving his Ph.D. from the University of Halle in 1877.[26] Charles De Garmo, with whom George James was in contact while acting as secretary to the American Society for the Extension of University Teaching, also received his Ph.D. from the same university. De Garmo became the first professor of psychology and pedagogy at the University of Illinois, where he introduced into the curriculum the Herbartian ideas he had learned at Halle. Frank McMurray of Teachers College, Columbia, was another Herbartian who had taken doctoral work not only at Halle but also at another leading center of Herbartian thought, the University of Jena, from which he received his Ph.D. in 1889.[27] While there is nothing to indicate that George James was a follower per se of either Herbart or Froebel, he did see great profit for educational theory and practice in late nineteenth-century German thought.

It would be unnecessary to say more of Froebel or Herbart were it not for the fact that James and a number of other prominent American intellectuals were so strongly attracted to them. Herbart was especially well thought of in this country; as one of Kant's successors at the University of Gottingen, he had an excellent reputation as an idealist philosopher. His *General Theory of Education* [*Allgemeine Pädagogik*] had been published in 1806 and won broad acclaim in educational philosophy for the remainder of the century. Because Herbart combined psychology and philosophy (while simultaneously anchoring his psychology firmly in ethics), his teaching was irresistible to a man like George James. The University of Halle was widely known as an institution where James and other Americans like him who were interested in post-Kantian idealism could go to study Herbartian thought and teaching based on that philosophy. They did not go there thinking that abstractions were to be their only course of study, however; Herbartians felt that they also knew the practical methods a teacher could use to build moral character in their students who, as possessors of free will, were able to choose between good and evil. The Herbartian method became famous, and there was much talk of *clarity, association, system,* and *method* — the four steps that became hallmarks of the Herbartian model for teaching. James was indeed in good company in terms of both educational philosophy and educational practice. Regrettably, the latter probably seemed all too "progressive" and impractical to many educators in Minnesota.

Others who were involved in university administration and extension across the country shared James's intellectual background. Both Harris and De Garmo, in addition to being administrators (Harris as U.S. Commissioner of Education, De Garmo as president of Swarthmore College) were also educational philosophers. Harris was the leading Froebelian and Hegelian scholar in the United States; his support for the timely introduction of the Froebelian kindergarten into the country was essential to its success. While there is no evidence that James had any personal contact with Harris, it is obvious that he shared Harris's enthusiasm for Froebelian thought. While acting as dean of the College of Education at Minnesota, James described Froebel as "one of the stupendous figures in educational history."[28] Froebel's mysticism also fascinated James, whose brief essay "The Basic Philosophy of Froebel" demonstrates an unusual grasp of a most abstract and abstruse concept termed *idealism.* Idealism emphasizes the primacy of the mind and of spiritual values over all other forces. It contrasts with *naturalism,* which sees both as being derived from nature and therefore reducible to the material. The writings of the post-Kantian idealists — especially of such German "absolute idealists" as Johann Gottlieb Fichte, Friedrich Wilhelm Joseph von Schelling, and Georg Wilhelm Friedrich Hegel are difficult, to say the least. It was a point in James's favor that he seemed to comprehend these complex ideas. Harris, too, was able to master this very recondite philosophic literature. Himself an idealist (or, more precisely, a post-Kantian idealist), Harris was this country's most renowned student of the post-Kantian school of thought. No former commissioner of education (and few who came later) was his peer — nor, for that matter, was any functionary in a comparable post.

James must have sympathized with Harris's stance. His own Halle dissertation had dealt with the idealism of the post-Kantian Englishman Thomas Hill Green. Although it is not particularly germane to the issue at hand, it is interesting that Green was probably closer in thought to Kant than Hegel, even though Hegel was considered to have been Kant's successor. Green's ideal for the individual was perfection through obedience to a moral law that might be interpreted as Platonism dressed in the intellectual garb of a well-tutored English cleric. He was considered to have been a social radical, a reformer, and a man of vision — but his vision posited the existence of a society whose citizens would be morally advanced. His emphasis on the necessity of social reform can be seen as having influenced James, who himself viewed moral and social betterment as going hand in hand with university extension. In short, then, James must have been far removed intellectually from the mundane challenges of the ordinary school. If Kiehle perceived himself as more advanced than his colleagues, it is easy to imagine how James must have felt. James was at home with Harris's thought — not with the more provincial educators and administrators of the state. One can view him as having been ideologically consistent with Kiehle — and, to reiterate, neither was perceived as being practical, and neither lasted very long at the University. It was not until America's entry into World War I (in fact, until after 1919) that the College received its first real taste of educational sociology, one which was heavily spiced with a social philosophy that would have appealed to Kiehle and James alike. Despite its social ideology, the educational sociology of Ross Finney, who taught at the University from 1917 to 1930, was an educational cut below what James had known in the writings of Green — even as Chautauqua was an intellectual cut below university extension, despite Bishop Vincent's claims to the contrary.

In its early years, the College of Education at Minnesota did not impress President Northrop as a public success, at least in its ability to attract teachers. A year before Vincent's arrival, the *President's Report* took a defeatist tone in its discussion of extension work: "Public school teachers . . . prefer something inspirational or popular . . . and from teachers these evening groups are generally recruited."[29] The report continued with this rueful observation: "It is scarcely possible that regular university courses . . . ever will be demanded by large enough groups to make them self-sustaining."[30] Vincent was more optimistic than Northrop, and his optimism was due in large part to the success of Chautauqua. While too much should not be made of James's having been personally acquainted with abstract and lofty thinkers, it can be assumed that Vincent was not overly impressed by this fact. It may have even contributed to James's eventual dismissal. Vincent's experience with Chautauqua had put him in contact with many people of the type who were not commonly found in university halls, and he was careful to avoid the educational elitism which many of his peers advocated. He envisioned Chautauqua — and, later, university extension — as being for the people in general, not merely for those who were seeking the benefits of higher education to further their own specialized careers. James might have benefited from a clearer understanding of Vincent's background and beliefs. As Gray describes him, Vincent was not a defeatist. He knew that the chief difficulty, faced by anyone who wished to create an extension program for a statewide university, was the implacable, snobbish hostility of the Brahmins of education within the institution itself. Such men were strongly inclined to believe that opportunity should be reserved for the elect. To encourage extension work was to open the citadel of culture to an invasion of barbarians. Destruction lay ahead for those who attempted to admit to the company of academic aristocrats any part-time, night-time beggars of scholarship.[31]

The same sentiments could have been voiced years later when there was a shift in emphasis from extension to the General College; an identical educational philosophy stood opposed to the entry of students to the former and subsequently to the latter.

James had been at the University of Minnesota for nine years, six of them as dean, before Vincent became president. To his credit, James had not coasted either as head of the tiny department of pedagogics or as dean of the College of Education. Neither job was an easy one, especially since the faculty was far from what one would call stable; its members entered and left the University with remarkable speed. For example, David Lloyd, a 1901 graduate of the University, remained with James for only one year. Charles Holt was another faculty member whose service proved brief. Originally hired as a "scholar in pedagogy" in 1902, Holt's title was changed to "instructor in education" when Chapter 120 of the General Laws of 1905 authorized the Board of Regents to "organize and establish . . . a teachers' college, or department of pedagogy."[32] This change of title, minor though it was, reflected a major change in education at the University. Since the *Fifteenth Biennial Report of the Board of Regents* stated that a department of pedagogy already existed, it was therefore assumed that "the legislature required the work already undertaken to be extended."[33] To that end, the regents voted on December 12, 1905, to establish a college of education and named George F. James as dean. In the same action, the regents authorized a "model school which was to serve as a training laboratory." A number of regents objected to this, however, voicing an old and often-heard complaint: "The majority of the board . . . seriously questioned the wisdom of conducting a model school in connection with the work done in the University, believing that provision . . . might better be made in the normal schools."[34] The regents who objected were overruled, and Alice Mott became the principal of the new school. (Incidentally, she was related to Willis West and somewhat more distantly to Professor West's daughter, Edith, who later directed the high school's social studies department.)

Although it had increased in size since 1905-06, the Education faculty was still small on George Vincent's inauguration as president. For example, while there were five faculty in Agriculture specializing in "sweet curd cheese work" and the same number in "cultures and starters," the College of Education had only six members, James included. It is interesting to read about them in older University publications such as the *Minnesota Alumni Weekly*.[35] Four years after James was placed on the faculty list, he was joined by Albert Rankin, whose mother, the *Alumni Weekly* states, was "of old New England ancestry." Rankin's father was a Scotsman — and that is all that is said of his family background.[36] There were no rules against nepotism then; Rankin's wife, Jean, joined the Education faculty in 1907, which was a busy year for appointments in the new college. Fletcher Swift also joined the faculty at that time, and his was the last appointment made before Coffman took over in 1915.

Albert Rankin was well-versed in the most avant-garde educational theory and practice, having visited with Colonel Francis W. Parker, a noted educator, at Quincy, Massachusetts[37] and having been in close touch with both G. Stanley Hall and John Dewey. He was also privy to the Minnesota educational scene, having served as superintendent of city schools and for eleven years as state inspector of graded schools. In addition, he had been president of the Minnesota state teachers' association and editor of *School Education*, a professional journal of some repute. All of this was duly recorded in the *Alumni Weekly*, which added to its description of Rankin by stressing that he had contributed to current periodical literature, been active in politics, served on committees and political clubs, and was a member of "the Society for the scientific study of education of the N.E.A."[38] The *Alumni Weekly* erred in only one respect; the National Society for the Scientific Study of Education was not a part of the National Education Association. Instead, it had evolved from the National Herbart Society, whose illustrious membership included such men as John Dewey and Charles De Garmo. When Dewey announced that the "Will" showed scientific investigation to be superior to metaphysical speculation for analysis of such faculties as the Will itself, the society changed its name to the National Society for the Scientific Study of Education. (That the study of education was to be scientific came to be taken for granted after World War I; today, the society is known simply as the National Society for the Study of Education.)

Fletcher Swift was another respected member of that first faculty. When he eventually left for a post in education at the University of California at Berkeley, Swift had been on the Minnesota faculty for eighteen years. If we assume that Rankin was in close touch with the cutting edge of educational practice, then we must consider Swift to have been a visionary. His interests also echoed those of past University figures such as Neill, Merrill, and Kiehle; specifically, he, too, felt that religion played an important part in education. He received a Bachelor of Divinity degree from Union Theological Seminary in 1902 and made use of it in his teaching at the University. According to the *Bulletin* for 1909-10, he offered courses in both the History of Religious Education and Principles of Religious Education.[39] In addition, his interests extended into secular concerns; before coming to Minnesota, he carefully researched the history of the school systems of the state of New York and in 1911 published *A History of Public Permanent Common School Funds in the United States, 1795-1905.*[40] Nor was his scholarship limited to relatively timely issues; he also translated German and Latin source materials on the history of education. Apparently, his ideology knew no bounds; he performed a comparative study of Buddhist and Christian doctrines of love in addition to authoring "Joseph: A Drama for Children" and "The Most Beautiful Thing in the World."

Obviously, Swift was a man with broad interests and talents. Not only did he have an extensive background in history, philosophy, and religion, but he also spent a year in Europe (from 1911 to 1912) and returned to Minnesota to add teaching in comparative education to his instruction on the history of education. In 1916 he published "Social Aspects of German Student Life," a series of articles which grew out of his European study.[41] Late in his stay at Minnesota, he effected a radical change in his career by entering the field of educational administration. Between 1922 and 1925, he published a four-volume series entitled *Studies in Public School Finance.*[42] The shifts in direction and interest demonstrated by Swift's life were both dazzling and inexplicable; his reputation as a creative thinker was well deserved.

James and Swift shared the responsibilities of lecturing on history, philosophy, and comparative education. This left the bulk of the preparatory work for elementary and secondary school teaching and administration to Rankin, who must have had difficulty in handling all of these areas at once. Fifteen credits in psychology and education were required for certification; students entered the College of Education as juniors, having first completed two years in CSLA. Before enrolling in the College, students were expected to take one course in general psychology; afterward, they were to take additional work in educational psychology (termed "developmental psychology") which was offered by the psychology department.

After the College had been under way for some two years, thirteen courses were offered. Seven were taught by James (or co-taught by James and Holt), five were given by Rankin, and one, in educational psychology, was taught by James Burt Miner of the psychology department. As is to be expected, James taught the History of Modern Education, the Theory [philosophy] of Education, and Comparative Education. He also offered a course in secondary education. For his part, Rankin handled courses in the Practice of Elementary Education, a similar course in secondary education, and instruction in administration and supervision. When Swift joined the faculty, the list of courses went from thirteen to sixteen, with Swift being responsible for the History of Education to the Reformation and Educational Classics. A hint of Swift's later concentration on issues in educational administration is found in the fact that he also offered a course entitled Problems in School Administration — described as a research course open to seniors and graduate students.

During the academic year 1908-09, James taught the Organization of Higher Education, the first course on higher education ever to be offered at the University. In the same year, three students in the College were granted the M.A. degree and eleven received the B.A. The College was growing, and James was ambitious for it. He lost no time in introducing and encouraging new emphases and directions. Holt's course, the Technique of Reading — another first — was followed the next year by the first of the College's "methods of teaching" courses — specifically, Methods in Elementary Teaching. This growth was reflected in the College's enrollment as well as in the widening variety of course offerings. Thirty-one students took the B.A. degree in 1910, and there was a parallel increase in general University enrollment. In 1912, forty-one students in the College received the B.A. degree, and one of the M.A. thesis titles was prophetic: "A Plea for an All-Year School."

Examining early College records, one cannot help but be impressed with how persistently James and his colleagues petitioned president and regents alike. Their first appeal was for a building of their own. As occupants of the chair of pedagogy in CSLA, Kiehle and James were naturally integral parts of that college and had willingly remained with it. However, as soon as the College of Education opened in 1906, James and other members of the faculty began thinking of establishing a separate identity which would be more visible if housed in a new building. This dream of a distinct facility to be designed for the College's specific needs has been a persistent one since the College's establishment. Before 1907, the department of pedagogy was located in Old Main, on the present site of Shevlin Hall. After the destruction of Old Main in 1904, the chair of pedagogy (and, later, the office of the dean of the College of Education) moved to Folwell Hall. The model or "practice" school was located on Beacon Street, immediately north of today's Experimental Engineering building. The hope for a new building rested on the development of a model school, presumably because the faculty of the College by and large had appointments (and established offices) in other colleges. It is impossible to tell how much the need for a separately visible organization and its accompanying autonomy influenced the development of a model school, if at all, but it is clear from early documents that the Board of Regents and the legislature were confused over the distinction between the facilities for a model school and college. The phrasing of the regents' report for 1908 — which grudgingly accepted the idea of a model school while challenging the legislature to finance it — is ambiguous about precisely what was supposed to be financed. Knowingly or not, James contributed to this ambiguity. Writing of the need for better facilities for the model school in a 1910 report to Northrop, he subtly shifted to talking about the College:

> The work of our practice school has increased in scope and improved in quality during the past two years, and, even though on account of very limited space, equipment, and teaching force we have hardly made more than a beginning, it is already recognized by the teaching profession of Minnesota as a vital part of our training. The school has so commended itself to the professors of the university that several

from different faculties have placed their children in it. The imperative need of adequate housing and equipment is more clear than ever. In consideration, however, of the uncertainty as regards the final conformation of our campus and of the impossibility of saying just now in what part of it the college may best be ultimately placed, I would respectfully suggest that our needs can be met for some years if we are assigned the present Chemistry building, with an adequate allowance for remodeling and equipping ($60,000). If, however, the school of Chemistry does not receive a new building from the present legislature, I would respectfully urge that a special building appropriation for the college be requested.[43]

In this context, it seems likely that the president and regents must have been making large-scale plans for expansion. During the same year, Cass Gilbert developed an ambitious model for the campus as a whole. James might have fared better had he proposed a College of Education building fitting Cass Gilbert's plan, but what he wrote to Northrop centered largely on his goals for the model school.

It appears from the *Fifteenth Biennial Report of the Board of Regents* (1908), that a model school was the rock upon which the College's hopes for a separate building were founded. Although the regents petitioned the state legislature to appropriate "not less than $150,000 for a new building . . . and to provide not less than $25,000 annually for its maintenance,"[44] their own opposition to the model school undermined the force of the request. At any rate, the request for a new College building was standard for every succeeding biennium. And just as standard was the compromise first suggested by James: if the College could not have a new building, then might it at least occupy an old one? In the *Sixteenth Biennial Report*, James rather pathetically suggested that if the legislature gave the School of Chemistry a new building, Education might take the old one.[45] The College had begun to play its standing role of the hermit crab that occupies the outgrown shell of a snail.

Finally, in 1913, toward the end of his deanship, James was allotted funds for renovation to make it possible for the College and the University High School to occupy the same building. As a result of this move, the College became inseparably allied with the model school. Working with the gutted shell of the School of Mines building, which had suffered a fire in February of that year, the designers were able to draw plans to fit the needs of both the high school and the College. If physical space and design can be seen as an expression of intangibles such as organization, administration, and status, the layout of the building was more important than any other in the history of the College. There is no way of knowing how much influence James had on the formulation of the building plan or how precisely his wishes were carried out. However, it can be presumed that, like other deans, he was concerned about it and did have some say in the matter. When Folwell Hall was being planned, for instance, Dean John F. Downey argued before the regents that the building occupants ought to know better than the architects how college buildings should be designed.[46]

The floor plan of the Education Building (which now houses part of the Institute of Child Development) shows that the entire basement was used for the model school. The principal's and dean's offices, located on the first floor, were identical to each other in space and configuration. A small room upstairs was set aside for the history and philosophy of education, and seminar or lecture rooms were provided in addition to a few offices for senior faculty. The *University Address Book* for 1914-15 lists James's office as 103 Education, where it remained until 1926, when the College moved into its more familiar site, Burton Hall. The early proximity of the dean's office to that of the principal of the model school, however, illustrates how closely the College of Education and University High School were allied philosophically if not administratively. As times changed, the high school became the sole occupant of the Education Building and a more hierarchical relationship was established between its principal and the dean, who called for annual reports on its operation and administration. Nevertheless, this early informal working relationship proved to be an important link between educational theory and practice in the College's history.

In the meantime, extension work, which had been financed since 1907 by the University, was continued by annual appropriation. An "appointment bureau" or placement service opened in 1911; according to the *President's Report* for 1912-13, the bureau helped a number of teachers to obtain positions, with "salaries varying from $65 for the inexperienced women graduates to $1200 or $1500 for the men with some experience in teaching."[47]

A number of other innovations were made during James's tenure at the University. In 1914-15, for example, instruction on the methodology of specific courses was given for the first time. These became the famous "teachers' courses," which were offered within CSLA but encouraged by the College of Education. August Krey taught the Teaching of History and Royal R. Shumway presented a comparable course in the mathematics department. The degree to which James was involved in these efforts is open to conjecture, but it is difficult to imagine that these "teachers' courses" would have come about without his leadership. He also stressed the need for the College — and the University as a whole — to become aware of and involved in new teaching fields. In the *President's Report* for 1911-12 —Vincent's first year as president— James is quoted in words that recall Kiehle's earlier plea: "The superintendents of Minnesota schools have for several years urged the University to provide them with teachers and supervisors of drawing, music, physical culture, manual and commercial training, household arts, and agriculture."[48]

In the same report, James is mentioned as having asked for "a traveling fund" to be used by faculty moving throughout the state with the purpose of keeping in touch with the public schools. While nothing came of the request, it initiated a statewide communication that was later maintained by such men as Willis Dugan and Wesley Peik. But James's original plea went unheard, despite the fact that Vincent was in favor of it:

> The university does not arrogate to itself the control of the educational system, but must take an intelligent and genuine interest in every division of the system. Through its College of Education the institution may render important service in studying the problems of the grade schools, the curriculum, organization, and administration.[49]

Although the College did not have a full-time specialist in secondary education until Dean Coffman managed to bring in Leonard Koos in 1919, it is obvious that Vincent realized the importance of the University's establishing some sort of relationship with the state high schools. He went on to insist that the University

> is immediately interested in the efficiency of the High Schools. It would have them not so much preparatory schools for the college as institutions serving the communities in which they are established and the majority of pupils whose formal education is carried no further than high school graduation.[50]

Vincent did not hedge; for him, the high schools were pivotal, and he saw the University's role in their progress as fundamental to their success. This makes it even more difficult to understand his failure to support James. Vincent continued:

The University can not do its duty by the High Schools until plans are perfected by which University teachers can visit these schools regularly, familiarize themselves with the problems of adjustment and instruction and thus become more intelligent and sympathetic with reference to the situation.[51]

For the moment, at least, James must have been pleased.

Even if James did not get his traveling fund, the College did mount the first of what became its very successful Schoolmen's Week sessions in 1914. During that year, which witnessed the outbreak of World War I, the first session had a relatively large attendance of 227. In the following year, the number almost doubled: 427 participants enrolled for a discussion of the topic "More Efficient Management of the Public Schools." It would appear that this theme reflected both widespread interest among area educators and the absence of any formal University course on the subject. The early "short courses," as they came to be called, were led by well-known educators: C.H. Judd from the University of Chicago; W.A. Jessup of the State University of Iowa; G.D. Strayer of Teachers College, Columbia; and F.E. Spaulding, superintendent of the Minneapolis schools. Lectures were given by nationally known leaders who were involved either in school administration or in work upon which the management of schools and school systems depended. Among them was Lotus D. Coffman of the University of Illinois, who would become the next dean of the College.

Vincent's rhetoric in support of the College of Education was fine, but the *President's Report* for 1913-14 betrays the dissatisfaction the faculty felt with what the president had actually done for them. Swift, writing as the College's secretary, was especially outspoken:

The designation "College" would seem a misnomer if viewed from the standpoint of the support that the College of Education has received in the past. It seems no exaggeration, speaking from this standpoint, to say that the College of Education has never been a college except in name. Its budget, if compared with that of other colleges, suggests little more than a poorly supported department.[52]

Salaries paid the staff were said to be "wretched."[53]

The penury that outraged Swift was not uncommon; pedagogy and education were traditionally the poor relatives who ate meagerly at the academic table. Clifford S. Griffin echoed Swift's sentiments in his history of the University of Kansas;[54] at the University of Illinois, the same financial deprivation prevailed.[55] As was the case with most colleges and schools of education across the country, funds were short, faculty few, and facilities less than perfect. These complaints were made so frequently at Minnesota that the administration may simply have been deaf to them by the time the 1913-14 *President's Report* was published. It concluded with still another longstanding request, this one for two positions — the first in school administration and the second in educational psychology. These appointments, however, were made not by James but by Lotus Coffman, who soon brought Leonard Koos to the former post and Melvin Haggerty to the latter.

James's record of solid accomplishment as dean of the College of Education was, in the end, not sufficient to save his career at Minnesota. For reasons not specifically known to us, he was relieved of his duties by President Vincent. Similarly, the events leading to James's termination are not clear, and the available records are inconclusive. In "Reminiscences of Faculty," Mary Folwell states — many years after the event — that Rankin had told her "a student going into James's recitation gave a look and shut the door and sent for President Vincent. He ordered James out of town before night."[56] On the other hand, it is clear from a 1915 faculty memorandum that Vincent had given James notice of termination at least a year before his departure and had, in the meantime, taken personal charge of the College's faculty meetings.[57]

Whatever the circumstances, James left the University in 1915 to become dean of education at the University of Nevada, a post he held jointly with the directorship of the State Normal School in Reno. Three years later, he became educational director of the Western Department of the YMCA's National War Work Council and in 1919 was assistant director of the Army Educational Corps of the American Expeditionary Forces. From that year until his death in 1932, he served as educational secretary and later national executive secretary for the Military Training Camps Association.[58]

Four

A New Emphasis on Professionalism

LOTUS COFFMAN spent only five years as dean of the College of Education, but they were important years. It is difficult to imagine any other span of time which witnessed more positive developments within the College, developments which were to deeply affect its later history. And, of course, when Coffman left the dean's office, it was not due to any perceived lack of ability on his part, or to his failure to get along with University faculty or administration; on the contrary, he went on to assume the presidency.

In spite of difficult odds, much was accomplished during Coffman's tenure as dean. The College began to take a specific direction and to develop a strong identity within the University. These steps were impeded somewhat by the American entry into World War I and the departure of many faculty members and students who answered the call for national service. Changes within the president's office compounded the problem. George Vincent stepped down in 1917 and was succeeded by Marion Burton, who in turn left Minnesota after only three years to assume the presidency of the University of Michigan. The effects of these various upheavals were not all bad, however; they actually may have served to make the University more conscious of its role. Students who returned from the war were generally more mature, more serious, and certainly less provincial and isolationist than they had been before. They also had higher expectations of what education should do for them. There were other, more tangible gains as well: across the country, increased attention was paid to physical education as a direct result of the war. The most handsome dividend, however, came in the form of the influence played by the Army Alpha-Beta Test, an intelligence measuring device which

57

had been used during the war to identify potential officer candidates. Donald Paterson, who joined the University's psychology department after the war, had had a great deal of experience in dealing with this test as well as with problems of selecting personnel in both business and industry. Pinpointing ways in which individuals differ became an inherent part of the selection process, and this technique carried over into the University as well.

This new emphasis profoundly affected the direction the College of Education would choose to take. While it would be more dramatic than historically accurate to say that the notion of distinguishing types of students became a dominant theme in the intellectual life of the University, adaptation of courses and curricula to individual differences was, in fact, a major focus of the activities of the College's faculty. A good deal of subsequent research involved minor, albeit important, variations on this theme. For example, the attention paid to remedial teaching in reading and arithmetic (with which Guy Bond and Leo Brueckner were associated) focused on teaching methods aimed at a distinct or "different" student population. Walter Cook's earlier criticism of the schools of 1900 was prompted by his wish that the individual differences teachers saw daily would not only be recognized but encouraged and used. After World War I, this concern was translated in part into a nationally recognized guidance counseling program at Minnesota.

Coffman's role in this new wave of thinking was minimal; he was involved in other equally important efforts. If anything, attention to individual differences tends to lead in the direction of instability or uncertainty, and Coffman represented stability first and foremost. While the College of Education was not exactly in chaos during the pre-war years, it lacked a clearly defined role. Without such role definition, stability was impossible. Coffman's great achievement as dean was to clarify and realize a clear-cut *professional* role for the college and to do this in the face of an unsettled presidency. Without a doubt, his outstanding maneuver involved having would-be teachers register in the College of Education. This significant move was unopposed by Presidents Vincent and Burton; more importantly, neither Dean Roscoe Thatcher of Agriculture nor Dean John Johnston of CSLA stood in its way. Coffman succeeded where others before him had failed; he managed to convince the administration that the College of Education did indeed have a professional function — and even a professional responsibility. No longer was it assumed that teacher training was a function better left to the normal schools. Kiehle had certainly attempted to point this out, and it stands to reason that James had, as well — although his arguments are no longer extant. Coffman, however, not only persuaded presidents and deans, but convinced the Board of Regents.

It may be said that Coffman had an advantage over his predecessors from the start. While Kiehle, James, and other early visionaries had carried on their work in spite of the administration, Coffman entered his deanship with the good will and blessings of President Vincent. For a year prior to James's sudden dismissal, Vincent himself had substituted for James as the presiding officer at College of Education faculty meetings. He must have been relieved when a man who seemed to meet all of his expectations was chosen as James's successor. James's precipitous leavetaking had, of course, left the College without a dean, and this occasioned a flurry of activity in the spring of 1915 to find a replacement.

Three letters sent out on March 12 of that year by Guy Stanton Ford, Vincent's chief ally and dean of the Graduate School, attest to the urgency with which the University sought a capable successor to James. They also unashamedly lay bare some of the College's problems. In his first letter, to Professor Frederick Meisnest of the University of Minnesota, Ford stated: "We shall need in our College of Education a man capable of taking hold of a rather disorganized college, [one] which has lost the confidence of the public schoolmen of the State, and put it upon its feet."[1]

This crucial admission of the demoralized state of the College was followed by another letter addressed to Professor B.F. Shambaugh at Iowa City. In it, Ford wrote: "We shall need a good vigorous man to take charge of things with a view, not only to strengthen the work on the campus, but in order to get it in touch with the public schoolmen of the State and regain their confidence."[2]

Ford's third letter was written to Professor C.P. Colgrave in Cedar Falls, Iowa. Here he not only restated the now-familiar set of basic qualifications — "vigorous leadership," the need to get the College back on its feet, and the need to "regain the confidence of the public schoolmen of Minnesota"[3] — but also hinted that the prestige and reputation of the College of Education at Minnesota had suffered during James's deanship. It is interesting to note that this search for a new dean was conducted without the participation of the College staff, which serves as a good indication of the College's status at that time.

While the University was thus engaged in active recruiting, the school year was rapidly drawing to a close. There was some anxiety over whether the College would indeed have a new dean by the summer. The first hint of success is found in the minutes of the meeting of the executive faculty of the College of Education on April 26, 1915: "The Secretary [Swift] was directed to arrange for a General Faculty meeting after consultation with Mr. Vincent, the time for calling such faculty meeting to be determined in part by the date when Mr. Coffman is expected in Minneapolis."[4]

Bringing Coffman to Minneapolis as a candidate had been no easy task. In a May 10 memorandum to the executive committee of the regents, Vincent told of Governor Hammond's opinion that "the university ought not to bid against other institutions for strong men."[5] Coffman was employed by another university at the time, and the question of whether it would be ethical to lure him to Minnesota may have triggered Governor Hammond's misgivings. (It is not clear how the governor thought the recruiting process was accomplished; nor is it known whether he offered any workable alternatives to the standard practice.) Vincent went on to assure the regents that a conference was being arranged with the governor "either to secure his acquiescence or to explain the reasons why the Regents feel it wise to follow the practice common to American colleges and universities."[6]

This communication was accompanied by another entitled "Memorandum Concerning the College of Education Deanship." This document outlined seven specific points which the regents were to consider; each reflected on some aspect of the College's history, needs, or policies:

1. The College, founded twelve years ago, has failed to take its place of educational leadership in the State. It is regarded as the most vulnerable part of the Institution.
2. The consensus of opinion in the University and outside is that a change in the Deanship is necessary. Notice was given to the present incumbent a year ago.
3. The Dean must be: (1) well-trained in modern scientific methods; (2) a strong teacher; (3) a good administrator; (4) a man of personal qualities which will inspire confidence inside and outside the University.
4. Such men are few and in great demand. It is vitally important to secure the right leader to give efficiency to a $100,000 plant and a $25,000 annual budget.
5. Dr. Coffman of the University of Illinois is regarded by the Univer-

sity men concerned and by the Superintendents of the State as singularly and peculiarly adapted to the needs of the situation. Success in securing him would be hailed as marking a new era in the educational development of the State.

6. Illinois has raised Dr. Coffman's salary from $4000 to $5000, which equals the first figure suggested by Minnesota. If Minnesota, following the recognized custom of educational institutions, can offer $500 or $1000 more for a Deanship than Illinois pays a regular professorship, Coffman will have reasonable ground for leaving Illinois for Minnesota. In the absence of any difference, he will be in the position of leaving without substantial reasons, an institution which has treated him well.

7. In view of the urgent demands of the schoolmen of the State, failure, on the part of the University, to do everything within reason to secure Dr. Coffman would be unfortunate. The Regents have an unusual responsibility with respect to this deanship.[7]

Two comments need to be made about this extended argument. First, the requirement that the new dean be "well-trained in modern scientific methods" was especially significant. No longer would a smattering of experience or a theoretical interest in education be sufficient; it was time for the College to be led by a well-prepared specialist in education. Second, whether Coffman was indeed treated well at Illinois, which had not yet proved that it was deeply committed to teacher education, is open to question. In *Teachers for the Prairie,* Johnson and Johanningmeier give ample evidence of neglect, and there is good reason to believe that Coffman would have been more than willing to consider other offers.[8]

Whether the contents of this memorandum managed to reassure Governor Hammond of the propriety of recruiting personnel from other institutions is not known. Regardless, the College today owes a debt of gratitude to those who helped to secure Coffman for Minnesota. The years of his deanship were good and fruitful ones. Above all, he was guided not only by a vision but also by a philosophy of education which rested on an empirical, scientific foundation. Early in Coffman's career as an educator, the scientific study of education had used as its primary tools surveys which focused on a variety of questions. Coffman had conducted more than his share of these, starting with his noteworthy doctoral dissertation, "The Social Composition of the Teaching Population."[9] Another example — and one closer to home — was the 1917 survey of the St. Paul school system which he coauthored with G.D. Strayer, an educational administrator, and C.A. Prosser, who would soon gain national recognition in the field of industrial education.[10]

Coffman's effect on the College of Education was especially remarkable when one considers how bleak the outlook was at his arrival. For almost a year prior to James's departure, the College had virtually been without a dean, and it had suffered as a result; not only had the lack of leadership been destructive, but internecine conflicts had also taken their toll. True, President Vincent had himself chaired the faculty meetings, and Fletcher Swift had agreed to serve as secretary to the Education faculty, but both men had other and more pressing responsibilities. They had done what they could, but it had not been enough; the College was foundering. Under Coffman's early leadership, however, a definite course — a new direction with a strong emphasis on research — became apparent.

One of Coffman's first actions as dean was to associate himself with the University's Bureau of Cooperative Research. Before long, its name was changed to the Bureau of Educational Research, a rechristening which indicated Coffman's efforts to bring the bureau into the mainstream of contemporary developments in education and in touch with educational research in the East, where William James and Edward Lee Thorndike were the shining stars of pedagogical studies. Though records are lacking, sometime between 1915 and 1920 (the bureau was renamed in 1919) a sufficient number of like-minded scholars existed across the country to charter an organization whose primary objective was the promotion of educational research. This new group would eventually evolve into that celebrated sounding board for pedagogical inquiry, the American Educational Research Association. However slight Coffman's own contribution to this fledgling organization may have been, he nevertheless set Minnesota's College of Education on a course of research from which it never departed and which would result in its later assuming leadership in the association. This new course was exemplified by the changes which took place at the University High School not long after Coffman's inauguration as dean: while the high school had formerly been preoccupied exclusively with demonstrating teaching techniques, it gradually shifted its emphasis to educational research. (Kenneth Anderson, who served as acting principal of the high school during the late 1940's, would become an early president of the American Educational Research Association, and the association itself would recognize Minnesota's contributions to education by creating its Palmer O. Johnson Award for distinguished research to honor this Minnesota faculty member.) Over the years, the concept of educational research would change, as would its various interpretations — but at least Coffman was able to plant the first seeds in reasonably fertile ground.

Coffman's own training in educational research began long before he embarked on his doctoral studies at Teachers College, Columbia. For one thing, he had previously served as supervisor of the "training school" of Eastern Illinois Normal School. (A generation later, another future dean of Minnesota's College of Education, Walter Cook, served as director of teacher training at the same school, which was renamed Eastern Illinois State Teachers College and then Eastern Illinois University. The evolution of such an institution from a normal school to a teachers' college, then to a state college, and finally to a state university occurred elsewhere across the nation and reflected the growing acceptance of American teacher training as a professional venture.) During his days at Eastern Illinois, Coffman's research was largely of a practical or applied type; theoretical research was another matter with which many people were not yet comfortable. It should be recalled that James and others were considered "impractical" and hence "undesirable" precisely because they were so interested in and committed to the study of educational theories.

Luckily, the prejudices against theoretical research were waning by the time Coffman arrived at Minnesota; his graduate studies in New York had suggested a promise of things to come. While at Columbia, Coffman was fortunate to have as his mentor Henry Suzzalo, whom Walter Cook described as a "pioneer in the sociology of education," a man who believed that "the art of teaching is the humanization of scientific knowledge and method."[11] Suzzalo was very interested in the influences which society has on the teacher, and Coffman's own doctoral dissertation (later published under its original title, *The Social Composition of the Teaching Population*) was consistent with that interest. Coffman's dissertation drew him to the attention of the faculty at the University of Illinois; it also helped goad administrators — especially those at the University of Illinois— into reevaluating professional teacher education and the university's role in it.[12] There was no disputing Coffman's inference that what had been done in the past to give

63

teachers — or, for that matter, school administrators — a good professional grounding had simply been inadequate. Johnson and Johanningmeier credit him with having had a significant influence on campus thought, and aptly summarize his scathing conclusions:

> The incredible characteristics of the teaching population which Coffman revealed were the general immaturity of the teachers, their inadequate or total lack of professional training, the brief time most teachers spend in the service of the schools, the poor status and even poorer salaries offered teachers, and the dreadful condition of the normal schools. Coffman had shown that the nation's schools were staffed by teachers who were, in large measure, inexperienced and either untrained or ill-trained for teaching.[13]

Other educators would voice concerns similar to those Coffman emphasized in his study, but they would approach the problem from differing perspectives. One in particular, George Counts, published a brace of books in the 1920's and 1930's, including *The Selective Character of American Secondary Education*[14] and *The Social Composition of Boards of Education: A Study in the Social Control of Public Education.*[15] These studies introduced an era when philosophers and scientists — primarily social scientists — became deeply involved in the fact-value controversy. (Basically, this consisted of a great deal of argument concerning which kind of knowledge was more valid and reliable — facts free of values or facts with values added. It paralleled the growth of science and often set those who advocated scientific data as the only true knowledge against those who preferred to engage in moral or philosophical speculation; in other words, it proved a battleground for subjective vs. objective data, for impersonal vs. personal statements and beliefs.)

Counts's monograph on the social composition of school boards was a mixture of survey results and ideological commentary. He was concerned about the role that class bias was playing in decision making about curriculum and other educational policy; this preoccupation was even more obvious in his 1932 publication, *A Call to the Teachers of the Nation.*[16] By then the Depression had engulfed the country, and Counts was one of the "reconstructionists" who believed that the schools should help prepare people to avoid depressions, wars, and other social disasters. Coffman's dissertation, on the other hand, had nothing to do with ideological reconstructionism. Again, Suzzalo's influence is evident. Suzzalo was at the other end of the liberal continuum. Lawrence Cremin, in his history of Teachers College, Columbia, links Suzzalo with David Snedden as characterizing John Dewey's particular brand of educational reform.[17] Essentially, Dewey encouraged cooperation and intelligence through educational experience. Suzzalo, who was neither a philosopher nor a sociologist, favored the study of problems in educational administration which demanded accuracy in data collection and interpretation while simultaneously calling for practicality in recommending policy. The Suzzalo-Coffman end of the fact-value continuum, then, was anchored in a desire to know something about the social matrix in which educational institutions are located. This concentration required *applied* research, which was characteristic of Coffman's scientific work throughout his entire career.

It is understandable, then, that over the years the College was to move away from the social *vision* personified by such men as Kiehle and James and toward a social *science* of education. The transition between these two approaches was effected by Coffman's hiring of Ross Finney, a pioneer in the area that came to be known as educational sociology. (Today's emphasis at Minnesota on the social foundations of education can be dated from this appointment.) Finney's hiring revealed Coffman's hope that a pledge of allegiance to a democratic philosophy of education could be put on a scientific footing. During the academic year 1916-17, Albert Rankin and Raymond A. Kent, who succeeded Alice Mott as principal of the University High School, offered a course together on the social aspects of education. It is likely that Coffman wanted to encourage the growth of this new approach to educational studies, and Finney's appointment was clearly intended to help it along. Although Coffman may not have been aware of it, the social idealism Finney promulgated was very much in tune with national developments of the time. It may not have been far enough removed from the democratic vision espoused by Kiehle and James, however, to satisfy Coffman's — and later Haggerty's — more scientific view of the empirical study of school and society. Though we have no evidence that the administration was unhappy with Finney, it was not until 1929, a year before Finney resigned from the University, that he was promoted to associate professor. While at the College, Finney found himself in the uncomfortable position of having to live in two worlds at once. Educational sociology was not his intellectual home, at least not quite. He was most at ease among "humanitarians" who "wanted to help bring about a better world in which to live."[18] The outlook was almost visionary; this time, however, the message was carried not by ministers such as Kiehle but by educators and economists such as Richard T. Ely. There were others, too, including Washington Gladden, who has been characterized as a "pioneer in the crusade of the social gospel."[19] Like Gladden, Finney looked for the birth of a new "socialized individual" — neither socialist nor rugged individualist — who would encompass the best and brightest characteristics of humankind. Had this doctrine been more widespread (it matured in the East and carried its greatest weight there), Ross Finney might very well have met with more approval and encouragement — not to mention professional recognition — at Minnesota.

Finney's spiritual membership in the group which ascribed to this "social gospel" was revealed in his 1913 publication *Personal Religion and the Social Awakening*.[20] (It is doubtful that Coffman read this book; if he had, he would have learned about an ideology similar to that of Chautauqua in that it was more a gospel than an ideology and more emotional than intellectual.) Finney's commitment to this social gospel movement might have seemed strange, but it was not idiosyncratic. He knew its vital history and what it meant, and he had carefully read its seminal writers. The first of these was, of course, Washington Gladden, whose *Applied Christianity* called for the application of the golden rule to the labor problem. Other books appeared in the 1890's; among them was *Social Aspects of Christianity* by Richard Ely, then professor at the University of Wisconsin. In this book, which Finney states was required reading for many young ministers, Ely applied the principles of Christianity not only to the labor problem but to other economic concerns as well. This approach delighted Finney, who wrote enthusiastically, "How that book set the young ministers of America to thinking as to what Christianity means to the world as well as to the individual!"[21]

That vision began to fade in the early 1900's, however, and secularization set in. Coffman was determined that the College of Education would have a respectable program in school administration, and he may have put pressure on Finney to conform to his wishes. Little wonder, then, that Finney followed his idealistic *Personal Religion and the Social Awakening* with such titles as *The Administration of Village and Consolidated Schools* in 1921 and, in the same year, *The American Public School*. He was in a

66

prolific phase, and he allowed himself to be bent in the direction Coffman had chosen. In 1922, he wrote a book which showed an unmistakable blend of the empirical and the ideological: *Causes and Cures for Social Unrest: An Appeal to the Middle Class*. A scant year later, his *Elementary Sociology* clearly identified him with a field of empirical social science and indicated that his thought had taken a quantum leap. Other titles followed, but one in particular reveals that Finney finally abandoned general sociology to apply himself to a more specific form of sociology whose data came from educational institutions. *An Introduction to Educational Sociology,* which he coauthored with L.D. Zeleny (and which was published in the year of Finney's death), indicated that Finney had made the long journey from the social gospel to the social science of education without turning his back on humanitarianism. It is apparent that Finney was trying hard to mold his views to those held by the College; what the administration thought of his willingness to compromise is not known.

With Finney's departure from the social gospel — if not from the desire to use education in helping to develop "socialized individuals" — the vision that lighted the way for Kiehle and James seemed to fade. It did not entirely disappear, however; the Depression provided the catalyst needed to give it new energy, and Minnesota faculty member Theodore Brameld's reconstructionism in educational philosophy and policy was to bring it fully to life once again. In the years between the wars, however, the College needed a respite from *all* gospel. This was a time of transition — and of almost no substantial research. The image of the College during this era was not one of which anybody could be proud. What the College needed was to gather strength and improve its reputation, and this is exactly what one of Coffman's first appointees, Leonard Koos, helped it to do. Armed with neither a social gospel nor any ideology other than a burning interest in the potential of the junior college concept, Koos helped to identify Minnesota as an important and influential force in professional education.

Koos has been called a "leader of pioneers," and rightfully so. He brought with him to Minnesota a number of innovative ideas, not the least of which concerned the development and implementation of the junior college. The course he taught during the summer of 1921 was the first anywhere to deal with this topic, and three years later, his two-volume study, *The Junior College,* proved to be the first significant analysis of that mode of education. Reviews were enthusiastic, and the work did not become outmoded. According to James L. Wattenbarger, *The Junior College* "has been the basic foundation for most of the later studies carried out by several generations of researchers in higher education."[22] To the charge that the junior college has now become passé, shouldered aside by the more contemporary community college, Wattenbarger has replied that Koos's 1921 "taxonomy of junior college purposes are valid for the 1976 community college as well."[23] Minnesota's own General College attests to Koos's perceptiveness and foresight; today, it embodies an idea which comes very close to Koos's educational philosophy. Its Associate of Arts degree validates the belief that two-year colleges can prepare students to apply the concepts of the arts and the sciences to both living and making a living.

Just as Edgar Wesley, Wesley Peik, Gordon Mork, and Willis Dugan were to do in later years, Koos traveled throughout the state, visiting and surveying high schools. Coffman had heeded the advice of such men as Fletcher Swift and realized that the University was in need of a specialist in secondary education. If anything, the new dean got more than he bargained for: Koos knew a great deal about high schools, having both taught in rural schools and having served as a superintendent in both Illinois and Minnesota for seven years prior to World War I. If Koos had a problem, it was the fact that he was very aware of his own capabilities. The challenge to any faculty member — or to any scholar-teacher who establishes a national reputation — is that the drive to maintain this reputation can interfere with one's teaching. Unfortunately, it is possible for one to become famous at the expense of his or her students, and Koos seems to have fallen into this trap. According to James Umstattd, a graduate of the College who himself became a national figure in the field of education, Koos had but one rival in his field, and he was determined "to remove all doubts as to which of them . . . [would] assume unquestioned leadership":

> Consequently Koos was too busy serving as chairman of national commissions and making speeches at conventions to give any thought to his teaching responsibilities. His classes were condemned to sit and listen as he read from his book.[24]

Happily, this tendency was not to be repeated in the future of the College; educational leadership did not have to be achieved at the cost of neglecting one's teaching responsibilities. The careers of such outstanding scholar-teachers of what might be called the College's Golden Age — Dora V. Smith, Palmer Johnson, Edgar Wesley, Ella Rose, Gertrude Baker, Leo Brueckner, Homer J. Smith, and Louis Keller — would prove Koos's unfortunate illustration to be the exception and not the rule. The myth of the ambitious scholar who ignores the needs of his or her students has also been dispelled by a number of other nationally visible University educators, including Emma Birkmaier in modern foreign languages; Fred Engelhardt or Mervin Neale in educational administration; Alvin Eurich and Harold Benjamin in educational psychology and adult education; James Umstattd in elementary education; Guy Bond, whose name is firmly linked to developments in reading; and Donovan Johnson, whose reputation is equally prestigious in the field of high school mathematics. Traditionally, the College of Education faculty has made it a policy to closely involve its graduate students in a number of significant research projects, often introducing the fundamentals and practices of research to men and women who later themselves joined the ranks of scholars.

It was not until after World War II, however, that research in the College was to begin on a truly grand scale. (It would achieve its full stature in 1957, when the Institute of Child Welfare joined with the College.) Early movements in this direction were often uncertain and frequently stymied. Coffman's reorganization of the Bureau of Cooperative Research nearly faltered for lack of funds; in a letter to President Burton dated October 24, 1917, Coffman complained bitterly that "with the survey movement widespread and with a willingness on the part of the public schools of this state to cooperate with us, as shown by the 170 schools that sent us data last year, we have been compelled to discontinue our work because we do not have the time to compile the results nor the money with which to publish them."[25] Luckily, Minnesota's potential had begun to be recognized in Washington, and the federal government rescued the research effort by choosing the University as a research station of the Federal Bureau of Education.[26] Funds for publication were supplied as a result of that action. Later, when Coffman became University president, he persuaded the executive committee of the Board of Regents to vote "that an item of $10,000 a year for each year of the biennium be added for the purpose of educational research."[27] (These were the first monies earmarked at the University for the continued funding of educational research.) Meanwhile the Bureau of Cooperative Research was renamed the Bureau of Educational Research in 1919; Coffman was by then its director and Koos and a relative newcomer named Melvin Haggerty were his collaborators.

Although the crowning achievement of the College was to be educational research, the vision of those who had the most to do with shaping the curriculum of the College was seldom limited to this or any other single concern. Coffman serves as a good example of the versatility which has been necessary to move the College into its present position. His ability to balance a number of seemingly contradictory demands is shown in the way in which he reorganized the College in 1919. Among the eight departments into which it was separated were Trade and Industrial Education, Agricultural Education, Home Economics Education, and Art Education. The first three were undoubtedly in response to public and administrative demands; there is no indication, however, that any outside force urged Coffman to set aside a department exclusively for art education. (The Minneapolis Handicraft Guild had been recognized by the Board of Regents in 1917, and the board had carried on a program in "normal art education" with the guild since that time. They had worked especially closely with Ruth Raymond, who joined the University in 1918. In no more than two years, the guild was absorbed by the College and became the Department of Art Education.) Coffman's new appointments also took music education into account, since T.P. Giddings was named lecturer in public school music in 1915. Admittedly, these were small beginnings — a modest fulfillment of the vision Kiehle had set forth following the turn of the century — but they were nevertheless significant. As President Folwell had said many years earlier at a banquet commemorating the first University graduation (for only two graduates): "A wolf upbraided a lion for bringing forth only one at a time. 'Yes,' said the lioness, 'one — one, but a lion!'"[28]

The staff grew in other areas as well. Four lecturers were added in 1914 and 1915 to the Department of Rural Training; high school methods instructors in mathematics, physics, English, and manual training were also appointed. Professor Haggerty was recruited to head a new department, Educational Psychology, and was followed a year later by Marvin Van Wagenen. (There was a potential third member of the educational psychology staff, W.S. Miller, but his principal function from 1916 to 1921 was that of administering the University High School.) Haggerty, who was not prone to wait for things to happen, made a reputation for himself almost immediately. He was such an ardent advocate of the College that Coffman occasionally had to restrain him. For example, he thought nothing of enlisting the resources of his own department — and later those of the entire College — for whatever cooperative effort appealed to him. In 1916 (in fact, at the very beginning of his tenure at the University), Haggerty's Department of Educational Psychology joined with the departments of Pediatrics and Mental and Nervous Disorders in the Medical School to launch the Psychological and Psychiatric Clinic. This clinic tested mentally retarded children, in addition to training students in a program that set a precedent for the Psychoeducational Clinic that opened its doors some years later.

With such a rapid increase in the College's staff — and with so many different types of personalities converging on the College almost simultaneously — precisely how serious conflict was avoided remains a mystery. One may assume that it was largely due to Coffman's efforts. He was not a man who aroused others' tempers; he had a strong presence, and he made his wishes known in no uncertain terms, but he managed to be firm without being abrasive. This blend of forthrightness and suavity proved especially valuable during Coffman's attempts to secure the registration of would-be teachers and other educational personnel in the College of Education, a stunning feat which was all but accomplished by the end of his deanship in 1920.

This validation of the College as *the* teaching organ of the University was more than the result of adroit political maneuvering on Coffman's part — it was also an idea which had found its proper time. This was recognized as early as 1914. The minutes of a College of Education meeting held on November 16 of that year note that the central topic of discussion was "Who will take responsibility for practice teaching mandated by the State Department of Education?"[29] It was clearly necessary to give someone this responsibility, and the College was a likely candidate (especially since it is doubtful whether any of the other schools wanted to assume it). Dean Johnston of CSLA had been asked earlier whether CSLA would give credit for practice teaching, and he had agreed that it would. Two days after the November 16 meeting, the College of Education High School Council convened and agreed to appoint a committee with members drawn from the College of Education, the University High School, the Agriculture and Home Economics Departments, and CSLA. This committee was asked to draw up a group of general proposals concerning what they felt should constitute a "teachers' course." The members wasted no time. On November 23, it was agreed that "the College of Education [should] control the choice of subjects [to be required for satisfaction of the mandated practice teaching]. It was pointed out that as a professional school the College of Education ought not to continue allowing the freedom of selection which heretofore has existed."[30]

This was a first step; University historian James Gray has pointed out the essential second step. According to his account, it was necessary "to persuade the regents to adopt a resolution recognizing the College of Education as the official agency for teacher training. The same statement provided that all candidates for teaching positions must be certified by the College of Education and that recommendations of candidates should be a university function administered by a bureau under the supervision of a committee named by the university Senate."[31] This reference to the University Senate set a precedent for involving other University units as well in the preparation of teachers.

For once, the College was not battling the University administration or having to defend itself against accusations that it was incompetent or simply unnecessary as a unit within the University. A spirit of cooperation was in the air, and it appeared to be the impetus the College needed to get it firmly established once and for all. Again, Coffman's diplomatic and political skills may be credited with effecting this change.

The way in which Coffman reorganized the College of Education faculty during his five years as dean proved in large part responsible for the College's new and respected role. A better appreciation of the effects of this reorganization, however, requires a glance further back at the way things were before Coffman's arrival. Prior to that time, it would have been impossible to convince the regents and the administration of the value of having prospective teachers register in the College without implying that the University as a whole would have a diminished responsibility or lose some of its powers.

The minutes of College faculty meetings between 1914 and 1919 indicate the progression of this reorganization and how radically it changed the College's role. For the first time, the faculty was grouped into two interrelated parts: the executive faculty and the general faculty. Expressed in this organizational division was the important idea that faculty members outside of the College were expected to share in the responsibility of preparing teachers. This concept was first outlined in a September 22, 1914, meeting of the College faculty. At this time, the plan for restructuring the faculty into these two groups — executive and general — was announced without explanation as to how 'they were to be selected or precisely what their responsibilities would be. After a series of weekly meetings, organizing principles were set down on February 1, 1915. Three arrangements were proposed: (1) that in any given year the general faculty of the College of Education was to consist of *all* persons giving courses designed to prepare teachers; (2) that this general faculty would include the deans of *any* college in which teacher training courses were offered; and (3) that the executive faculty would be made up of the dean of the College of Education, College faculty of professorial rank, the principal of the University High School, and two members from the general faculty. In the meantime, "teachers' courses," which had blossomed within several University departments, were to be surrendered by their respective departments to the College of Education.[32]

In the College's executive faculty meeting of March 25, 1918, Coffman stated that he would promote the reorganization of these various courses, hoping to make them somewhat more consistent.[33] And, finally, on December 9, 1919, Coffman suggested that the executive and general faculties be reorganized in such a manner that "the Executive Faculty shall consist of the Dean of the College of Education; one representative of each department located wholly within the College of Education; one representative of the Department of Home Economics; one representative of Agricultural Education; [and] two representatives of the College of Liberal Arts, the latter two elected by the general faculty of the College of Education.[34]

Many of the details discussed in these early faculty meetings have unfortunately been lost to us, but one overriding fact is apparent: over one-half of the teaching of students registered in the College of Education was conducted by CSLA,[35] and not a little of what CSLA taught was technical or professional. Dean Johnston addressed this issue in a letter to Coffman composed during the fall of 1915. The letter "showed that the B.A. degree was being offered for widely different types of work ranging from definitely vocational to general cultural courses, and that the traditional distinction between the B.A. and other degrees was 'in grave danger' of 'being entirely lost unless speedy action [was] taken to correct the present condition.'"[36] After recommending that only one-tenth of the credits required for this degree be allowed for technical courses, Dean Johnston went on to recommend that "the training of prospective teachers should be recognized as the function of the College of Education and not of the College of SLA."[37] Finally, he concluded that "the College of Education should be requested to change the degree now granted to B.A. in Education."[38]

Coffman could not have asked for better cooperation. Not only was CSLA willing to relinquish some of its control, but it was transferring that control to the College of Education — a college which had had its very existence challenged only a few years before. Johnston went on to reemphasize his support of the College in a letter written in the middle of December 1915, in which he repeated that the College of Education should take the initiative for planning preparatory work for teachers.[39]

This background is essential to a better understanding of the important resolution passed by the Board of Regents on June 7, 1916, the second article of which states unconditionally that "the College of Education is the University Organ upon which responsibility for teacher training is placed."[40] The CSLA faculty would have to be represented in the College's executive faculty in order that CSLA might be held accountable for "proficiency in subject matter."[41] (This clarified the otherwise puzzling statement with which the resolution begins: "Teacher training is a function of the University and not of any one college or department.")[42] Other colleges — principally CSLA — would share in the preparation of teachers, but the College of Education was to guide that participation. A well-organized mechanism for effecting this joint undertaking had not yet evolved, however. It would be a generation before the need for a comprehensive plan of professional-academic counseling to guide would-be teachers enrolled in CSLA courses would become apparent.

The regents went on to insist that "all instructors and courses of a professional nature . . . shall be instructors and courses in the College of Education, which shall assume administrative responsibility in the usual acceptation of the term; that is, for recommending appointments, promotions, and increases in salary, [and] supervision of work."[43] This was easier said than done, however.

Even with the regents' support, the struggle over registration did not end. Though Johnston was certainly accommodating, he was still concerned about the role the College of Education would play and whether it would be capable of assuming its new responsibilities. Making and implementing policy were two very different matters, and Coffman had to argue this issue for nearly three more years before it was satisfactorily resolved. Although in November 1916 Coffman told the general faculty of the College of Education that he and Dean Johnston had "come to the conclusion that every prospective teacher should be required to register in the College of Education,"[44] the issue was not yet settled — at least, not as far as the CSLA faculty was concerned. The CSLA advisory committee recommended in April 1917 that students be given a choice of registering either in CSLA or the College of Education, even though they were seeking the University Teacher's Certificate. Coffman responded to this suggestion in no uncertain terms:

> As far as the law is concerned, the College of Education has complete and independent jurisdiction over all matters pertaining to the training of high school teachers. We wish to do what is best for the university and our students, but we do not assume that it is necessary for the College of Education to submit its policies to the consideration of the Arts College.[45]

No matter how many concessions were made to Coffman and the College, then, there were still those who worried that it might not be able to perform its new role. At the root of this matter was the fact that the policies of George James had "established prejudice" against the College of Education and had "created in the Arts College a general attitude of suspicion and distrust."[46] Although there was "increasing satisfaction and confidence in Coffman's administration," it was still commonly held that "education generally speaking has not commanded universal respect."[47] Coffman found it difficult to disassociate himself from the effects of James's tenure, yet CSLA representatives eventually came to see that it was unfair to judge the present dean by the deeds of the previous one.[48] Coffman's performance spoke for itself.

This brief altercation occurred during an April 2, 1917, meeting of the executive faculty, and Coffman took matters into his own hands. While earlier in the meeting he had shown his willingness to compromise on the matter of registration by allowing two more years to elapse before requiring all candidates for the teacher's certificate to register in the College of Education, the resistance of CSLA faculty led him to suggest just prior to adjournment that if CSLA objected to the registration proposal supported by the College of Education, then it should present its case to the regents. There was no doubt, of course, that the regents would rule in favor of Education.[49]

Another joint meeting was held on April 23, 1917, although Coffman indicated that he thought further discussion of the registration issue would not be profitable. At this meeting, he again made his position clear:

> If we approach the question of registration from the standpoint of the rights of the College of Education, [it] could prepare its own curriculum and . . . require all students who are to receive the University Teacher's Certificate to register in the College of Education. It could do this without consulting the faculty of any other college in the university.

He stepped briefly away from this hard-line position by going on to point out the need for cooperation and assistance from the CSLA faculty.[50]

The registration issue remained unresolved as late as the autumn of 1917. Meanwhile, Coffman and the new president, Marion Burton, had discussed the matter on August 30 and had exchanged a number of letters on the issue during September and October. Coffman wanted the College of Education to receive the recognition it was due as a professional school on a plane with those of law and medicine. To this end, he believed that (1) the dean of the College of Education should have some control over the selection of College faculty, (2) students desiring teachers' certificates should be registered in the College of Education, and (3) the College should receive more liberal financial support. With respect to registration, Coffman wrote to Burton in October:

> In my opinion we should announce to the students of this university in our bulletin this next year [1918] that in 1919, certainly by 1920, all those expecting to receive teachers' certificates from this institution should be registrants in the College of Education."[51]

In September 1917, Coffman had been assured by Burton of his support on the registration issue when the president wrote, "I wish, therefore, to say to you that I am heartily in accord with the resolution as adopted by the regents [concerning registration — June 1917], and want to express to you my purpose and intention to cooperate with you in every possible way for the full realization of the aims set forth in that resolution."[52]

76

Coffman had every intention of holding President Burton to his pledge. After all, everything that Coffman had outlined in his October letter to Burton had been guaranteed to the College of Education by the regents' resolution of June 7, 1916. Coffman was simply asking that this resolution be cemented into University policy. President Burton, Dean Johnston, Dean Thatcher, and Dean Coffman gathered in conference to discuss this issue in December 1917. At this meeting, it was agreed that, beginning in September 1918, notice would be prepared and published announcing that henceforth students preparing to teach were to register in the College of Education. These notices were inserted into the bulletins of the College of Education and CSLA. The College of Agriculture needed some additional prodding on the matter,[53] but for all intents and purposes the registration question had been settled. This final outcome was due in no small measure to Coffman's prestige, diplomacy, and determination.

Coffman's tenure as dean was brief, but during these five years he accomplished more for the College than any of his predecessors. The University was no longer standing in the College's way and was willing to support it wholeheartedly. This was most evident in the registration issue; allowing the College this measure of control proved crucial. Not everything was to proceed smoothly from that point on, however; conflicts still arose over registration and power, and each was dealt with in turn. Melvin Haggerty, who succeeded Coffman to the deanship, found that his years as dean would not be easy ones, despite the groundwork Coffman had laid. Haggerty was nevertheless greatly assisted by the fact that while Coffman had to turn his attention to the entire University, he would still prove a friend to both the new dean and the College he had himself done so much to build.

Five

The Haggerty Years
and the Maturing of the College

WHEN MELVIN HAGGERTY assumed the College of Education deanship in 1920, he was loathe to permit any of Coffman's hard-won victories slip away. In contrast to Coffman's experience on his arrival in 1915, Haggerty must have known that the College was in better shape than ever before, and he meant to see that it grew even stronger and more independent. Furthermore, as Coffman had had Vincent's friendship and support, Haggerty in turn had Coffman's. He was thus free to guard the reputation and rights of the College, and he took every opportunity to fortify its professional autonomy and power. Coffman could no longer focus exclusively on the College's needs — his new duties as University president demanded a wider perspective — but Haggerty could and did. Yet, even while serving as a vigilant guardian of his own office's interests, he nevertheless played a leading role in Coffman's larger plan to see that educational research would be directed toward overall University concerns.

Like Coffman, Haggerty was a man of many interests and capabilities. A.C. Krey, a long-time friend of Haggerty's and a professor of medieval and renaissance history at the University, recalled his strengths in a statement written not long after Haggerty's death in the fall of 1937.[1] Krey's "In Memoriam" is the most adequate and informative summary of the Haggerty story available to us; it attests not only to the warm friendship between the two men but also to the respect which Haggerty rightfully commanded from his colleagues and peers.

Krey began by discussing Haggerty's teaching experience in rural Indiana and moved rapidly to an examination of his graduate studies at Harvard. "In college," Krey wrote, Haggerty's "consum-

78

ing interest was in psychology and philosophy, although history, English, architecture, and science were ever a challenge to him."[2] No one ever accused Haggerty of being intellectually narrow; neither his vision nor his mission was confined to a single emphasis. Although his first teaching experience was in English, he took advantage of the resources available at Harvard to probe "deeply into both philosophy and psychology, stimulated by such scholars as William James, Royce, Palmer, Muensterberg, Yerkes" — under whom Haggerty performed his doctoral research on animal behavior — "and Santayana."[3] Haggerty was especially devoted to the psychological and philosophical thought of his teacher, William James — so much so that he later named his own son William James Haggerty.

Krey went on to discuss Haggerty's professional forte, educational psychology, with a particular focus on testing: "The development of educational measurement under the brilliant leadership of E.L. Thorndike attracted [Haggerty's] attention, and he soon became a leading worker in this field."[4] He was convinced that testing was a valuable educational tool and carried this conviction with him to Minnesota. Prior to his arrival at the University, *Indiana University Studies* published his "Arithmetic: A Cooperative Study in Educational Measurements";[5] a year after assuming the deanship of the College, he contributed to the Virginia Education Commission's publication, *Virginia Public Schools*,[6] as the director of the Division of Tests. By this time, the *Haggerty Intelligence Examination* was already well known and respected. In 1924, he became chair of the University Committee on Educational Research, "under whose auspices the scientific study of instructional and curricular problems as well as educational testing and measurement was applied to college teaching in nearly all parts of the University of Minnesota."[7] Haggerty's grasp of the role measurement could play earned for him a national reputation; as Krey recalled, "It was doubtless because of this interest that he was able to take so large a share in the study of the evaluation of higher institutions of learning in the North Central Association of Colleges. The three volumes on this subject published by the University of Chicago Press mark the climax of his work in measurement."[8]

Haggerty's commitment to and advocacy of testing did not always meet with approval, however. In 1934 the Commission on Social Studies in the Schools, sponsored by the American Historical Association and headed by his friend Krey, attacked testing and measurement in its publication *Conclusions and Recommendations.* In a letter written on September 21, 1934, Haggerty fired back at Krey that "this volume either directly or by innuendo condemns practically every activity in which I have engaged in the last twenty years."[9] He simply could not understand the commission's attitude, having never believed that there was anything anti-intellectual or anti-humanist in working on and using tests. He elaborated on this topic in an article entitled "The Low Visibility of Educational Issues,"[10] published in 1935 — less than a year after the commission's report and only two years before Krey would write his "In Memoriam." In the meantime, Krey may have had a change of heart — or he may have wished to memorialize Haggerty in exclusively glowing terms; at any rate, Krey remembered this disagreement in the following way:

> While [Haggerty's] attack upon the *Conclusions and Recommendations* of the Commission on the Social Studies in the Schools, largely provoked by that Commission's attack upon educational measurement, will long remain a masterpiece of invective in educational discussion, few educators strove more clearly to realize the goal of true educational statesmanship which that very Commission recommended, than he did in his last few years."[11]

Krey's tribute to his friend only partially records the accomplishments of the man who served the College as dean for seventeen years and began his career at Minnesota prior to that as a professor of educational psychology. Today, Haggerty is seen as occupying a central place in the University's history — and this in spite of the fact that he was not the College's first choice when it went looking for a new educational psychology professor. Haggerty may well have known that others had been considered for the post as well, but it seems to have made little difference to him. Letters from Dean Coffman to President Vincent written during the spring of 1915 mention several other possible choices, among them Stephen Colvin, who was then at Brown University, and Guy Whipple of the University of Illinois.[12] The opinions of Charles H. Judd of the University of Chicago and Edward Lee Thorndike were also consulted regarding this decision. At the end of June of that year, Coffman contacted Haggerty, and on the first of July was able to write the following to Vincent:

> I wrote a letter of inquiry yesterday to Professor M.E. Haggerty of Indiana University. You may know that Indiana University has the custom of permitting its men to teach during the summer session with-

out pay but with [the] understanding that an equivalent amount of time can be taken during the college year. It has been reported to me that Professor Haggerty has a year's leave of absence coming to him. If this is correct, and if we are unable to get Whipple, at this time, I think that we can afford to make him a proposition to help us out this year.[13]

Haggerty agreed to Coffman's invitation — and ended up staying for well over a year. It was natural that he would want to establish a reputation for himself in the field of educational psychology, and Minnesota seemed to afford him that opportunity. He was soon respected both on and off campus. By dint of his unquestioned abilities as an educator, combined with the strength of his ego and simple persistence, Haggerty became the man whom Coffman chose as his successor once Coffman assumed the University presidency in 1920. Haggerty had shown himself to be self-assured, assertive, and well-organized. These qualities occasionally exacted a somewhat stiff cost in human relations — Haggerty lacked the subtlety and sense of diplomacy that were among Coffman's strongest points — but the College itself was amply rewarded.

The registration controversy had not been settled by the time Haggerty entered the deanship, but he was quick to involve himself in it. He did not waver for an instant from Coffman's original insistence that future teachers and school administrators be registered in the College of Education. Though most of the needed steps in this direction had already been taken, it still remained for the bulletins of the College of Education, CSLA, and the College of Agriculture, Forestry, and Home Economics to carry the same announcement that all students intending to teach had to register in the College of Education. In a number of letters — most of them written during January 1921 — Haggerty cleared this with Dean Johnston of CSLA and Dean Freeman of Agriculture, Forestry, and Home Economics. By 1922, all teacher candidates were required to register in the College of Education, and all special methods courses were likewise transferred to the College.

Haggerty was not merely satisfied with winning the registration victory, however; he was also determined to see the College stand on a professional par with those of medicine and law. To this end, he was concerned that it be adequately structured internally. For example, he saw it necessary to differentiate the preparation of graduate students who had chosen *research* careers — as, for instance, educational psychologists — from that of those who had chosen *administrative* careers. He felt keenly that this distinction ought to be recognized. Although he himself was pledged to research, he never gave the impression that he looked down upon the type of study that was directed to the improvement of technical skills used by teachers, school principals, or superintendents. In a lengthy letter to Coffman on August 27, 1926, Haggerty asked that master's degree programs designed for those choosing administrative careers be placed under the control of the College of Education.[14] Then Haggerty advanced a radical proposal for reorganizing the College as a whole. He suggested that after a two-year junior college experience (the two years of work in CSLA required for admission to the College of Education), students should enroll in a three-year College of Education program. Haggerty felt that "this would give [the College] the same status as the Law School. In my judgment, this is a statesmanlike procedure in university reorganization and one that ought not to be too long delayed"; he ended this thought by pointing out that "such reorganization should give complete freedom to the faculty of the College of Education . . . for the mapping out of curricula for the training of public school workers of all sorts."[15]

Haggerty went on to pinpoint the types of training the College would undertake:

> The proposed move would . . . allow us to map out three-year curricula based on two years of junior college work for those particular specialities for which there now appears to be a demand. The outstanding . . . curricula would be those for training superintendents, for training principals of high schools, for training supervisors of instruction, and the new curriculum which we have in mind for training teachers in normal schools.[16]

At the end of three years in the College, the student was to receive a Master of Education degree.

It especially annoyed Haggerty that his college did not have the autonomy he felt it deserved. In the same letter to Coffman, he reminded the president that the College's faculty was "required to submit its curriculum for the professional training of public school administrators and teachers to a group of men [faculty of other colleges] who have no experience in this field and have no real interest in it."[17] In Haggerty's mind, the College had been monitored long enough: "With all deference to their scholarship in their own fields, it is clear that [outside faculty] are no more qualified to determine curricula in education than is our faculty to determine curricula in law, medicine, or engineering."[18] What Haggerty was claiming — as Kiehle and Coffman had claimed before him — was nothing less than that pedagogical careers were to be taken seriously. Teacher training was to be treated as a professional endeavor — not merely an offshoot of the University's major efforts.

One might assume that Coffman would have been in complete agreement with Haggerty on this issue, but it was not that simple; Coffman had presidential responsibilities and could not look solely at the College's needs. Dean Ford of the Graduate School was one of many who viewed Haggerty's claims for independence with some disapproval. On November 19, 1926, he wrote to Coffman that he had "read with interest, tinged slightly with irritation, Dean Haggerty's letter of August 27th."[19] The gist of Ford's letter was that he did not believe it necessary to alter the requirements for the master's degree. As far as he could tell, College of Education master's students should be able to satisfy the requirements asked of all University students, and he did not see why it would be advisable to change these demands. In the end, Ford's view prevailed over Haggerty's.

The matter was laid to rest for nearly two years. Late in the spring of 1928, however, Haggerty took up the cause of professionalism again. This time, he chose to concentrate on the issues of library training and preparation in physical education. In a May 23 letter to Coffman, he wrote:

> So long as these instructors are appointed and their appointments and promotions made without any reference to whether or not they are satisfactory to the administration of this college, we shall be without the necessary authority to encourage improvements and changes looking forward to better teaching in these fields."[20]

A recommendation brings this letter to an end:

> It would be a distinct [advantage] if the appointment of all those people in physical education and in library training whose business is fundamentally the training of teachers, should be made only with approval of this office. To carry out this program would be nothing more than the logical evolution of the program for unification of teacher training begun in the University in 1916.[21]

Haggerty's persistence — normally a quality of which Coffman approved — may have distressed the president in this particular instance; at any rate, his reply was sharp. While admitting that the library and physical education departments did indeed train a great many future teachers, Coffman nevertheless insisted that as a matter of policy I am clear as to one thing and that is that the University should not authorize or grant by executive action to the College of Education jurisdiction and control over any of the departments in the College of Arts or over the departments of Physical Education or Library Training. The principles governing the organization and establishment of the College of Education never intended that that type of control would be granted to the dean of the College of Education or to the faculty of the College of Education. The extent to which the College of Education can influence conditions within departments which lie largely outside of it, will depend upon the confidence which the College of Education can establish in such departments and upon its ability to convince these departments of the desirability of such cooperation.[22]

Coffman went on to say: "Each of the departments whose work is offered in a public high school is, I believe, entitled to a representative in the faculty of the College of Education."[23] The letter ends with a stern injunction:

The most disastrous and unfortunate thing the University could do would be to issue some sort of a ukase requiring the various departments whose subjects are taught in the public high schools of the state to submit lists of their appointees to the dean of the College of Education for his approval for appointment or dismissal. I am sure that the success of the College of Education depends upon the confidence and good will it may create and establish rather than upon authority and coercive power which may be granted it.[24]

Coffman was a friend, but he was also in command. Haggerty realized this, and recognized that his argument had been in vain. (The only time when anyone could remember Haggerty as being docile was during his official visits to President Coffman.) An unanswered question, however, remains: Was Haggerty simply looking for greater personal control, or did he sincerely wish to establish a principle of professional autonomy and responsibility for the College? Regardless of the answer, he accepted Coffman's stricture, although it is probable that he did so with a great deal of discontent.

There were other ways of ensuring that the College of Education would present a fine image to the rest of the University, and Haggerty was quick to grasp and utilize them. For one, he began to involve faculty from other colleges in the guidance of undoubtedly superior graduate students in education. This new approach was discussed in a lengthy letter addressed to Coffman on November 28, 1927, a few months after their unhappy exchange concerning the physical education and library study faculties. Haggerty was not really opposed to the idea that other colleges would have some say in his college's policies, but he was determined that Education would lead the way in research. He accomplished this goal in large part by overseeing the preparation of graduate students who would later become the core of an impressive faculty. His correspondence with Coffman shows that Haggerty fought hard on behalf of his faculty and took pride in its accomplishments. He did his best to see that they got research grants and made certain that they were properly paid and rapidly promoted.[25] By involving the faculties of other colleges in Education's activities, Haggerty automatically ensured that they would have a stake in its future faculty. This established a precedent for all-University involvement in the College of Education's research and the preparation of its graduate students. It was a natural result of these efforts that the College would play an important part in such later curriculum developments as Project English and Project Social Studies during the 1960's. In particular, Stanley Kegler, a key figure in research that was basic to Project English, was a student (and later a colleague) of Dora V. Smith, one of Haggerty's first appointments and coauthor with Haggerty of *Reading and Literature*.[26] Likewise William Gardner, one of the principal investigators in Project Social Studies,[27] had as his adviser Edgar Wesley, another of Haggerty's appointees.

Haggerty was determined to answer Coffman's reprimands by raising a generation of educators of whom the entire University community could be proud. This may have been in the back of his mind when he wrote a lengthy letter to Coffman in November 1927 following a conference with the deans of Agriculture, the Graduate School, the Law School, CSLA, and the Institute of Technology. Discussed at this conference, he stated, were "the methods by which the University of Minnesota could provide training for present and prospective college teachers."[28] He proposed further conferences with groups concerned with languages, mathematics, natural sciences, social sciences, and "possibly" English. (His hesitation about English was not due to anything other than "the opinion generally expressed in the conference that English should be made a common subject for the general meetings.")[29] Haggerty suggested to his fellow deans that graduate students be allowed to assume the leadership in this cooperative venture: "In the field of history," for example, the graduate student "would probably take a major in the field of history, a minor in education, and do his thesis on the problems of the college teaching of history."[30]

Haggerty then reminded Coffman that a system resembling this was already in operation within the University. In chemistry, for instance, Victor Noll had done a master's thesis which was "an experimental study of the effectiveness of different methods of teaching in the beginning university classes in chemistry."[31] Chemistry professor M. Cannon Sneed had taken part in this effort, along with Earl Hudelson in education and W.S. Miller in educational psychology. Haggerty cited another case, that of A.W. Hurd, who was doing his research on the teaching of physics. "He is working . . . with Professor Erikson of the Department of Physics and is carrying through some experimental studies in attempting to evaluate the relative value of laboratory versus lecture instruction."[32] W.S. Miller was also working with Hurd and Erikson on this project.

Palmer Johnson was the third case Haggerty referred to in his letter. Haggerty's pride in the promise of this graduate student — who as a faculty member in the College later directed the science education program — was evident as he reviewed Johnson's background for Coffman:

> He is a graduate both of the University of Wisconsin and of the University of Minnesota, having studied here in the field of agriculture. He has had extensive teaching experience, the most recent being head of the Science Department in the Peoria High School, Peoria, Illinois. He came to the University at the beginning of 1925-26 as a graduate assistant in Education, working with Professor Hudelson. Being a teacher of science and well-trained basically in science fields, he became interested in the work of the Sub-Committee of the Committee on Educational Research on the Teaching of Science, and for a year now he has been working under the joint direction of Professor Hudelson and Professor Freeman, studying the curricula in the field of biology, I think with special reference to the problem of prerequisites for advanced courses.[33]

The fourth student to be mentioned in Haggerty's letter was Alvin Eurich. Like the others, he illustrated how wisely Haggerty chose his graduate students. Eurich was to become a scholar of international reputation and in the meantime served as Haggerty's assistant dean. Eurich's training followed the form which Haggerty proposed as the model for all promising graduate students. Like Haggerty, Eurich had chosen a discipline that Edward Lee

Thorndike made famous in this country — educational psychology. Haggerty detailed Eurich's background for Coffman's benefit:

> Mr. Alvin Eurich is a graduate of North Central College and the University of Michigan. He received his master's degree from the University of Maine, working out his thesis with President Little on the scholarship of fraternity and non-fraternity students over a period of fifteen years in the University of Maine. He came to us in the fall of 1925-26 as an assistant in Education. He has served in many capacities as an assistant, has pursued his graduate courses in psychology and educational psychology, and has taught classes in the summer session and will teach again the coming year. He is now teaching undergraduate courses in educational psychology for half time. Under my general direction, he is serving with the committee which is studying the reading problems of college students. This committee is now composed of Dean Thomas, Professor Willey of Sociology [later vice president for academic affairs], Rottschaefer from the School of Law, Miss Brown from Home Economics, Tinker from the Department of Psychology, and Krey from the Department of Social Studies. [Although Krey was officially a member of the Department of History, it is plain that Haggerty thought of him as a colleague in social studies education.] He is working towards his doctor's thesis under the general guidance of this committee.[34]

The paragraph ends with Haggerty's customary spotting of a graduate student's status: "He has passed his preliminary examinations."

There is no reason to doubt that Haggerty hoped to develop a team of staff and students in educational psychology that would give Columbia Teachers College respectable competition while simultaneously doing what Teachers College did not do — that is, leading the way in the study and improvement of the educational problems of the host university. He probably had this goal in mind when he managed to bring Marvin Van Wagenen to the Minnesota faculty. Van Wagenen had apprenticed with Thorndike and had fulfilled his early promise. In later years, he was to be remembered as the man who devised the C-score in the measurement of reading achievement. But Van Wagenen never quite came up to Haggerty's expectations — perhaps in part because of the unfortunate hostility which existed between the two men.

At the end of the war, the College budget supported two positions in educational psychology: Haggerty as professor held one, and Van Wagenen as assistant professor held the other. When Haggerty later hired W.S. Miller as an educational psychology professor — without promoting Van Wagenen — the latter might have felt as if he were being shouldered aside. Years later, in a May 26, 1928, letter to President Coffman, Van Wagenen complained that Dean Haggerty had denied him essential materials for summer instruction, despite the fact that student fees were supposed to be used for such purposes. Haggerty had withheld a hundred dollars' worth of supplies from Van Wagenen, who claimed as a result that Haggerty was directly interfering with his research. He wondered in his letter to Coffman "whether an instructor's life work is to be taken so lightly."[35]

The Coffman-Haggerty correspondence also leaves little doubt that Haggerty and Van Wagenen were not on the best of terms. Earlier, in October 1926, Haggerty had written to Coffman that "an attitude of non-cooperation has persisted through all the years that I have been dean of the college, [Van Wagenen's] relations with this office and with the administration of the work in educational psychology growing more and more remote."[36] In response, Coffman urged Haggerty in an October 19 letter to talk with Van Wagenen: "I think you owe it to Mr. Van Wagenen as well as to yourself to sit down some day and discuss these matters which you have outlined in your letter with great frankness, candor and sincerity."[37] Coffman wrote Van Wagenen on the same day telling him that he was making available some $400 for his research in the field of biology. Haggerty was far from pleased about this; he felt that what Van Wagenen proposed to do was already being done: "Relative to [Van Wagenen's] request for a special subsidy to study the work in Animal Biology," he wrote Coffman, "I would say two things. First, the University already has an agency for this purpose and is now paying the salary of an individual, Mr. Hurd, whose business it is to serve in exactly this capacity."[38] His resentment toward Van Wagenen's independence was painfully clear: "The second thing I desire to say is this: to accede to Mr. Van Wagenen's request . . . will probably have the effect of confirming him in his growing tendency to disregard his administrative relationships."[39]

It had been — and still is — generally assumed that a faculty member of the College could conduct his or her research on a fairly independent basis, and that funds from the graduate school would be made available for this purpose. Haggerty obviously did not think that this was a good idea; he felt that it contributed to strained relations if not to downright insubordination:

> The freedom with which he [Van Wagenen] has received aids from the graduate funds in past years has, without doubt, already tended in that direction [that is, Van Wagenen's apparent lack of cooperation] much to

the lessening of his usefulness in this college. Year by year he has been subsidized more continuously and I think more generously than has any member of the Education Faculty excepting Mr. Koos. Despite that fact and the further fact that his teaching duties have always been light, so light that he has had ample leisure to teach elsewhere during the college year, it is now true that he is less useful and necessary to the work in education than at any time in the past.[40]

In 1926, Haggerty did manage to convince Coffman that Van Wagenen should leave his post at the University. From his summer place in Battle Lake, Minnesota, Coffman wrote Haggerty a letter containing the following statement: "I wired Van Wagenen that I could not agree to increase his rank and salary. This should bring about his resignation."[41] It did not — but neither did Van Wagenen enjoy a good rapport with the University administration for years to come.

Haggerty's goals for the College were somewhat impeded by the fact that he tended to alienate people — Van Wagenen was not the only one — and often mismanaged personal situations. Some people disliked him so intensely that they literally crossed the street to avoid him. Edgar Wesley, one of Haggerty's appointees who later became a national educational leader in his own right, described him as "a remarkable man, rather stubborn, opinionated, conceited, dogmatic, arbitrary, [and] self-sufficient."[42] In one instance, Haggerty's inability — or unwillingness — to cultivate good relations with others sorely affected the College. During World War I, Haggerty took a leave from his teaching to conduct a program of rehabilitation for the army. There he crossed paths with Richard Elliott, who was to become chair of the Department of Psychology in CSLA. Both men had been graduate students at Harvard in psychology and philosophy; while in the army, Elliott grew to dislike Haggerty to such a degree that he nearly refused to come to Minnesota when he learned that Haggerty was there. Their estrangement gravely handicapped the possibility of collegial cooperation between the Department of Educational Psychology in the College of Education and the Department of Psychology.

Despite his ongoing feuds with Elliott and Van Wagenen, among others, Haggerty was not without friends; he could be a warm and sympathetic human being. Even though he was not an easily liked or likable person, he managed to maintain close relations with A.C. Krey and Lotus Coffman for many years. Some of Haggerty's own correspondence reveals a side of him which has not often been seen— witty, humorous, empathetic, and kind. For example, he wrote such a letter to Coffman in the summer of 1937, not long after the University president had suffered a heart attack. Haggerty, too, lived with a heart condition — it would claim his life later that same year. Aware that Coffman, who had been an avid sportsman and an enthusiastic participant in University affairs, would find it most difficult to remain in bed, Haggerty addressed him in a gentle vein:

> Dear Friend:
> Of course we know that a born fisherman like you would suffer mental depression in the absence of a good [strike] but it is surprising to find you calling in doctors and nurses just to make a vacation interesting. And how quick you do things! Here I am who have been playing around with "a tired heart" since late January and all the excitement I have been able to create is the occasional inquiry as to why I don't play golf. It is good second news to hear that you are resting, that you are in competent professional hands and that you have agreed "to take orders" meekly from the head of the family. If your experience is at all like mine you are getting much advice about everything from the simple daily activities to the proper control of your bank account and the maintenance of your moral character. I have gotten reams of advice and admonitions from doctors, from the children, and most constantly from the boss. When Laura runs short she pulls out another volume of the Brittanica and reads up on something new . . . .Incidentally, in an occasional free interval I have learned a few things myself, particularly that my heart is a pretty good organ still if I give it a break. It won't respond as quickly as it used to do but it will keep pumping away and will catch up with my ambition if the eagerness to do things is definitely restrained. It is amazing how many things affect it. I can't eat big meals, walk fast, quarrel with my colleagues, argue with the administration, or resist family direction very far. All these things that have always given me "a big kick" seem definitely out of my pattern if my heart is to have an easy quiet life. Part of the time I feel like a man whose teeth have all been pulled out but most of the time I feel fine.[43]

Haggerty could be affable toward others as well. By chance, a long letter the dean wrote to a campus reporter who had asked him to send her a "dean's statement" testifies to Haggerty's sense of humor:

> Is it not so that your proper title is Miss? At least, your annual appearance in my office is in the guise of a young woman whose request for a photograph and page has all the atmosphere of a feminine imperative. The reproving look which you shot across my desk this morning at my halting admission that the page was not ready would not have been accepted from a masculine gopher. I would have twisted his neck and dropped him from the window on the stone steps below.

What dean knows how to compose a "page"? I, for one, have failed at it six years in succession. I have also read what the other deans have written and have no high opinion of their efforts. I suppose you keep coming back year after year in the hope that some day you will get a picture and a "page" that is worthy of the junior class. Your efforts are hopeless. No dean can really measure up either in appearance or performance to the standard of his juniors. You are both too handsome and too clever.[44]

Haggerty's warmth extended to his students; he tried to become almost a father figure, although his personality made this a bit impracticable. He wanted the College to have a family quality. One of his efforts in this direction resulted in a longstanding tradition which began in 1920: the singing of Christmas carols by faculty and students during the holiday season. As Haggerty told it, "memory is none too accurate in recalling the individuals who came together in those first years. There were the Swifts, the Sears, the Kooses, the Finneys, the Millers, the Storms, the Reeves, and soon many others came, children always."[45] What Haggerty neglected to mention was the fact that many young faculty members were unable to buy train tickets home on their small salaries. The Christmas carol sing helped to alleviate their homesickness:

> The new President and Mrs. Coffman found time to join the group lending, as always, the rare joy of their companionship. When the group seemed too large for a single home we borrowed a key to Shevlin Hall and there about the big fireplace we sang and imagined the flaming Yulelog of olden times. One Christmas morning dawned over a deep blanket of snow and until well past noon the flakes drifted down.[46]

Haggerty described his own role in an almost tongue-in-cheek manner:

> The Dean was janitor for the day. In his old Dodge car he carted a load of wood and a little later the family with apples and nuts to Shevlin Hall. Other families came ploughing through the deep snow; Mrs. Finney marshalled her three boys with violin, cello, and cornet into an orchestra with Mr. Koos at the piano, and about the roaring fireplace we sang once more the songs of Christmas.[47]

Over the years, students and faculty contributed their own favorite holiday songs, and quite a collection ensued. In 1932, the Schmitt Music Company published for the College a book of its favorite carols; by that time, the sing had become a major holiday affair. The College sold copies of its carol book and realized a profit of twenty-seven dollars during the first year. Someone had the idea that the money should be used to start a "student emergency fund," and the first loan went to a student from Lake Minnetonka who had been hitchhiking to the Minneapolis campus every day. He was awarded $6.25 for bus fare.

Personal qualities aside, it cannot be denied that Haggerty made his mark on the College and on the University. He had a fine faculty and staff working for him, and he made it a point to put together the first managerial group ever to administer the College. This was neither a quick nor a simple task; the College was growing in numbers and influence, yet it took seven years for Haggerty to convince the administration that he needed an assistant dean. Harold Benjamin filled that post for four years, after which time he left to become the director of the new Center for Continuation Study. Alvin Eurich then stepped into Benjamin's former position. He did not remain for long, however; the practice of raiding other universities for excellent faculty members (which, of course, had brought Coffman, Haggerty, and many others to the University) was hardly unique to Minnesota, and Eurich was himself persuaded to leave for Northwestern University in Illinois. Haggerty asked Coffman to bid against Northwestern, but Eurich did not stay, and Minnesota lost the man who was later to edit *The Changing Educational World,* a book of essays written to honor the twenty-fifth anniversary of the College.[48] Eurich's career would progress to ever more challenging positions, including the presidency of the State University of New York, until he finally retired from the Ford Foundation's Education Division.

The period of staff expansion which followed World War I witnessed the addition of many notable faculty members and saw a number of curricular innovations. Prior to this time, for example, women had led the way in physical education; in 1922, the first class of women to graduate with this area of study as a major was advised by Gertrude Baker. A year earlier, the College had boasted a new department — Physical Education and Athletics for Men. Up until then, men had been taught athletics but not physical education. English benefited as well: Dora V. Smith of the University High School supervised student teachers and teachers of English from 1917 to 1928. Another promising young University High School staff member, W.S. Miller, served as its principal from 1916 to 1921. These two are ample proof that the high school played an integral part in the College's development, and Haggerty recognized their contributions.

Miller left his principalship in 1921 when Haggerty hired him to teach educational psychology full time. It is clear why Haggerty was so interested in Miller; Miller was equally convinced of the value of testing, and would make the measurement of the cognitive grasp of students his specialty while at the University. By the time he left the College to become acting dean of the Graduate School, his Miller Analogies Test was a nationally recognized screening device. The process of determining student aptitudes and abilities for different programs — and even different colleges — became a hallmark of the Coffman administration, and testing and measurement were major emphases of the College of Education. In 1922, Coffman appointed the University Committee on Educational Guidance and named as its chair his friend Dean Haggerty; after two years, the committee regrouped under the name of the Committee of Seven, which was chaired by W.S. Miller and included various state educators and administrators as members. The committee concentrated primarily on determining what preparations and qualifications were necessary for college entrance, and testing, of course, played a crucial role.

The year 1922 also saw the addition of Leo Brueckner, another advocate of testing, to the College faculty. Brueckner had attained national stature in the area of elementary school arithmetic, but what drew him to Haggerty's attention was his ability to conduct statewide surveys on the topic. Haggerty himself had undertaken a number of similar studies in both reading and arithmetic, and he was especially impressed with Brueckner's professional competence in the area of measurement. Haggerty and his faculty were deeply concerned with and involved in educational research; they not only wanted to keep up with what was being done, but also wanted to stay informed as to what preparations had been made concerning specific studies and under what conditions these studies had been carried out. They believed that this information could help them to improve the achievement of students in general. Before improvement could be made, however, it was essential to know the status quo — and there was no better tool for determining this than testing.

The College faculty reached unusual heights of excellence during Haggerty's tenure as dean — and this in spite of the fact that many of its members left Minnesota to take positions elsewhere. By the 1930's teacher education was recognized nationwide as a professional undertaking and a common university responsibility; it was no longer the exclusive property of eastern universities or scattered colleges. Thus, more educators were involved in this field than ever before — and more institutions were looking for competent and qualified personnel to add to their faculties. Minnesota was not the only university which openly recruited faculty who already held posts elsewhere — nor was its own staff immune to offers from the outside. Eurich's successor at the State University of New York, William Carlson, was a former member of the College of Education who came to Minnesota in 1937 as director of the University High School; in less than a decade he had become director of the Office of Admissions and Records at the University. He then left Minnesota to become president of the University of Delaware and subsequently to preside over the University of Vermont, the State University of New York at Albany, and the University of Toledo. Both James Umstattd and Nelson Bossing came to Minnesota in 1928; both departed for other positions in 1937. Bossing later achieved honors in secondary school curricula, while Umstattd became a national figure in education. Similarly, Harl Douglass left Minnesota to become dean of the College of Education at the University of Colorado at Boulder, and Fred Englehardt of the Department of Educational Administration was appointed president of the University of New Hampshire. The fact that so many faculty members went to other institutions after sometimes lengthy stays at Minnesota appears troubling only if one neglects to consider that the number of people who are sought by other universities and colleges testifies to the quality of one's faculty.

Haggerty fought these losses, and he was often successful. When he discovered that the University of Iowa had made a handsome offer to one of his new appointees, T.R. McConnell, Haggerty immediately wrote the ailing Coffman:

> McConnell is in my judgment one of the most promising men now on our staff and he ranks well up in promise with the best men we have. He is well-trained [and] has had unusual experience in college administration and in university teaching. I should like very much to be able to retain him.[49]

His plea was successful; had it not been, the loss would not have been limited to the College, since McConnell went on to become dean of CSLA. Eventually he departed Minnesota to become chancellor of the University of Buffalo and later accepted an offer from the University of California at Berkeley to chair its Center for the Study of Higher Education. Nevertheless, Haggerty's effort to retain him if only for a while had lasting effects. In the meantime, although these faculty losses were hard to accept, the image of the College was enhanced by its contribution to the country's deans of education. Among these were such notable persons as Ernest Melby at New York University, Ernest Teigs at the University of Southern California, Henry Kroenenberger at the University of Arkansas, and Henry Harmon, who became president of Drake University.

One of Haggerty's appointees stayed on to serve the University throughout the duration of her professional career. Marcia Edwards was an especially fortunate choice on Haggerty's part; there seemed to be nothing she was incapable of doing, and she played many roles during her University service, ranging all the way from secretary to acting dean.

Haggerty had been dean for thirteen years before he named Marcia Edwards as his assistant. She had come to Minnesota from the state of Washington as a graduate in English from the College of Puget Sound. As has been shown, Haggerty had a strong personal interest in English literature in addition to an excellent command of the language, and he found Edwards an able secretary and an even abler graduate student. Although she had not come to Minnesota intending to work as Haggerty's secretary, the Depression made a job in his office seem most attractive. In fact, she had been granted a year's fellowship by the American Association of Collegiate Registrars, and had come to Minnesota in part because the chair of the national award committee, Rodney West, was registrar of the University of Minnesota. Once she had earned her M.A. in educational psychology — under a Carnegie Foundation grant for a study that carried the title "The Accreditation of Colleges on the Basis of the Success of Their Graduates in the Graduate School" — Haggerty convinced her to continue on with doctoral work, and she earned her Ph.D. in 1935.

Meanwhile, E.G. Williamson, who had learned so much from Donald Paterson, taught Edwards enough personnel-guidance philosophy to equip her to offer the University's first course in guidance. In the fall of 1934, she joined the faculty of the College of Education and taught educational psychology as well as guidance. Academically, she suited Haggerty's notions of proper training, and her appointment was much to his credit. One of the most skillful moves he made during his seventeen years as dean was to persuade Edwards to become his assistant and eventually go on to become assistant dean. Haggerty could not have chosen a more suitable companion in his work: Edwards was acquainted with a number of academic areas, including sociology and social philosophy. She had a social conscience as well as a social vision, and she not only championed a program in personnel-guidance psychology but also befriended a number of graduate students and faculty members who needed help. Without her, it is doubtful whether Haggerty would have been able to establish the esprit de corps within the College that he so yearned after. His own personality grated on too many people's nerves; Edwards was a willing and graceful ambassador.

In a college where economics was limited to school finance, Haggerty must have been pleased when Edwards chose to do her master's thesis on the relationship between college enrollment and economic cycles. Her doctoral dissertation on the graduate level of higher education brought her into close contact with Guy Stanton Ford, historian and dean of the Graduate School. Her fellowship with the Carnegie Foundation for the Advancement of Teaching made it possible for her to visit eleven other universities around the country, and she learned a great deal about developments in the teaching of the arts and sciences elsewhere. As a result, no one was better able than she to relate to faculty members outside the College of Education, which Haggerty must have appreciated.

Haggerty was not the only dean, however, to profit from Edwards's expertise and diplomatic skills; Wesley Peik and Walter Cook also found her invaluable. Immediately following Haggerty's death in 1937 — which left the College temporarily without a dean and in earlier days might have signaled the sort of crisis which characterized the beginnings of the College — she prepared the way for Peik, who did not arrive until 1938. When Peik died in 1951, she served as acting dean until Walter Cook took over in 1952. And, when Dean Cook died in 1963 — thirty years after Edwards had been named an instructor in the College — it was President Morrill's wish that she succeed to the deanship. However, thirty years was not long enough for attitudes about women in higher education to change; Edwards believed that it was not yet time for a woman to be dean of the College of Education and was content to serve as acting dean until Robert Keller accepted the deanship in 1964.

Marcia Edwards stands as one of the foremost managerial figures within the College and a testimony to Haggerty's perceptiveness. She has never been one to accept praise, however, and is content even today to describe her role as one which simply "kept the clock ticking."

Throughout Haggerty's deanship, Coffman remained convinced that he had made a wise choice. He needed no reassurance that Haggerty intended to increase the College's strength and influence within the University and nationwide. He realized that if the College prospered, so would the University, and he was grateful for Haggerty's enthusiasm and dedication. Nor did Coffman have to worry that Haggerty would incline the College toward a lopsided emphasis on empirical research alone, most of it in educational psychology. Haggerty's interests and commitments were more diverse than that. For one thing, he was very aware of the sad educational results of the Depression. His *Children of the Depression*[50] preceded the invitation that came from his office on March 5, 1934, to "more than five hundred prominent citizens and officials of Minnesota to attend a 'Citizens Meeting' on behalf of education on March 30 on the University Campus."[51] James Umstattd later recalled the conditions which Haggerty must have known about:

> School revenues in the state had decreased 30% between 1931 and 1934; tax delinquencies had increased to 17%; numerous public schools had been forced to close; important services for pupils had been curtailed in almost all schools, the amount per pupil in Minneapolis had dropped from $93 in 1928 to $78 in 1934; teachers' salaries had dropped to rock bottom, and only one in four of our Minnesota University teacher-education graduates had been able to find jobs during the Depression.[52]

Haggerty himself was no stranger to a bleak environment. The part of rural Indiana in which he had grown up had little to offer either body or soul; in his *Children of the Depression,* he recalled his own impoverished youth. He had a strong desire — which echoed both Kiehle's and Coffman's — to make art available to people in general. He was especially concerned with finding the roots of the folk art which had been replaced by machines. This commitment to art in education and everyday life was to result in Haggerty's last and greatest effort on behalf of the University. In his book, *Enrichment of the Common Life,* which was published posthumously, he wrote:

My father's mother had completed the homemade linen supply with a counterpane fashioned by her own hands from raw flax and wool, dyed and woven into a spread of color. But in my early boyhood I saw the homely art of my parents and grandparents give way to quantity production . . . .I saw the turn-top table my grandfather had fashioned from clear yellow poplar broken into kindling wood and replaced by a badly glued but highly varnished extension table from the store . . . .As these works of the early handicrafts disappeared, I saw the inexplicable whatnot with its load of bric-a-brac come to relieve the tedious monotony of our bare rooms and of our lives, hungry for some touch of beauty.[53]

It is little surprise, then, that Haggerty held Ruth Raymond in such high esteem. Dean Coffman before him had added Raymond to the faculty when the University absorbed the Minneapolis Handicraft Guild.[54] University historian James Gray recalls:

In a day when fundamentalists believed that the three R's were all that a satisfactory teacher need understand, [Ruth Raymond] and Robert S. Hilpert developed a formidable array of courses ranging from Knowledge of Textiles to Art Appreciation. A culminating expression of her missionary spirit was the Owatonna Study, a large cooperative project under the direction of Dean Haggerty, in which university men and women explored every aspect of the impact of art in the life of a typical small community.[55]

Gray implies that the Owatonna Study (also called the Owatonna Art Project) was Raymond's idea; in fact, it is more likely that it was Haggerty's. The dean was more than willing to recognize Raymond's value to the College, however, and once, having learned that Northwestern University had invited her to head its Department of Art Education, immediately wrote to Coffman:

To lose Miss Raymond from the university would be more significant, I think, than the mere loss of a single instructor or department head. This University has few persons on this staff of the rich personal qualities of Miss Raymond. Her influence reaches very much beyond the mere matter of instruction in Art.[56]

The Owatonna Art Project crowned Haggerty's professional career in the sense that it gave him room to explore one of his lifelong and passionate interests. He had long believed that art had a rightful place in every person's life, and he once wrote to Coffman expressing his opposition to "the nineteenth century cleavage between art and life that has done so much to degrade art and to impoverish life itself."[57] If Haggerty had one wish for humanity, it was that its routine life and surrounding environment be touched in some way by art. That is the point of his book *Art, A Way of Life*,[58] the first in a series of volumes on art which included A.C. Krey's *Florence, The City that Art Built.*

Art, A Way of Life describes the Owatonna Art Project, including its funding by the Carnegie Foundation and the Carnegie Corporation. Henry Suzzalo was then president of the Carnegie Foundation for the Advancement of Teaching,[59] and it is not unreasonable to assume that he already knew about Haggerty from Coffman, his one-time graduate student and advisee. Haggerty tells of an address he gave before a convention of the Western Arts Association in which he described the salient features of art as a way of life. Suzzalo was in the audience, and Haggerty took the opportunity later on that day to speak with him: "I recall with great vividness an after-midnight conversation with Henry Suzzalo . . . during which he proposed that the educational implications of this address be tested in a typical American community."[60] The year was 1931; Suzzalo went on to propose that "the College of Education undertake research studies in the field of art education."[61] In 1932, the Carnegie Board of Trustees granted $12,000 (to be supplemented by $20,000 a year later) to the University of Minnesota "for support of researches into the validity of psychological and educational assumptions now prevalent in the field of art education."[62] The project was to develop a novel curriculum in art education for public schools — "this to be the outcome of a study of the art needs and interests of a typical American community of moderate size."[63] Haggerty, in turn, intended that the project seek to "discover and . . . clarify the art interests and the art needs of modern American life, and to fashion the school curriculum so that these needs and interests may be made effective determinants of educational practice."[64]

Haggerty's dreams became reality in September 1933, when the Owatonna Project began. The study made a profound promise to the people of the community: that art could be made available to everyone — in their homes, their public buildings, their dress, and all of the other objects that are designed for human use. Haggerty's conception of art, as it is here expressed, would have pleased John Dewey, among others:

> It does not occur to . . . a person when he selects a good-looking chair in preference to an ugly one, when he arranges the windows in his house to give pleasing lights and shadow in his rooms, or when he plants a vine to thread its way over the rough corners of his garage that he is giving play to impulses to enrich his life which are akin to those that prompt an artist to paint and draw.[65]

It was a view that was impatient of the sharp distinction between "fine" and "applied" art; Haggerty went on to say: "Yet the kinship of these simple and seemingly remote activities to the work of the professional artists is the reality upon which we must build an understanding of any art that is to be vital in education."[66]

Edwin Ziegfeld was one of three people who worked under Haggerty on the project. Looking back at the experience, he was to affirm its practicality. Born in the years of the Depression, the project "was, in a very real sense, Depression-oriented and the emphasis on practicality was almost inevitable at that dismal time in our history."[67] As was to be expected, the Owatonna team had been instructed by Haggerty to assume that art could be thought of as *objective*, not merely as the subjective expression of an individual who could not be expected to communicate many of his or her inner feelings to others. The products of art were assumed to be subject to measurement and grading. Haggerty may well have been moved by the beauties of art, but he was not about to be talked out of his original dedication to testing.

He was not to have his own way entirely, however. According to Ziegfeld, Owatonna was seventy-five miles away from Haggerty's office, which meant that "he could not carry on close supervision and that those of us working on the Project were able to introduce subjective and individualistic undertakings as part of the school program to a degree that Haggerty might not have approved of."[68] It should not be assumed that Haggerty's preference for tests and measurements blinded him to the subjective, however; after all, he himself wrote poetry (some of it extant) and many of his letters obviously could not have been penned by a man whose veins were filled with ice water. Nor did he fail to recognize the outstanding qualities of Ruth Raymond, whose description as a "mystic" was not inappropriate.[69]

A delightful exchange of letters between Coffman and Haggerty reminds us that the belief both men had in educational research did not mean that they were insensitive. Haggerty had visited the new Fine Art Room in Northrop Memorial Auditorium and had sent his "reflections" to Coffman. In the cover letter of February 7, 1936, Haggerty acknowledged that he had written "in a bad temper" because "some activities about the university cut so clearly across the general philosophy of our departmental program in the field of art that I have attempted to express myself more emphatically than you will feel is justified."[70] Haggerty was upset about the mere existence of the Fine Art Room; he felt that it implied a difference in esthetic worth between the type of art which was locked away in museums and the type of art that graced daily life. "Let the university buildings be beautiful," Haggerty suggested. "Let students live in an environment that is not drab and pedestrian. That will have an effect on their lives far greater than a Fine Art Room."[71] A week later, Haggerty had his friend's reply. The president was accustomed to the dean's strong reactions to things that displeased him, and wrote lightheartedly: "I think there may be something to your surmise that you got out of the wrong side of the bed the morning you wrote your reflections on visiting the new fine art room in Northrop Memorial Auditorium."[72] Coffman agreed "that we should create an environment which will be artistic and attractive," but admitted that he and Haggerty had very different opinions on art in general:

I do not believe that all art is associated with utility, just as I think that many researches are carried on without the researcher having any thought or conception of their value or use. I should have pictures and other forms of art about the campus even though I don't understand them, just as I would have a beautiful chapel on the campus even though no one ever worshipped in it, or ever went there for prayers, or to hear the Scriptures read. I would have fine music played on the campus [Coffman eventually succeeded in having the Minneapolis Symphony Orchestra housed in Northrop] and I would reduce the rates, if I had my way, to a point which made it possible for the poorest to attend . . . I would have people live in an environment every feature of which makes some artistic contribution and I really would try to teach students as much as possible about these features, for I believe that appreciation and genuine understanding are closely related.[73]

In other words, Coffman — unlike Haggerty — believed in the distinction between fine art and everyday art; he also believed that fine art should be made available to the people, and it is doubtful that Haggerty disagreed with him on this point. In reality, then, the philosophies of the two men did not differ to any significant degree. Both men recognized the importance of art; both advocated its availability to the public at large. Haggerty may simply have been more vocal in expressing his views, but this should have come as no surprise to Coffman or anyone else who knew the volatile dean.

Many years later, when George Olson wrote his "Department History: Art Education Program,"[74] Haggerty was given credit for holding "a conviction that nothing surpassed the potential of art as a dynamic force for educational development."[75] Olson felt that Haggerty's *Art, A Way of Life* "functions still as a slogan which stirs and unites art educators throughout the country."[76] Haggerty's commitment to art was echoed by others; the art education department flourished under the benign guidance of Ruth Raymond, and Edwin Ziegfeld collaborated in the late 1930's with Ray Faulkner, another faculty member, on a class syllabus that became the basis of their widely used text, *Art Today*.

The dramatic increase in art courses at the University during the 1930's and continuing up until World War II attests to the practical form which Haggerty's influence was able to take even after his death. While there had been only one course in art appreciation in 1934, there were sixteen by 1942. During the same eight-year period, the number of courses in handicrafts doubled. Haggerty also lent his support to music education, although it must be admitted that the visual arts proved the most interesting to him.

It is impossible to adequately detail the career of a man like Melvin Haggerty when one is concerned with presenting a larger picture, that of the College as a whole. His mind has been compared to Joseph's Coat of Many Colors — it seldom focused on one topic for long and was constantly veering off in a number of seemingly disparate directions. Charming one moment, domineering the next, he made both friends and enemies who held equally strong opinions about him. Regardless of the picture one chooses to paint of Haggerty, however, it cannot be contested that the College of Education finally came into its own under his leadership. It acquired a faculty which had never before been seen at Minnesota, and it gained a reputation which could only improve as the years passed.

Six

The Haggerty Faculty

THE DIRECTION in which the College of Education at the University of Minnesota has moved since the 1920's is due in large part to the influence of Melvin Haggerty. Not only did he strongly affect the College during his seventeen years as dean, but he also managed to select a faculty whose members would continue to fulfill his hopes for them long after he himself was gone. Although the outward appearance of an educational institution may be molded by its administrators, its success or failure rests on its faculty. Haggerty chose his appointees astutely. Those who did not measure up to his standards, or who chose to run counter to his expectations or aims, quickly discovered that Minnesota could be a difficult place at which to work. Those who readily acceded to Haggerty's opinions, or who at least did not contradict him to the point where communication became impossible, were amply rewarded — whether they decided to remain at Minnesota or pursue careers elsewhere. Under Haggerty's leadership, Minnesota became a good place to be and to be from. A close look at Haggerty's faculty goes a long way toward explaining how and why the College of Education gained its national reputation.

From the earliest days of the University, each of its colleges was designed with one primary objective: the training of practitioners. The College of Education had a similarly singular mission, but with two focuses: it aimed at preparing and graduating both teachers *and* administrators. Of these twin purposes, the latter was apparently considered to be the more important, judging from the relatively large number of faculty who were appointed in educational administration. There was a further subdivision within these two focuses, however, which sometimes meant that the College's goals seemed more complex than they actually were. For instance, the professional preparation of administrators and superintendents seemed to carry more weight than the preparation of principals, and the education of secondary school teachers was thought to be a more worthwhile pursuit than the education of elementary school teachers. The latter was the case in most colleges of education across the country in Haggerty's day; elementary school teachers were trained not by colleges within universities but by the separate teachers' colleges into which most normal schools had developed during the first half of the twentieth century.[1] Haggerty himself paved the way for the emphasis on secondary school training at Minnesota. Granted, the three R's were not ignored by the College's faculty (at any rate, reading and arithmetic were studied), but they were generally approached via "pure" or unapplied research; that is, the studies had little if anything to do with readying elementary school teachers. In his own surveys of reading and arithmetic, Haggerty observed that student achievement could be divided into different levels, but at no time did he read into his results any indication that professional training programs for teachers should be changed. Again, he and most members of his faculty were primarily concerned with determining the status quo — they wanted to know what students were like. What students *could be* if exposed to different teaching techniques and practices was a subject that fell beyond the realm of Haggerty's concerns. At that point, research was generally confined to measurement and testing and did not extend into prediction or hypothesis.

Haggerty's appointees usually fit his image of the good and capable researcher. Even though it later turned out that Haggerty and Van Wagenen did not get along, Van Wagenen was initially hired because he was a specialist in elementary reading who confined himself to studies of measurement. Leo Brueckner was another faculty member who seemed to fit the mold. He came to the University in 1923 as associate professor of education and director of tests and measurements, and held these positions until 1927, when Haggerty named him professor of elementary education. Brueckner's new job title did not mean that he would have much to do with preparing elementary school staff, however. His publications — including *Scales for the Rating of Teaching Skill* in 1929 and *Diagnostic and Remedial Teaching* in 1931 (which he coauthored with E.O. Melby)[2] — were aimed at an audience which consisted not of young men and women who were studying to be elementary school teachers but of supervisors and principals. Even though the College was concerned with the preparation of elementary school teachers, it had already begun outlining a mission that would make such teacher training secondary and instead emphasize the nurturing of future educational leaders.

The College itself was divided. Its undergraduate program was designed for would-be classroom teachers, while its graduate program was aimed at those who would someday be contributors to educational theory rather than practice. These two aims were not always complementary. For years, the College suffered a bad conscience because so many of the faculty at the University High School were also graduate students who were taking courses, collecting data, and writing their dissertations. To make matters even more complex, students of the high school were being observed by student teachers who were enrolled in the undergraduate program of the College, and these undergraduates were in turn supervised in part by that same high school faculty (who were certainly busy enough without these additional duties). Low salaries and inadequate facilities only compounded the problem. When Haggerty pleaded with Coffman on behalf of the high school's staff, Coffman refused to go along with the dean's request that salaries be increased: "The [instant] this paying higher salaries is done," he wrote to Haggerty in 1931, "its program [that of the University High School] will tend to become formal. Whenever you create the impression that permanency of staff is secure, then the High School will cease to be a place of intellectual ferment."[3] As a result of this attitude, the salaries of University High School staff members would not catch up with those of other faculty in the College for many years.

No other professional college at the University of Minnesota had as many seemingly contradictory responsibilities as Education did. There were compensations, of course; a few of the University High School faculty also held positions within the College, and graduate student teachers at the high school could often go directly to department heads with questions or problems. The lines of communication within the College at least were clear. Many of these graduate students may very well have had the opportunity to consult with such outstanding figures as Edgar Wesley in social studies or Dora V. Smith in English. These two department chairs, along with a powerful roster of industrial arts heads, including

Homer J. Smith, William Michaels, and Howard Nelson, gave the College such leadership that its reputation continued to grow. It was even more enhanced after 1940 by a new generation of University High School department chairs — Emma Birkmaier, a pioneer in curricular and pedagogic innovation in the study of modern foreign languages; Stanley Kegler in English language arts; Clarence Boeck in science (especially chemistry); and Donovan Johnson in mathematics. Many administrative heads of the University High School, including W.S. Miller, William Carlson, G. Lester Anderson, and Robert Keller, went on to become deans of collegiate units or university presidents.

The dual focus of the College meant that it had to balance what might have ended up being two opposing forces: research and teacher preparation. In addition, Haggerty and his faculty had to keep in mind that indefinable concept known as "service." After all, the University was (and still is) a state institution, which meant that its responsibilities extended beyond the bounds of the campus itself. Which would prove more useful to the community — research or teacher preparation? Which would provide the most obvious benefits to the College and the state educational system as a whole? Over the years, research has been the dominant emphasis — in the meantime, however, teachers have received excellent preparation, and College graduates have made their mark as teachers as well as administrators and theorists. The fact that the College has succeeded in maintaining a balance between these two goals may be credited to the early example set by Haggerty's remarkable faculty.

One practice begun during Haggerty's day which has consistently contributed to the College's growth and success has been the institutionalization of research. In brief, this has meant that graduate students have been able to share in the research of senior faculty. This "apprenticeship program," carried on in a collegial manner, has formed a common bond of cooperation in research between senior and junior investigators, one which has also influenced the undergraduate classes and introduced them to the spirit of inquiry. Thus, undergraduates as well as graduates have benefited from the College's concentration on research — and this has held true regardless of whether they were planning to go on to teaching positions or were aiming instead at continuing with graduate studies.

Ernest O. Melby, Brueckner's collaborator on *Diagnostic and*

Remedial Teaching, serves as a good example of the College's tradition of training its graduate students in such a way that they could work together with senior faculty on research projects. Melby received his master's degree in 1926, and Haggerty saw such promise in him that he immediately appointed Melby an instructor. Not long afterward, Haggerty named him assistant director of the Bureau of Educational Research. All of this happened within a span of two years, between 1926 and 1928 — and all of it happened while Melby was still a graduate student. When he later went on to assume the deanship of the School of Education at Northwestern University, Melby's graduate training was recognized as having been in the best Minnesota style.

In the years between the two world wars (which roughly marked the extent of Haggerty's tenure at Minnesota), educational research primarily concentrated on secondary and higher education. Equal status for elementary education would have to wait for the attention of such a leader as Wesley E. Peik, Haggerty's successor. A cursory glance at Leo Brueckner's work may seem to refute this claim — he did, after all, write about the elementary school-age youngster — but a closer look bears it out. Rather than focusing on elementary education, Brueckner instead pursued a theme that often recurs during the College's history: the attention to individual differences. Brueckner was especially concerned with handicapped youngsters, and they were frequent subjects of his long career in educational research. Two publications which reflected his interests were his *Adapting Instruction in Arithmetic to Individual Differences* and *Diagnosis and Treatment of Learning Difficulties*.[4] On the latter book, he collaborated with Guy Bond, who was to become Minnesota's foremost student of learning and the teaching of reading. These two titles, along with many others which could be listed here, fail to do justice to the fact that Brueckner's research was a blend of the practical and the theoretical; it centered on real problems whose results could be transferred to populations of real students. One of his first positions was with the newly created Research Bureau of the Minneapolis Public Schools;[5] it was arranged that Brueckner would allot half of his time to the bureau and the other half to his appointment in the College. He continued in this dual role for five years, and it allowed him to develop a lifelong habit of thinking in terms of the learning difficulties of the average student.

A brief examination of a few of Brueckner's books reveals the

107

range of contributions which Haggerty's faculty made to educational theory. *Scales for the Rating of Teaching Skill*, published in 1929, distills an idea which was accepted by many American educators of the early twentieth century — namely, that any skill, whether it be as simple as typing or as complex as teaching, could be measured and often scored in terms of a scale of numbers or letters. In his book, Brueckner looked for a measure which would take into account both the types of students being taught and the methods being used to teach them.[6] The scales he arrived at were aimed at helping administrators to "secure a reliable rate of teaching ability" by measuring the skill with which a teacher used a given method that he or she deemed appropriate to a given situation. What was important about Brueckner's study was that he gave weight to the *teacher's* assessment of what was appropriate, thus showing an appreciation for professional competence that was not always demonstrated by others who did research in similar fields.

Diagnostic and Remedial Teaching, published two years later, reflected more of Brueckner's innovative thinking. It was common practice at the time for teachers to treat an entire class as though all the students had equal capabilities — an approach which Brueckner rejected outright. In itself, his departure from the norm was not extraordinary. Rather, its significance lay in the fact that it reinforced a fledgling Minnesota tradition: that of noting and heeding students' individual differences. The practice of paying scientific attention to these differences would become the hallmark of the College of Education. Later, when Walter Cook advocated the principle of teaching the individual child rather than the group, he would stand on the solid ground of precedent. Nor was it simply a happy accident that Guy Bond pursued in elementary school reading what Brueckner had begun in arithmetic; the individual student was fast becoming a prominent focus of Minnesota's approach to education. Eventually, Bond and Brueckner would collaborate on *The Diagnosis and Treatment of Learning Difficulties*, published in 1955, the year in which Brueckner retired. Fourteen years earlier, in 1941, Brueckner's *Adapting Instruction in Arithmetic to Individual Differences* symbolized what was about to happen. Elementary education would become vital and would champion the ideal that education should be adapted to individual differences. Brueckner's national reputation gave credence to his ideas, and his professional visibility aided in promoting them. In 1936, for example, he was invited to become director of a study on elementary education in the state of New York entitled *The Changing Elementary School.*[7]

Marvin Van Wagenen was another important contributor to measurement based on the study of elementary school children. He had been a student of Thorndike and was much influenced by him.[8] No one on the College faculty was able to match Van Wagenen's statistical competence during the early years of his Minnesota appointment. Reviews of his Unit Scales of Attainment with their use of C-scores, a way of pinpointing a child's achievement in reading, uniformly praise his technical skill in constructing items for the Minnesota Pre-School Test.[9] One of Van Wagenen's major interests was the discovery of a reading measurement scale that would be capable of determining students' reading levels at the beginning of the school year and again at its end. This objective was to form the basis for his *Statewide Testing Program Study,* which occupied much of his time from 1933 to 1940. Unfortunately, Van Wagenen and Haggerty were soon at odds and this undoubtedly impeded what Van Wagenen was able to do at Minnesota. Had circumstances been different, the College may have had an early national reputation for the measurement of reading achievement and the prediction of a child's competence in reading. This would have to wait for Guy Bond's arrival, however.

Looking back on his Minnesota years, Bond wrote that "the main questions . . . that most concerned me all centered around the children who get into learning difficulties in spite of the best efforts of school systems."[10] Bond centered his activities on four major questions: (1) How can we educate children in the necessary basic skills without limiting their potential creativity? (2) What causes very capable children to have trouble in learning to read? (3) How can we correct reading and other educational disabilities so that children can realize their full educational potential? and, finally, (4) What can we do to adapt instruction to overcome the devastating personal effects of children who have reading problems? Bond was not satisfied with merely asking questions — he did his best to answer them, or at least to make inroads. In response to the first, he gave thirty years of his career to the preparation of students and graduate students so that their curiosity about this matter would also be aroused; it became the leading theme of his book *Teaching the Child to Read.*[11] In answer to the second question, he sponsored some sixty Ph.D. dissertations and 1,200 colloquium studies centered on this topic. His own research in the area is best typified by *The Auditory and Speech Characteristics of Poor Readers*,[12] which served as his Ph.D. thesis. He pursued the solution to the third question by starting the Psychoeducational Clinic and eventually publishing the famous *Reading Difficulties: Their Diagnosis and Correction*.[13] Originally coauthored with Minnesota psychologist Miles Tinker, this book remained a vital part of the professional literature in the field; a fourth edition was prepared as late as 1978. In addressing the fourth question, Bond wrote *Adapting Instruction to Individual Differences in Reading*.[14] In a way, this final title summarizes all that Bond stood for during his continuous quest to modify the instruction of reading to each child rather than teaching children as though they made up a faceless, nameless group.

It cannot be said that Bond was Van Wagenen's successor, even though this may appear to be so at first glance; the two men were simply too different and their assumptions too disparate. Those who succeeded Bond, on the other hand, tended to pursue studies which were variations on Bond's original themes. Van Wagenen's theories, though significant, were apparently not explored further, although the reason for this is not known. In the 1940's, for example, Bond and other prominent scholars of elementary school reading stressed sight reading; Van Wagenen, on the other hand, held to linguistics. His strong background in Latin, German, and English grammar led him to believe that the elementary teacher ought to depend on linguistics rather than on the sight reading of words in a "controlled vocabulary." Nor was Van Wagenen willing to compromise; his staunch adherence to his own ideals was reflected in his *Primary Reading Scales*, published in 1953, the year of his retirement.

Van Wagenen's audience was so limited that he had to publish his own materials; it became impossible for him to find a commercial publisher. Nonetheless, his probing was fundamental and in the best tradition of testing and measurement. His ideas may not have endured, but some of his tests have. For example, Buros's *Tests in Print II* of the Minnesota Pre-School Scale, which Van Wagenen helped to design (in collaboration with the well-known psychologists Florence Goodenough and Katherine Maurer), was still in use well into the 1970's.[15] It is regrettable that little else of Van Wagenen's work has been deemed important enough to continue during subsequent years; his conflicts with Haggerty and the University administration had worse effects than even he might have been able to imagine. His ideas were not really that far removed from College concerns of the time; he, too, focused on individual differences and was one of the first to suggest that gifted students were being grossly neglected. It is interesting to speculate about what he might have been able to do for Minnesota and for education in general had not unhappy relations with his peers played such a prominent role in his career.

Meanwhile, the College was growing, and its growth made for such bureaucratic complications that Haggerty finally decided that he needed an assistant dean. Harold Benjamin was appointed and remained in that position from 1932 to 1936 (he later went on to become dean of the College of Education at the University of Maryland). This growth also made it possible for more College staff to do research on pedagogical subjects. The possibilities inherent in the increased emphasis on research were obvious to President Coffman, who in 1931 suggested that a subcommittee of the University Committee on Educational Research initiate a study of the examinations being used throughout the University. Palmer Johnson and A.C. Krey were immediately involved, Krey with the social sciences and Johnson with the natural sciences. Two years later, they coauthored *Differential Functions of Examinations*.[16] Similarly, a modified version of Dora V. Smith's doctoral dissertation was published in 1931 under the title *Class Size in High School English: Methods and Results*.[17] This particular piece of research typified the College's methods during these years: it was a large survey, and its objective was to report the results of prevailing practice. Smith's research was timely and of such quality that when the U.S. Office of Education undertook a national survey of secondary education in the early 1930's, with Leonard Koos as associate director, Koos asked Smith to lead the survey of instruction in English. She did so immediately after the publication of *Class Size*, and the bulletin that resulted bore the simple title *Instruction in English*.[18]

Although the onset of the Depression resulted in radically lowered budgets, the College did not suffer from a lack of curricular innovation. The financing of E.G. Williamson's statewide testing of high school students was a sample of Coffman's willingness to invest in his confidence that Williamson, a student of Donald Paterson, would be able to help select the kinds of students who would be most apt to profit from a university education. In addition, such a statewide testing bureau could also help to determine where students should be placed within the University. If all students could not be expected to succeed in CSLA, for instance, alternative experience might be just the thing for them; this sort of thinking served as Paterson's rationale for what became the educational vision of General College, which opened in 1932.

Attention to University testing was also an integral part of the wish to utilize tests and measures for the improvement of educational technology. This was the foundation on which Dora V. Smith built her career. Except for a year in England during 1920-21, she had been supervisor of student teachers and a teacher of English at the University High School since 1917. Though she was not a test-and-measurements person per se, this did not mean that Haggerty deemed her unworthy of his attention; she had, after all, undertaken a type of research he admired. In 1927-28, the three volumes of their collaborative work, *Reading and Literature*, was published by the World Book Company.[19] Haggerty keenly wanted young people to read — and not just in "readers." Despite her association with literature, it would not be fair to claim that Smith followed a career apart from research. Unlike Leo Brueckner, she never chaired the board of directors of the National Society for the Study of Education, but she was elected president of the National Conference on Research in the Teaching of English and was also a member of the American Educational Research Association, in which Kenneth Anderson, Palmer Johnson, and other members of the College faculty became prominent. Like Brueckner, Smith took part in the New York State inquiry into elementary education and published *Evaluating Instruction in Secondary School English* [20] as a result. Haggerty recommended that she be appointed in 1928 as an assistant professor in the Department of General Education (which he chaired as dean of the College). Immediately after her appointment she spent a year at Teachers College, Columbia.

Smith returned to Minnesota to begin a stunning career. From 1929 until her retirement in 1958, she directed the training of English teachers and the College's program in elementary school language arts. She also directed graduate students and contributed to research in the teaching of English, earning the coveted W. Wilber Hatfield Award of the National Council of Teachers of English. There were many good reasons why she attained this recognition. For one, she had served as director of the organization's

Commission on the English Curriculum, which would eventually publish a five-volume study of the English curriculum from kindergarten through college.[21] Communications in general, along with dramatics and speech, flourished at the University in no small part because of Dora V. Smith's boundless energy. Hers was a cosmopolitan career, unrestricted by national or ethnocentric frontiers; she visited many parts of the world and carried her knowledge of children's and adolescent literature to any number of countries.[22] It was also a focused and effective career, however. One of her most notable contributions to the College and the University was Book Week, originally conceived by her and begun under her direction in 1941 with the theme "Book Institute for Parents and Teachers." The opening of Coffman Memorial Union made space available for a large public dinner, a part of the program that has continued until the present day. The dinner program features as guest speakers noted illustrators, authors, or others who have made recognized contributions to the field of young people's literature. Among those who have spoken at past dinners are Maud Hart Lovelace, Carol Brink, Walter Havighurst, Robert McCloskey, John Ciardi, Natalie Babbitt, Jean George, and Gerald McDermott. In addition, an annual review of children's books, *New Books for Young Readers,* is compiled and published by the College and sent to all schools in Minnesota. The intent of the book program, which is always sponsored by the College of Education, is to provide a forum for discussion among the several organizations and agencies whose goal it is to encourage young people to read.[23]

Many of Smith's colleagues exhibited equal professional stature. One in particular deserves mention: Edgar Wesley, the head of social studies education. Wesley, like Smith, was at the University High School but had an appointment in the College of Education. He arrived in Minneapolis during the summer of 1930 as an assistant professor. Prior to that time, he had worked under A.C. Krey's direction, compiling tests for the Commission of Social Studies of the American Historical Association.[24] Wesley and Krey had met at a conference of the Mississippi Valley Historical Association, and Krey had invited Wesley to Minnesota at that time.[25] This was Wesley's first experience in the construction of tests and resulted in his "Wesley Tests on Political Terms."[26] While Wesley, like Dora V. Smith, cannot be considered a test-and-measurements person in the Haggerty-Brueckner-Van Wagenen mold, his desire to see student competence measured objectively was in the

Minnesota tradition. Krey recommended him to Haggerty, and Haggerty in turn invited Wesley to join the College faculty. Wesley directed social studies education at the University High School until 1948, when he officially moved to Burton Hall and turned the leadership of social studies at the high school over to Edith West.

Twenty-one years of teaching and research followed, years that were "on the whole a very happy, busy, industrious period."[27] For many of those years, Wesley remained a close intellectual companion of A.C. Krey. "Krey was remarkable in being a historian of Florence," Wesley recalls, "of medieval life, [and] even. . .American history."[28] His respect for Krey never waned. Once, when Wesley was participating in a doctoral examination for Horace T. Morse, a student of both Krey and Wesley who would later become dean of Minnesota's General College, "they had to ask me whether Morse was majoring in history or education." Wesley admits that he "imitated Krey in that I got the University to establish the Ph.D. major in the social sciences and bestowed that degree on five or six persons." The "imitation" of which Wesley speaks was in reference to a unique multidisciplinary doctoral program which Krey had established and which was designed to prepare social studies teachers in such a way that they would be knowledgeable about more than one or two of the social sciences. Thus, he constructed a demanding curriculum for his students, and managed to convince two key historians — Krey and Theodore Blegen, dean of the Graduate School — to support the degree. Participants in the program were required to take a major in one of the social sciences, supporting programs in two other social sciences, and a minor in education. When Wesley left the University in 1951, the administration of this program was farmed out to *six* different faculty members.[29] Wesley's own comment on this arrangement is typical of him. As he wrote George D. Heiss, his biographer,

> The idea of dividing my work among six people instead of getting a successor is an example of administrative stupidity hard to match; the wonderful freedom and help that I had enabled me to build the best single place in the U.S. for the training of experts in the social studies. This whole structure was with blindness and possibly a touch of malice allowed to disintegrate fast.[30]

The breadth of study Wesley urged in his students seems natural when one considers that his own undergraduate major at Baldwin-Wallace College (from which he graduated in 1914) was in modern languages, with minors distributed among English, history, and political science. While his most solid academic background would prove to be in history, he veered toward English literature during the early stages of his career. He began his commitment to teaching by conducting English classes at Jackson Academy in St. Louis from 1917 to 1922, and a summer of graduate study in English at the University of Wisconsin was followed by another year of teaching English, this time at Maplewood, Missouri, from 1922 to 1923. During that year, Wesley went on with his graduate study in English at Washington University and wrote a master's thesis on the narrative poetry of the seventeenth century.

While at Washington University, Wesley met Thomas Maitland Marshall, and this was a turning point in his career. He moved easily from English to history and, under Marshall's guidance, wrote a second master's thesis, "The Fur Trade of the Southwest." By the outbreak of the Depression, Wesley was ready for his doctoral examination, and he was awarded the Ph.D. shortly after the stock market began its disastrous fall. His dissertation, "Guarding the Frontier: A Study of Frontier Defense, 1815-1825," was published by the University of Minnesota Press in 1935, when Wesley was a member of the faculty of the Minnesota College of Education. In the meantime, he had taught at high schools in Ohio and Kentucky and enrolled in Greek and philosophy at Yale graduate school, emphasizing the history of ideas. Wesley was not a test-and-measurements person; his perspective on education had a humanistic background, and his social conscience and sensitivity to social issues were important elements both of his personality and of his teaching.

Wesley had joined the College faculty during December of 1930. During the winter quarter, early in 1931, he visited other University classes, talked with his colleagues, and prepared to learn for himself what social studies education was all about in Minnesota schools. He spent the spring quarter driving around Minnesota and visiting dozens of schools — at University expense. Haggerty felt that a "survey" of the firing line — that is, the Minnesota public schools— could only benefit the College, and Wesley seemed to be just the person to carry it out. These informal surveys, conducted in a casual, friendly, and sociable manner, were the natural complements of the formal survey reports in which Haggerty and so many others had such confidence. Wesley taught his first University class during the 1931 summer session;

115

by that time, as he himself admits, he "probably knew more about Minnesota than most of the faculty."[31] He acknowledged the generous role Haggerty played in his preparation: "Few deans would have invested so much in a new faculty member."[32] In fact, Wesley's statewide visits were very much in line with Haggerty's own empirical philosophy; in addition, Haggerty recognized early what a boon someone like Wesley could be to the College and, true to form, was willing to support him in whatever way he could.

Interestingly, Wesley had a mind of his own — which he made very clear to Haggerty at the outset of their relationship — and yet managed to avoid the personality conflicts with the dean that victimized so many others. Haggerty was not about to be bullied, but he did respect those who confronted him directly and spoke their minds; Wesley was one of the few who won the dean's admiration almost immediately. He recalls: "When I had my first interview with [Haggerty] I (not he) listed and suggested what I proposed to do . . . . [Haggerty] gave a little startled jerk as he took my notation but so quickly entered into and commented upon my proposals that I saw at once I had won his approval and I never lost it."[33]

When Wesley recommended that the University attempt to influence education in Minnesota by regularly meeting with state educators and administrators, Haggerty forwarded his recommendation to President Coffman. Coffman, however, did not agree, and replied: "I am of the opinion that [the University's] prestige in the long run, resides in the quality of its intellectual effort rather than in the personal contacts which an official member of its staff may make with the schools of the state."[34] Coffman also maintained that the University's impact upon state schools would be strong enough if the faculty's publications were of high quality. Regardless of Coffman's feelings on the matter, however, Wesley maintained his contacts throughout the state — and simultaneously won national leadership in social studies education because of his publications.

Wesley may have felt that Coffman was a bit narrow minded. After all, the president had refused to encourage University faculty visits to other schools and had also been adamant about not raising University High School staff salaries. About the latter, Wesley probably felt that it was unjust — and he believed that one should not take injustice lying down. He was one with George Counts in holding that schools were responsible for helping to reconstruct the social order. In this sense, Wesley belonged to that other College tradition of the "social gospel." The idea that the schools reflect society struck him as "so much monkey chatter"; instead, he was convinced that "schools make society; they are not mere echoes and reflections, consequences and effects."[35] This attitude was nothing new for Wesley; one of his first publications, a joint venture in 1925 with Grove Dow, was entitled *Social Problems of Today.*[36]

Like numerous others before him at Minnesota, Wesley was a visionary, and his vision served as the foundation of his writings. His methods books, published in several editions, were widely used; while the sheer number of his texts is a sign of the appeal they had for social studies teachers, he was noted as much for being a trailblazer as for being a popular writer.[37] *Teaching Social Studies in Elementary Schools*, published in 1946, was the first book ever written on the topic.[38] Many social studies educators saw Wesley as making two major contributions to the field: he built a social studies education organization, and he helped to bridge the gap between academicians and educators.[39] It was during his presidency of the National Council for the Social Studies that the organization ceased being merely a "poor relation" of the American Historical Association and began holding its own national conventions.[40]

Surprisingly, Wesley's desire to see social studies education become something more than an appendage of the study of history did not mean that he was defensive in the presence of historians. On the contrary, he fostered cooperation between educators of several different persuasions. His own warm relationship with A.C. Krey serves as only one example of Wesley's belief that education need not be separated into a number of warring factions. As Heiss states, "possibly the most outstanding example of Wesley's role as an activist in bringing about cooperation between academicians and educators was his relationship with the Committee on American History in Schools and Colleges, which was the joint creation of the American Historical Association, the Mississippi Valley Historical Association, and the National Council for the Social Studies."[41] According to Heiss, it was Wesley "who repeatedly urged [the committee's] creation, helped secure its formation, acted as its director, and wrote much of its Report."[42]

Wesley's influence and excellence as a teacher is reflected in the fact that so many of his own graduate students went on to become educational leaders in their own right. Edith West, who succeeded Wesley at the University High School, rose to genuine prominence and remembers other social studies teachers at the high school who became presidents of the national social studies council, such as Dorothy McClure and Edwin Carr. Others went on to become professors of social studies, like Ellen Modisett, who joined the staff of San Francisco State College. Stanley Wronski, one of Wesley's finest students, was another who made a reputation for himself and coauthored with Wesley the widely used *Teaching Secondary Social Studies in a World Society.* Wilbur Murra went on to a distinguished career after a long period as a student and then an associate of Wesley's; in fact, he had been a student in Wesley's first course at Minnesota in the summer of 1931.

When he first arrived at the University, the Depression was near its lowest point. American society was grievously troubled, and Wesley knew it. By nature he was an activist and an outspoken advocate — as no one who has read his history of the National Education Association would doubt.[43] Even Haggerty with his ire fully aroused could not match Wesley at the peak of his anger; among those who most often felt its force were educators who believed that the chief responsibility of the high school was to prepare students for college. Other ideas which Wesley saw as impractical or foolish were not immune; his vision was often tantamount to sighting down a gun barrel.

Nevertheless, no one could presume to label Wesley a romantic optimist. He did not take issue with the surging tide of empirical research in the College, and he supported a number of causes that were sometimes at variance with one another. Even in the face of conflict, he maintained his professional integrity, and he went on to win a place for himself among the foremost ranks of American educators. It is much to Haggerty's credit that, although (in Wesley's words) "stubborn, conceited, opinionated, dogmatic, [and] arbitrary," the dean accrued for the College a faculty that included such persons as Wesley, Dora V. Smith, and others — some of whom were equal to Haggerty and some of whom surpassed him. Whatever else might be said or written of him, Haggerty was not a petty man; his vision extended beyond his own interests to encompass the College of Education as a whole and ideas far beyond its boundaries.

Seven

Vision and Research:
The College
Becomes a Community of Values

BEGINNING with Coffman's deanship and continuing on through Haggerty's, the College came into its own as an educational unit within the University. In 1938, when Wesley Peik was named dean, it was no longer necessary for the College to fight for survival; deans and faculty members alike no longer had to expend precious energy on simply justifying their existence. Now that the College was a strong and viable entity, it could turn its attention to more important matters. What direction would it take? What would its responsibilities be? What would determine its priorities? What role would it play — not only within the University, but within the community, the state, and the nation? As these and other questions had faced Haggerty and his faculty, they now faced their successors, and they were not easy questions to answer. This is not to say that nobody was willing to hazard an answer; rather, it was difficult to find a single solution to any problem, especially when such diverse individuals as those within the College were all eager to offer their own opinions.

Almost everybody was willing to agree that the College could not be an island and that it had responsibilities which extended beyond its own immediate bounds. Perhaps Edgar Wesley said it best: "The idea that education could and should contribute to social progress is as old as the institution of teaching."[1] While no one was going to argue with the idea behind this statement, a fair number of both educators and administrators were willing to contest its precise meaning. What exactly constituted "progress"? On whose terms?

It is doubtful that questions like these have been — or ever will be — resolved to everybody's satisfaction. The point that it is necessary to make here is that they were asked with increasing frequency during Peik's deanship and by increasing numbers of people within the College. In general, the College consisted of men and women who were liberal-minded and concerned with society at large. Thus, they had a common ground, but this ground was divided into opposing camps. The College had become a "community of values"; while most of its members voiced similar viewpoints, their vocabularies and methodologies differed radically from time to time. While some, in the tradition established earlier by such men as Kiehle, held to a *vision*, others, following in Coffman's and Haggerty's footsteps, advocated a *scientific* approach to education. For want of a more appropriate metaphor, this community of values which existed within the College at that time can be described as a *spectrum*, with such visionaries as Theodore Brameld at one end, empiricists like Palmer Johnson at the other, and men like Nelson Bossing and Harl Douglass toward the center. What held these educators and others like them together was their common concern for society and the individual. The Depression and the war years had made it clear that all was not right with America and, by extension, with its educational system. What could be done? Which was the best approach to solving the very evident problems which existed at the time — the visionary or the scientific? Wesley Peik, a deceptively unassuming man, would oversee during his tenure at the University a time in which these approaches could begin to meet via a common "bridge" which Bossing and Douglass built between those like Brameld and Palmer Johnson. For the first time in the history of the College, visionaries and scientists would learn to work together. Before we can begin to understand how this took place, however, we must first look closely at the scholars who figured so importantly during this period.

Theodore Brameld's eight-year stay at the University as a professor of the philosophy of education from 1939 to 1947 was often tumultuous. No one could ever say of him that he was in the least bit hesitant to express his own opinions. His beliefs were so forward-looking, however, that they raised the suspicion and ire of those who were not quite as eager as he to credit the future with as much importance as the present. Brameld summed up many of these beliefs in his 1945 publication *Design for America*,[2] a controversial book which reported on the findings of an equally controversial educational venture, the Floodwood Project.

Undertaken in Floodwood, Minnesota, during 1944, the project was provocative in a way that the Owatonna Art Project had not been. While the Owatonna Project had embodied Haggerty's beliefs that art could be significant to the "common people" — that it was "practical" as well as "pure," and that it formed an "integral part of the whole of democratic evolution"[3] — the Floodwood Project caused a furor because it looked beyond the present into a much less comfortable future. It presumed to ask high school students to formulate a "blueprint for society." Both the Owatonna and Floodwood projects aimed at progress through education as a principal mode of change; the essential differences between them were the meanings ascribed to the word "progress" and the types of research which were employed to facilitate it. While Haggerty was content to measure *what society was* in the hope of exposing weaknesses in the system, Brameld was eager to suggest *what society could be* with the help of properly attuned schools. For Brameld, those who defended the status quo in society, especially the "lords of the press" — as George Seldes had labeled (or libeled) them[4] — were, in effect, propagandists. Therefore, anyone who had a rational commitment to democracy had a right, if not a duty, to use counterpropaganda — that is, to be *partial* in defense of democracy.[5] This belief of Brameld's was termed "defensible partiality."[6] In 1950, he wrote out his reasoning on the issue,[7] condemning the sort of propaganda which was not open to challenge, along with the type of teaching which did not invite critique:

> What we learn is defensible simply insofar as the ends we support and the means we utilize are able to stand up against exposure to open, unrestricted criticism and comparison. What we learn is partial insofar as these ends and means still remain definite and positive to their majority advocates after the defense occurs.[8]

Brameld took Wesley's social conscience one step further into what became known as his theory of reconstructionism. In essence, this theory posed that public education had a twofold responsibility: to be aware of the findings of the behavioral sciences, and to use these findings to dramatically alter society. He looked hard at public education and saw that it was not all good. He was not alone in his beliefs — Mary Ann Raywid's *The Axe-Grinders*[9] describes a number of books and organized groups which were harshly critical of the day's public education — yet he nevertheless became a target of many groups who were particularly sensitive to what they perceived as his "left-wing" tendencies.

The Floodwood Project provided such persons with a focal point, but Brameld's other activities, including his teaching at the College, were not immune to criticism.

Brameld's outspokenness put the College in an awkward position. Although it was by that time firmly established, the College was still very much concerned with projecting a good public image. But while Haggerty undoubtedly would have been firm with Brameld, his successor, Wesley Peik, was seemingly mild and accommodating. He supported Brameld in most of his controversial ventures, and Brameld never forgot this fact. Peik recognized the value of Brameld's vision and was willing to let it run its course. As a result, the College came under fire from a number of persons and groups who saw Brameld's views as inappropriate if not dangerous.

A cursory glance at the times provides some clues as to why Brameld met with such difficulties. World War II had aroused considerable anxiety in America about anything foreign, especially anything which looked even remotely like communism. The Floodwood Project asked students to contrast fascism with democracy. Brameld and those who were friendly to his position (including Wesley) were advocates of democracy; to them, fascism represented racism, thought control, and general repression. They were not chauvinists, however, and believed that even the best system merited occasional close scrutiny. Thus, they posed questions like this one to their students: "Do fascist attitudes and practices exist within as well as without America?" This was hardly a popular question to ask during that era, when Americans were infused with a sense of patriotism and righteousness. The sort of self-examination which Brameld proposed was admittedly justified, but it was ill timed. In addition, Brameld stood with John Dewey in thinking of the world — and, as a corollary, America — as a system of interdependent nations and states which had to work together in order to avoid depressions and wars.[10] Americans had just come through a major war; not many of them wanted to look beyond their own immediate needs, much less plan for the future.

The Floodwood Project began simply. Dean Peik allocated a modest sum of $600 for the project's expenses, and, in Brameld's own words:

> One morning . . . fifty boys and girls, members of the junior and senior classes in a small, fairly typical rural community school at Floodwood, Minnesota, met for discussion with the superintendent of schools, the

English teacher, the social studies teacher, and a visiting member of
the University of Minnesota faculty. The students were asked whether
they would enjoy embarking upon an educational adventure. Instead
of studying literature of the past, the institutions and practices of yes-
terday and today, why not turn to the future for a change? Why not try
to answer the question, "What kind of society do we as young citizens
want to build for tomorrow?"[11]

The program continued for over three months, during which time
the students and their teachers met for two hours each day, five
days a week.

Brameld encouraged his young students to think of a *reconstructed* future[12] — not one that would be more of the same, and
not one that would promote the status quo, but one that would
truly be a "brave new world." The Floodwood Project may have
been the first example of educational futurism. Perhaps because it
was so innovative, or perhaps because Brameld's timing was off, it
was not well received by all members of this small Minnesota
community. As Craig Kridel states:

> During the war years, several new and returning businessmen moved
> into the area, an influx which created a division, and subsequent fight
> for school board power. Growing criticism of the High School's
> general education program ("too much general and not enough educa-
> tion") and charges of subversive activity as a result of Brameld's cur-
> riculum project, led this new and vocal business-interest group to form
> the Committee for Better Education.[13]

This quarrel was not provincial in nature; many innovative school
programs came under attack during this time.[14] Brameld did, however, serve as a sort of lightning rod. For example, such prominent
philosophers of education as John Childs of Teachers College, Columbia, and Boyd Bode at Ohio State University felt that Brameld's "defensible partiality" involved indoctrination of values.[15]
Both men could be considered as existing within the orbit of John
Dewey's thought; they were "experimentalists," not "reconstructionists." And, although no one spelled it out precisely, experimentalism made a good intellectual fit with the honor paid
empirical research at the University's College of Education. Few
of Brameld's colleagues had any idea as to what could have
spurred him toward reconstructionism; they had forgotten the
challenge of George Counts's *Dare the Schools Build a New Social Order?* along with the vigorous reaction to the Depression, a
reaction which had embodied a new look at what social con-

science should mean. Childs himself had been a social reconstructionist,[16] yet he was critical of Brameld, whose own thought had developed along a continuum that never lost touch with social reconstructionism. In fact, Brameld had a predecessor at Minnesota, but nobody there bothered to look backward to discover him; earlier, educational sociologist Ross Finney had voiced a similar kind of reformist outlook.[17]

Brameld's views should have come as no surprise to his colleagues at Minnesota; the direction he was taking was clear long before his hiring in 1939. In 1931, for example, when Brueckner and Melby published their *Diagnostic and Remedial Teaching*, Brameld was at the University of Chicago finishing up "A Philosophical Approach to Communism." While he did not advocate Marxist-Leninist thought, he was radically disturbed by the social ills of a country which could be stricken by a drastic economic depression. Later in his career, such distorted articles as "Putting Over Communism at Floodwood, Minnesota"[18] (which referred angrily to the "un-American" ideas contained in Brameld's curriculum) would be triggered by what some saw as his communist leanings. This incipient fear of anything "Red" grew later, of course, into the McCarthyism of the 1950's; Brameld was perhaps fortunate in having proposed his Floodwood project a decade earlier, when it was not quite so perilous to do so. At any rate, the "communist" label was never applicable to him; instead, he was a man of social conscience and vision. He demonstrated his commitment to improving society by such diverse acts as joining the picket lines of striking St. Paul teachers in November 1946[19] and making continuous efforts on behalf of workers' education.[20] His ties with the American Federation of Teachers, adult education, and workers' education culminated in the Conference on Workers' Education held in Washington, D.C., September 28 and 29, 1945, sponsored by the Department of Labor.[21] At that conference, he spoke as chair of the Adult Education Committee of the American Federation of Teachers (AFT). He had an equally long-lived interest in the education of minority groups[22] and worked closely with Jewish community groups who were concerned with the lives of minorities. "This," he later recalled, "led me into anthropology and human relations activism."[23]

Although Brameld has spent the majority of his life as a politically involved activist,[24] his years at Minnesota focused largely on academic issues. A philosopher first and foremost, he intended his philosophizing to serve the reconstruction of society. A good place to begin with this project, he felt, was with the academic curriculum. With this end in mind, he proposed an experiment in the social studies: a three-hour course which would be shared by six professors — Wesley and Brameld from the College of Education, Millard S. Everett from philosophy, Elio D. Monachesi from sociology, Henry Villard from economics (then a part of the School of Business Administration), and either Asher N. Christensen or Evron Kirkpatrick from political science. In a long letter of January 26, 1940, to CSLA Dean John Tate, Brameld described the initial impetus for the experiment:

> [It] came from a desire on the part of the Dean of the College of Education [Wesley Peik] as well as others in the college to prepare our education students somewhat more adequately in appreciating the major issues of contemporary society — the assumption being that teachers are in the last analysis servants of democracy who can perform their functions adequately only as they realize that teaching is not a mere self-sufficient occupation, but is intimately related to the conflicts and purposes of the social order.[25]

It should be recalled that Edgar Wesley had earlier expressed an interest in instilling within future social studies teachers a lively and informed concern for social problems; this in many ways paralleled Brameld's educational philosophy, although Wesley cannot be labeled a reconstructionist. In fact, the course Brameld proposed to Tate was similar in thrust to Wesley's joint Ph.D. in the social sciences. The two men may well have had complementary viewpoints; they were not similarly received by the public, however. While Wesley was highly respected as an educator, Brameld was often criticized as a communist. He writes, for example, of being "attacked by a red-baiter state senator who tried to get me fired (but President Guy Stanton Ford and the strong AFT local in St. Paul came to my support and the bill was defeated."[26]

A particularly vehement written accusation was leveled at Brameld less than a year after he joined the faculty. The letter observed that "the Political Science department is full of Socialists, which is bad enough; but the College of Education ... is composed of rabid revolutionists. And the worst of them all, the one who is admired by all other College of Education instructors, is Professor Brameld."[27] The writer went on to suggest that Brameld held to a utopian design for America:

Brameld says that there are two ways of getting this "Utopian" form of government; one method is violent revolution; the other is to teach and indoctrinate the Americans, particularly the children with the dogmas of Communism so that some day we can have a "peaceful revolution".... Brameld himself preaches Communism. The textbooks used in his courses are written by Communists.[28]

The letter had been written by a man whose sister was taking a course from Brameld; she "didn't keep her lecture notes," but was ready to produce a witness who did should it be necessary. It was not necessary. Again, Peik stood firm in his defense of Brameld, and Brameld himself wrote University president Ford to explain what the course in fact entailed. The accusation was not pursued.

Peik was not entirely in favor of Brameld's teaching methods, however, and occasionally said so. In one such instance, Peik wrote a number of "reactions" to Brameld's paper "Educational Philosophy: Its Need and Function in the Training of Teachers" indicating his disagreement with Brameld's point of view. In short, Peik felt that Brameld had underemphasized "systematic study or research" and was concerned that the means Brameld proposed to use to reach socially desirable ends were not informed by a study of psychology:

> These must be known to the philosopher through thorough study of psychology, particularly social psychology, just as the psychologist must also be concerned with values and objectives originating in the culture. As you know, I do believe in the great importance of a philosophy of education in its best sense, and as a thorough-going discipline for the functional educationist. I do deplore the deprecating remarks of many philosophers on the place of the modern evaluation and measurement movement, just as I deplore a similar attitude on the part of some educationists or psychologists toward the contribution of philosophy. The two must not be separated; they must be emphasized together. They must be thoroughly studied as foundations.[29]

Brameld admired Peik's stance, but he was not convinced that it would ever reach fruition at Minnesota. With that in mind, he decided to accept an offer from New York University. A year earlier, he had written Peik that "the rather peripheral position of educational philosophy here as compared with the central position it is expected to occupy at New York University continues to disturb me."[30] For some time, Brameld had been pressing for "a *requirement* in the [social and philosophical] foundations of education."[31] He did not see this request as anything out of the ordinary; in another letter to Peik written early during the fall quarter of 1944, Brameld cited evidence that in "nine leading institutions" there often was such a requirement "on both the undergraduate and graduate levels...and that *all* of [these institutions] have a requirement on one level or the other."[32] Two years later, a three-credit course entitled School and the Social Order (retitled School and Society in 1953) was indeed introduced as a requirement for graduation from the College, but by this time Brameld had left Minnesota for New York, where his reputation would continue to grow and the criticism leveled at him would lessen.

During his relatively brief and often controversial stay at Minnesota, Brameld managed to leave his mark, and two men — Miles E. Cary and Robert Beck — were appointed to take up his former responsibilities in the history and philosophy of education. In the meantime, Brameld had disturbed the collective conscience of many College faculty.

It should not be assumed, however, that no one but Brameld felt this way. He was not the first College faculty member to speak out for progress and change, nor would he be the last; he simply had an extraordinarily high profile. Again, most members of the College's community of values had similar viewpoints even though they expressed them in different ways. The College's social conscience had not merely been in the keeping of a few philosophers; the Depression had aroused more faculty members than Wesley and Brameld. In 1933, Haggerty himself had written *Children of the Depression* from his position in educational psychology. In that book, he called upon educators to organize nationally and to fight for the improvement of social conditions in America; after all, "chambers of commerce, taxpayers leagues, economy commissions, and municipal leagues are organized upon a national basis, and there is every evidence that they enjoy adequate financial sinews of war."[33] Like many others (who in later years would be apt to be labeled Communists), Haggerty saw that the country's enemies were its own rich and well-born. Recalling that President Woodrow Wilson had made a distinction between the deceptive German leadership and misled German people, toward whom he held no animosity, Haggerty pointed out that

> leadership in certain quarters [in America] is driving hard against an adequate support of education, and now, as then, we need to distinguish between the demands of great masses of citizens for relief and those of powerful leaders who would find economic betterment through curtailment of school support.[34]

In 1934, Walter Cook, who would one day succeed Wesley Peik to the deanship of the College of Education, sounded the same note. The Illinois Teachers College newspaper for February 20 of that year carried an article by Cook whose subhead read: "Tax Slashing Balks Education." The article opened with a strongly worded pair of sentences: "It takes time, energy, and intelligence to understand the causes of a depression, to modernize an out-of-date, unfair, and graft-ridden tax system, to remodel ox-cart forms of local government, and to remedy bad banking practice. But any member of a Taxpayers Association or Citizen's Committee can help slash school budgets."[35] Cook went on to tell his readers that "over one-fourth of the teachers, principals, and supervisors in the United States are receiving a yearly salary of less than $750 in 1933-34. This amount is below the minimum annual wage provided for factory hands under the Blanket Code of the National Industry Recovery Act."[36] He ended the article with an even more devastating statistic: "One teacher in ten is receiving a yearly salary of less than $50."[37]

A liberal social philosophy has colored policy in the dean's office of the College of Education almost since its inception. For example, although documentation is lacking to verify this opinion, there is every reason to think that George James's experiences in the area of university extension, combined with his study of education in Europe, made him a firm believer in a democratic and liberal philosophy of education. Similarly, Coffman held to a liberal position even though he met with strong opposition at times. Not only did he resist allegations that the faculty was infiltrated by Communists, but his own *President's Report* of 1934-36 voices concerns similar to those expressed by Haggerty in his *Children of the Depression*.[38] The report opens with a section entitled "Unsolved Problems of Youth" and is followed by another labeled "Exploitation of Youth." In the latter section, Coffman points out that such exploitation is being countered by study and by social programs recommended by organizations like the American Youth Commission of the American Council on Education (to which Coffman himself belonged).[39] A strong supporter of democracy, Coffman told the regents that he opposed loyalty oaths and considered them to be components of that evil domain of "restrictive pressures that hamper education." Early in his Minnesota career, Coffman took his stand with "a large and growing body of liberal-minded men and women who want the truth and who are willing to be guided by it."[40]

128

A habit of scientific inquiry inclines one to liberalism, although it does not, of course, guarantee that one will be a liberal. It is not unlikely that precisely this habit was what led Wesley Peik to advise Brameld to honor the picket lines of the striking St. Paul teachers. Nor did Peik discourage Van Wagenen and Brameld from walking with them in support of the strikes.[41] Ironically, the commitment of University personnel to their communities sometimes runs counter to the communities' desires; it cannot be assumed that St. Paul citizens were overjoyed to discover Van Wagenen and Brameld marching along with their striking teachers.

The same liberal conscience led Peik to support another controversial faculty member, John Rockwell. Long before it became popular for academics to devote time and energy to minorities, Rockwell recognized the educational predicament of the American Indian.[42] He has left little trace in the annals of the College; it is a matter of record, however, that Haggerty hired him as an assistant professor of educational psychology in 1923. Rockwell was then thirty-one years old and held a doctorate from the University of Chicago; in addition, he had experience as superintendent of education in Nebraska. After eleven years in the College, Rockwell resigned and later became Minnesota's state commissioner of education. His tenure in that post ended abruptly when he was discharged in 1941.[43] On the surface, it may seem as if the College was not involved in this particular incident. In a sense it was not, except for the fact that Rockwell had achieved the post as commissioner partly due to Peik's efforts on his behalf. The fact that Rockwell had left the University eight years earlier reinforces the belief that Peik actively supported him.

Peik's feelings for Rockwell in spite of the latter's unpopularity were made evident at other times as well. In writing to Chancellor Deane W. Malott of the University of Kansas in early 1941, Peik acknowledged Rockwell's "liberal social views" and informed Malott that Rockwell's specialties were "the psychology of learning, the psychology of individual differences and the education of the gifted, subnormal and other atypical types."[44] Peik went on to praise Rockwell: "He has done the best job of Indian education in our nation according to Washington authorities."[45] In this instance, Rockwell had managed to combine a scientific concern for individual differences with a social conscience aimed at bettering the conditions of a minority group. His research had not been faulty either. As Peik wrote,

129

in all these areas, Dr. Rockwell is a thorough-going scholar and research worker . . . . On educational problems he is thoroughly scientific. On social, economic and civic problems he is quite far to the left, yet not as extreme as many. I am writing thus frankly about a man who has blundered politically and therefore can probably not return to the University of Minnesota for his own good, but who is too great a mind and too great a scholar to be the victim of such circumstances as politics bring about an office of the Commissioner of Education when it becomes a football between conservatives and liberals.[46]

It is to the College's credit during this period that liberalism and vision could coexist with scientific inquiry and empiricism without tearing the fabric of the community apart. This fact attests to the common goal which served as the College's underpinnings — social concern. Again, while each faculty member may well have felt differently about how this concern should be voiced and acted upon, these differences were more superficial than fundamental. During the years following the Depression, a reconstructionist philosophy of education anchored one end of the philosophic continuum that held the College in tension between scientific research and social vision. What kept the tension from becoming too great was mutual respect. Brameld, for instance, held experimentalism in high esteem while, apparently without exception, the scientific wing of the faculty exhibited liberal sympathies. This meant that a reconstructionist like Brameld could plead for defensible partiality without fear of reprisal; likewise, experimentalists could ask reconstructionists to restrain themselves if only slightly by conducting scientific inquiries. There were no confrontations between those holding such polar positions. This surprising and fortunate set of circumstances was due in large part to the unconscious achievements of two men, Harl Douglass and Nelson Bossing. The former set an example by gently reminding the researchers of their limited vision, and the latter coordinated reconstructionism with a secondary school curriculum that was both novel and suggestive of scientific research that could be done on adolescent needs.

It was a happy accident that Douglass and Bossing respectively spent enough time at Minnesota to serve as effective ideological mediators. Even more fortunate was the sequence of their appointments. Douglass came to the College first, joining the faculty in 1929, just prior to the Depression. He left in 1938, on the eve of World War II. In the year of his resignation, Bossing joined the faculty, and remained until his retirement in 1961. In the meantime, the College became more cosmopolitan and less provincial.

With the passing years, an ever larger number of faculty members studied overseas and had foreign students in their Minnesota classrooms. It became impossible to view the College's program as insular; it was time to break out of the confines of the "provincial predicament" and become aware of the world beyond the College's walls.

One development which led to this maturation was presaged by the publication in 1933 of an essay by Harl Douglass expressing the need for the integration of educational science and philosophy. In "Does the Future of Secondary Education Depend upon Statistical Research in Foundational Thinking?" Douglass expressed a simple and straightforward message.[47] In brief, he claimed that educational science and philosophy had to inform one another — mutual respect and a laissez-faire attitude were no longer sufficient. He himself spoke from the scientific stance; his 1927 doctoral dissertation, "Experimental Study of Two Plans of Supervised Study," was a classic example of the early design of paired comparison. Douglass earned his doctorate at the age of thirty-five and had enough practical experience to make him credible as an authority on secondary school supervision. Thus, he was just the person to urge that the social and cultural qualities of democracy be introduced into and utilized within the American secondary school. And the more he reflected on the possibilities for participatory democracy in classrooms, schools, and school systems, the more he realized that it was necessary to contrast his vision with the status quo not only in American education but also European, which had been presumed to be "the best education for the best." In the end, he posed a two-part challenge to the College and to education in general. Technology and communications were bringing nations closer together, and provincialism was no longer acceptable. It was time for the American educational system to take democratic principles and ideals seriously.

By the time Nelson Bossing came to Minnesota in 1938 — as Harl Douglass left to take up an administrative career that eventually led to the deanship of the College of Education at the University of Colorado — Douglass had also prepared the College to take the reconstruction of the secondary school curriculum seriously. He did so by daring his students to think of teaching and the supervision of teaching in a reconstructed curriculum as enhancing the maturity of high school students. Bossing slipped easily into the role Douglass had vacated and moved on to specify how a reconstructed secondary school curriculum should be designed. His plan became known as the "core curriculum" and was the model Brameld used in Floodwood. Bossing and Brameld worked closely together; it might appropriately be said that each was partial to democracy.

Minnesota's acquisition of Bossing was a combination of luck and sheer stubbornness on Peik's part. None of Bossing's publications during his fourteen years at the University of Oregon had particularly impressed President Coffman despite Peik's suggestion that Bossing be given a permanent appointment in the College. When Peik submitted a list of names to Coffman for the president's consideration during the summer of 1938, Coffman replied, "After reading the material you left with me, I wish we might delay making a permanent appointment until we have had time to canvass the situation further. Not a single one of the names on your list quite measures up. Can't we temporize, find a substitute, and look a little further? We may come back, of course, to someone on your list."[48] About Bossing in particular, Coffman wrote that he "seems to be a well-meaning person of ordinary ability, of agreeable habits and likable disposition, but who, as far as I can tell, has achieved very little so far."[49]

The new dean held fast, however, and proved in the long run to be correct; Bossing's views on secondary education earned him a name that became known nationwide. His "Core and Common Learning Program" proved especially significant.[50] To put this program into perspective, it is necessary to compare it with other curricular designs which evolved during the 1920's. At this time, the idea of a *core* curriculum was not being investigated at the University of Minnesota, whose faculty were more interested in testing and measuring educational outcomes. A curriculum as such was viewed as nothing more than a program of studies. Gradually, however, the concept grew and evolved until it came to be viewed as including *all* school-directed activities; in short, everything that was seen as promoting the maturity and development of students. Under prodding from the Herbartians, even the staunchest subject-matter specialists began to try new arrangements in their classrooms to enrich their students' learning experiences. The most obvious approach entailed the teaming of natural allies, or complementary subject areas, such as geography and history or literature and history. A bit more radical were the innovations that much later became known as "strategies for teaching and learning." These included "projects" in which subject matter was submerged in activities and "problems" whose solutions required the use of skills and knowledge that were not locked up in any one subject area. In addition, there were entire units that held more than one problem within their boundaries. As Wesley explained it, "the core curriculum was an attempt to organize several subjects into a single sequence of units. The concepts of common learnings, popularized by an Educational Policies Commission report in 1944, was an arrangement by which two or more teachers cooperated to teach a double-period class the elements of several subjects."[51]

Bossing added to this approach the idea that educators should do their best to determine the interests of adolescents and incorporate their findings into their teaching — in other words, that teachers should gear their instruction to the needs of their students. When this idea was combined with Brameld's insistence that the school be perceived as playing a significant and lasting role in society and culture, the Minnesota view of curriculum was born. It was not a unique view, of course; John Dewey's little book *School and Society* had earlier laid the foundation for the Brameld-Bossing philosophy of curriculum. But Minnesota went further than Dewey or that chief architect of the Project Method, William H. Kilpatrick of Teachers College, Columbia, because it drew on *research* into child growth and development, adolescent growth and development, and the school's potential for guiding the adolescent.

Due to the work of Bossing and Douglass, then, the *vision* of a democratic social order which could also embrace individualization was made secure. All that was needed was a reconstruction of the scientific, or *empirical*, mode of looking at education. This was not to prove an easy task, however; the old ways of testing and measurement had quite rightly gained a good reputation, and there were those who saw no reason to change techniques that worked. The idea that experimentation could be just as valuable as surveys was a novel one, and only someone who had had experience and qualifications in the classic research models could persuade such a person as Haggerty to give it a try. Fortunately, Haggerty himself had seen to the training of the man who was to effect this reconstruction in research — Palmer O. Johnson. Haggerty placed his confidence in Johnson and was willing to go along with his plans to recast educational teaching and research using statistical analysis. Johnson's career, which spanned thirty-four years, left an impression on educational research at Minnesota that remains unmatched today.

Haggerty recommended the appointment of Palmer O. Johnson in 1926, two years before Johnson was awarded his doctorate for a dissertation entitled "An Evaluation of the Courses in Elementary Botany as Projected into Sequent Courses in the College of Agriculture and Forestry."[52] The year of his appointment, 1928, witnessed several events that would help to establish Johnson as a leader in the field of educational research. *The Journal of Educational Research* published his "A Comparison of the Lecture-Demonstration, Group, and Individual Methods of Laboratory Experimentation in High School Biology," and Johnson was appointed director of the Land-Grant College Survey for Minnesota.[53] When Johnson later wrote his memoirs of a half-century of service at the University, he began by commenting on what it had meant to be the executive director of that survey, whose "chief purpose was to portray and appraise the land-grant college type of education."[54] The results of the survey were published in 1934.[55]

The vision of a land-grant philosophy — a vision that reached back to the democratic social philosophy that had moved David Kiehle during the early days of the College and the University — was a motivating factor for Palmer Johnson. Due to his efforts on behalf of the Land-Grant College Survey, this vision was finally wedded to empiricism. In this way, a further bridge was built between the College's philosophical past and its scientific present. Johnson's early immersion in empirical studies, as shown by his involvement in such classic types of studies as surveys, comparisons of effectiveness in teaching, and evaluation, legitimated him in the eyes of men like Haggerty. What gave his professional future a unique quality, however, was his exposure and commitment to agriculture, botany, and biology. As his colleagues knew, Palmer Johnson "began his professional career in science teaching and . . . maintained his interest in this area all through his life."[56] His scientific way of looking at and thinking about agricultural production was still another trait which brought him closer in spirit to the College's founders, especially Kiehle.

Johnson chose to combine his undergraduate majors — science and agriculture — with a career in education. His first teaching experience was in Dassel, Minnesota (a community not unlike Floodwood), where he taught agriculture, biology, and chemistry from 1914 to 1916. For the next decade, he taught science exclusively and spent five years as a biology teacher at the senior high school in Quincy, Illinois. Twenty years later, Johnson aided the College's efforts to break away from provincialism by spending the year 1934-35 at the Galton Laboratory in England, where he studied the logic of experimentation. Subsequently, he was able to teach the College of Education that standard American procedures for the scientific study of education were not exclusively those worth learning.

During this crucial year in England, Johnson was associated with Sir Ronald A. Fisher, for whom he developed a great deal of respect. His enthusiasm is reflected in his own recollections:

> Professor Fisher's work at the Rothamsted Experimental Station in Harpenden, England, revolutionized the science of statistics and the technique of biological experimentation. He attracted a constant flow of workers from all over the world to learn to apply the new methods to problems in their particular fields of research. On October 1, 1933 Professor Fisher left Harpenden to take up new duties as Galton Professor of the University of London. I considered myself indeed fortunate when in October 1934 I was admitted as a volunteer worker at the Galton Laboratory. The period of 1934-35 was the most interesting I had ever spent. There were about ten or twelve other volunteer workers from different parts of the world in addition to English students, among whom were Mather, Stevens, Irwin, Welch, Jackson, and Cochran. Their zeal burned bright. J. Neyman and Egon Pearson also attended the lecture-seminar by Fisher on "The Logic of Experimentation." Another course of Fisher's was "The Genetics of Quantitative Characters." In addition to these courses, the laboratory work given over largely to the design, execution, and interpretation of quantitative research was most stimulating . . . . I should add that I profited greatly from two advanced courses in statistics given by Professor Egon Pearson and the course in the "Advanced Theory of Probability and Statistical Inference" by Professor J. Neyman. These courses ran throughout the year. The meetings of the Royal Statistical Society were especially attractive. I heard, for example, Professor Fisher give his classic paper on "The Logic of Inductive Inference" and Professor Neyman on "Statistical Problems in Agricultural Experimentation." There was also the thrill of meeting here such dignitaries as Professor Karl Pearson, Professors Bowley, Isserles, Greenwood, Yule, and others.[57]

When Johnson returned from London in the fall of 1935, Haggerty asked him to prepare an outline for a course in modern statistical methods. The resulting year-long course became famous, and Johnson referred to it in an essay he prepared for the fiftieth anniversary of the College in 1956: "From the start, it was my purpose to present a course, unencumbered by obsolete materials, keeping pace with the dynamic development of statistics as a science and particularly designed for the practitioner who needed statistics in his work."[58] From the beginning, Johnson intended that the courses he taught — and the department in which he taught — were to consist of *applied* scientific principles; once again, his own background in science education kept him from yearning for the misleading respectability of "pure science." To him, a science which could not be utilized in day-to-day practice was as useless as a vision which could not be realized. A devotion to theory was well and good, but Johnson had to be convinced that the theory was feasible and useful. Thus, as he wrote of his own course, "while an attempt was made to build a strong theoretical foundation, special emphasis was laid on the statistical craftsmanship needed to put theory into application."[59]

Palmer Johnson was very much at home in the theoretical foundation of statistics. In 1936 — the same year he began teaching his course in modern statistical methods — he published a landmark paper, "Tests of Certain Linear Hypotheses and Their Applications to Some Educational Problems" along with statistician J. Neyman.[60] This paper reported a new statistical concept and technique which soon became known as the Johnson-Neyman technique.[61] In addition, when Johnson could not find a text for teaching purposes which satisfied him, he wrote his own, and his *Statistical Methods in Research* became well known. He also continued to add courses to his list of offerings; for example, his course in statistical methodology was soon supplemented by instruction in experimental design. This course was not commonly taught in the United States then, and it attracted students not only in education but from other parts of the University as well. Many psychology students could find the carefully designed research-oriented courses they needed in the area commanded by Johnson. They and others were fond of repeating his favorite judgment against ill-designed statistical studies: "Cremate the data!" It is likely, in fact, that Johnson may well have wished the Floodwood data gathered by Brameld to be cremated; he had not helped in its collection, and he was annoyed when he found his name among the acknowledgments at the beginning of *Design for America*. Throughout Johnson's career, there would be a certain degree of tension between his scientific philosophy of education and the reconstructionism advocated by so many others. The conflict between vision and research, between philosophy and empiricism, would not be resolved during his lifetime; again, it is to the College's credit that this ideological disagreement proved to be a motivating rather than destructive factor.

Johnson was not satisfied merely with conducting classroom work and research. He also introduced to the University the idea of the statistical laboratory. This laboratory — which eventually, under Douglas Anderson, introduced students of the 1970's to the use of computers — was only one of the legacies Johnson left behind when he died suddenly and unexpectedly in 1960. Another was the group of dedicated and brilliant graduate students who had benefited from Johnson's tutelage and would continue to spread his influence both within the University of Minnesota and across the country. One in particular, Cyril Hoyt, was among a group of twelve graduate students who took Johnson's first year-long course in statistical methodology offered in 1936. Later, Hoyt would serve as director of the Bureau of Educational Research. He progressed rapidly from student to colleague[62] and wrote his own classic paper, "Test Reliability Obtained by Analysis of Variance."[63]

Graduate students have always been attracted to such scholars as Palmer Johnson, but ideally their professional preparation has extended beyond research and coursework alone. Minnesota has consistently offered its students opportunities for learning and for gaining experience outside the classroom. Such places as the University High School or the Bureau of Educational Research — and its all-University twin for many years, the Bureau of Institutional Research — have provided priceless training in a number of areas. Johnson's immediate successor, Raymond O. Collier, is a case in point. Collier came to Minnesota to study with Johnson but first went to work for Hoyt in the Bureau of Educational Research. When Collier thought back on those years, he sensed that the most important part of the professional maturation Hoyt encouraged was the informal interaction with other graduate student employees of the bureau.[64] Hoyt did not allow his graduate student employees to learn only as apprentices or as participants in informal discussion; instead, he worked patiently and carefully with each student, always calling attention to the practical. Discussion was, however, an important element of Hoyt's teaching. Collier recalled talks with Clayton Stunkard, who became a professor at the University of Maryland; with Cletus Cummiskey, now at Mankato State University; with Roland Buchman, later statistical director for the Forestry Research Service of the U.S. Department of Agriculture; and with Mildred Kosaki, who became a key figure in the organized educational research of the University of Hawaii. Hoyt supported any number of graduate students, not only psychologically but also financially.

The Bureau of Educational Research helped many faculty members with investigation that called for sophisticated statistical techniques. In time, it would be expected that new faculty possessed competence in these techniques, and the bureau was no longer needed. Gradually, the College's image came to be one in which research — or "scholarly inquiry" — was a top priority. Ruth Eckert, a leading figure in research and the first important Minnesota scholar to pose a systematic approach to curricular patterns in higher education, asserted in her "Working Statement on the Place of Research in the College of Education" that the College was pledged to advancing research by enlisting a faculty dedicated to its promotion.[65] The way was at last clear for the College to devote its efforts to educational research. Rather than *supplanting* the vision which had earlier kept the College alive, however, this emphasis on research and scientific inquiry would *supplement* it. The example set by the community of values in which such men as Brameld, Douglass, Bossing, and Palmer Johnson could all work toward a common goal would serve as a standard from that point on.

Eight

A New Focus on Higher Education

EVEN IN the midst of internal problems and growing pains, the College never lost sight of the fact that it was a part of a greater entity — a state university which would eventually become one of the largest and most respected in the nation. This consciousness of belonging to a whole and of having concomitant responsibilities was in part a result of Lotus Coffman's move in 1920 from the deanship of the College to the presidency of the University. Even when facing larger questions than those in the College of Education, Coffman was still very much interested in his former academic and administrative home. Thus, its difficulties and its goals were in no danger of being ignored by the administration. On the contrary, many of its aims — especially research — were seen as integral to the University as a whole.

Appropriately, the focus of research changed with the times. While such College faculty members as Melvin Haggerty, Theodore Brameld, Dora V. Smith, and Marvin Van Wagenen emphasized the study of problems common to the elementary and high schools, the concerns of higher education also demanded attention. In "A Half-Century of Progress in Higher Education" (a report written for the fiftieth anniversary of the College), Ruth Eckert and Gerald Erickson defined this field as "the systematic study of college and university problems."[1] Through coursework and experience in the University High School, many students in the College were being prepared to teach and supervise high school and the lower grades. It was also necessary to teach others to function as administrators and educators in colleges and universities as well.

This emphasis surfaced early in the College's history, but it took time to reach maturity. For example, the *Bulletin* for 1908-09 listed a one-credit course taught by Dean James called Organization of Higher Education. Known as "Ed. 17," this was the first course offered in higher education by the College. The *Bulletin* described it as follows:

> This course is intended for students who are interested in the general problems of educational administration, and who look forward later to college teaching. It includes an historical sketch of the development of the American university, with discussion of modes of organization and administration, problems of departmental management, and questions of class instruction.[2]

As early as 1918, Coffman felt that the staff of the College of Education should include a professor of higher education. It was not until the 1930's, though, that a genuine alliance between the University and research in higher education would be achieved. During this period, Coffman spoke for the University, and Haggerty represented the College's interests. Both men shared the same ideological language; both were devoted to empirical pedagogical research. Coffman expected his successor to support him, and Haggerty seldom failed — except for those times when Haggerty's own autonomy was threatened. For instance, Coffman felt that a person should be appointed within the University to coordinate the study and improvement of higher education. With support from Dean Johnston of CSLA,[3] he suggested that such a person be hired for the specific purpose of professionally training college teachers. Haggerty opposed this appointment, and the subject was dropped for the time being.

Coffman still maintained that a professor of higher education, if not a coordinator, should be hired; Haggerty was not particularly happy about this idea, either. During his own term as dean, Coffman had written President Burton to suggest that a then-substantial salary of $4,000 be budgeted for a professor who could "offer courses in the organization and administration of higher institutions."[4] This, he emphasized, was an "undeveloped field."[5] As though anticipating the functions of the Committee on Educational Research (begun in 1924), the Bureau of Institutional Research (begun in 1948), and the Administrative Research Unit (begun in 1956), Coffman attempted to strengthen his case by telling Burton that such a professor "could also be of service to the President, if it were desired, in studying the extent to which the university plant is being utilized," as well as in determining "the salary schedule, teaching schedules, entrance requirements, [and] college requirements for graduation" and in overseeing the "standardization of affiliated institutions."[6] In the *President's Report* for 1918-19, Coffman pointed out that

> progress in higher education is made largely on the basis of cut and dried methods when it ought to be made on the basis of carefully made, scientifically conducted studies. Some one should make such studies and offer courses covering various aspects of the administration of higher institutions.[7]

Unfortunately, nothing came of that recommendation. Nor was Coffman any more successful in later years when he tried to convince Haggerty that such a position should be established. In 1923, Coffman appointed a committee to study the "Professional Training of College Teachers" — obviously yet another attempt to get the College (or Haggerty) to agree to a professor of higher education. Apparently nothing came of this tactic, either. However, Coffman would not give up easily; in 1926, he suggested to Haggerty that a director of University instruction be appointed and charged with supervising the teaching of faculty members. Again, Coffman's prodding proved unsuccessful.

No one knows precisely why Haggerty was so stubborn about this matter. A likely guess is that he did not perceive such a person — whether hired as coordinator or professor of higher education — as falling under his control. He may have felt that the position was in danger of being filled by an outsider who would have insufficient knowledge of the College's needs. In response to Coffman's suggestions, Haggerty recommended that the College merely continue with the research projects that had been started in 1924, when Haggerty himself had chaired the University Committee on Educational Research. It is also possible that he felt that the College was rightfully the University's leader in the area of research into educational topics; with his unfailing interest in building the College's reputation, Haggerty was hardly going to bend his will to anyone who might not be under *his* direction.

After a time, Coffman ceased to press the issue. The existing system, after all, seemed to work well enough. The University Committee on Educational Research was his creation, and it functioned superbly. This committee was the culmination of almost ten years of effort on Coffman's part. One of his first acts on assuming the deanship had been the organization in 1915 of what he called the Bureau of Cooperative Research, which was supported initially with funds from the State Board of Education. Writing in 1956, Cyril Hoyt (then director of the College's Bureau of Educational Research) recalled that early studies of the Bureau of Cooperative Research consisted of a series of bulletins on educational testing and scoring for state schools. These bulletins were so successful that "one hundred and five cities and schools responded . . . by ordering material for making educational tests in their school systems. When the results of these tests were summarized by the Bureau, norms were set up for the city of Minneapolis in both arithmetic and spelling."[8] While these norms were subjects of bureau study — as was the cost of high school education in the state — the bulletins increasingly centered on the preparation of Minnesota high school students for coursework at the state university.

It was not long before the new Bureau of Cooperative Research attracted the attention of the United States Bureau of Education and became a federal research station. This move gave Coffman's project enough prestige that he could finally convince the Board of Regents to underwrite it. In 1919, its name was changed to the Bureau of Educational Research (BER), and in 1920, when Coffman assumed the University presidency, he was able to persuade the regents to award it an annual budget of $10,000. Another decade passed before the bureau had a central office; in the meantime, it functioned informally, with Coffman as director and Koos and Haggerty as associate directors.

Precisely where the BER fit into the College — and, by extension, into the University — during these early years remains something of an enigma, as does its history. For example, the 1922-23 *President's Report* shows the College as having a new "Department of Educational Research" with a budget of $7,825,[9] and Hoyt's "Historical Sketch"[10] notes a paper which Haggerty published in the 1922 edition of *Educational Monographs*[11] in which Haggerty reported that a "Bureau of Educational Investigations" was one of the ten departments of the College. (In fact, the Bureau of Educational Investigations and the Department of Educational Research were one and the same.)

While these variously named organizations came and went, however, the original BER remained strong. It had been created to serve the College, and it performed its duties admirably. Dorolese Wardwell, who served as the office manager for both the BER and the University Committee on Educational Research (whose workings were later formalized as the Bureau of Institutional Research, or BIR), recalls that the BER had three primary functions: (1) to perform pioneering research important to education, (2) to stimulate research activities among College of Education faculty, and (3) to provide internship experience for graduate students.[12] The BER, then, aptly reflected the main concerns of Coffman, its founder and director, and Haggerty and Koos, its two associate directors. Haggerty and Coffman were especially committed to educational research, and both were determined to see it flourish at Minnesota. As Haggerty concluded in his first report on the College to the president, "the continued prosecution of educational research is of very great importance to the life and welfare of this college, and properly organized and conducted, should render a great service in college teaching and to the public at large."[13] The subsequent two president's reports show that Haggerty's wishes and efforts were not in vain. In 1922-23, twenty-nine separate faculty research projects were reported; among the principal investigators were William S. Miller, Leo Brueckner, Homer J. Smith, M.G. Neale, and Marvin Van Wagenen. In addition, Leonard Koos was able to complete a study of junior colleges with the help of a $10,000 endowment from the Commonwealth Fund. The 1924-25 *President's Report* also summarized new research which was being carried out in the College's own curriculum using the techniques of occupational analysis (which were then in vogue in industry, along with time-motion studies). Three years later, Haggerty noted that Wesley Peik had completed what may have been "the most detailed and comprehensive study ever made of a college curriculum."[14] Haggerty was certain that Peik's study would be of "inestimable use to the faculty in the improvement of our requirements in the training of educational workers."[15] Even this level of activity was not enough to satisfy Haggerty, however; he still felt that educational research in the College was inadequately supported and inefficiently organized.

Nevertheless, progress was evident in the number of research-related publications which appeared during these years. Between 1923 and 1930, for example, the College published two series of research bulletins as a part of the official *Bulletin of the University of Minnesota*. The main series, termed the *Educational Monograph Series*, listed seventeen titles. Parallel to these monographs was a series under the title *Educational Research Bulletins*. While the monographs (the main series) were targeted to particular school systems or to the statewide system, the bulletins were directly related to the program which Haggerty termed the Bureau of Educational Investigations. Among the former were *Supervisory Organizations and Instructional Programs in Albert Lea* by Fred Engelhardt and Ernest Melby, along with Homer J. Smith's *Industrial Education in the Public Schools of Minnesota;* the latter group contained such contributions as Haggerty's *The Training of the Superintendent of Schools*[16] (published in 1925) and Dean Schweickhard's *A Guide to the Supervision of General Industrial Education.*[17] By 1929, the *Bulletin* was no longer used as a vehicle for the College's research publications; instead, they were published by the University Press.[18] The fact that the College's publishing responsibilities were delegated to this all-University agency reflects the important role which the College had come to play in educational research.

It was logical that the BER would gradually affect not only the College of Education but the University as a whole. After all, Coffman was its first director, and he was more than willing to work with his associates in the College to see that its resources for research were used to benefit the entire University. As it turned out, this new emphasis on organizational research would prove to be not only beneficial but also timely. With the end of World War I, enrollment increased sharply, bringing with it an increased demand for admission to professional programs. The enrollment of growing numbers of both undergraduate and professional students might have been handled haphazardly had not the resources of the BER been available. Both Coffman and Haggerty were convinced that the University could handle the influx of students and guide them appropriately — provided that adequate research into problems both real and potential was conducted. Even so, the situation grew critical by 1922, and Louis B. Wilson, director of the Mayo Foundation, suggested to Coffman that "the University hold a conference to discuss the improved selection of students who desire to enter medicine and other professions."[19] As a result of Wilson's prompting, yet another agency, the BIR, was born, along with the guidance-counseling movement for which both the College and University would become famous. A first step in the founding of this new and important institutional research bureau was a familiar one — the appointment of a committee. In this instance, Coffman named a special "Committee on Educational Guidance" in 1922. According to Walter Cook, "it did not take the committee long to discover that it knew very little about students, either before, during, or as a result of, their University training, and even less about testing or educational and vocational guidance."[20] In fact, it took almost a year before the committee issued a report which included a recommendation that

> the president of the University appoint an educational research committee which shall promote the study and investigation of educational problems within the University. Such agency should not . . . have administrative functions, but should be for the purpose of investigation, experimentation, publicity, and cooperation among administrative agencies now existing.[21]

"The immediate purpose of such a research committee," he stated, "would be to provide means of coordinating research now being done by individuals in the University, of advising in regard to the direction which research should take and the methods to be employed, and in promoting the dissemination of resulting information throughout the University."[22]

In 1924, Coffman responded to this prompting by appointing the fourteen-member University Committee on Educational Research. This prestigious committee had great influence within the University, at least in part because it was composed of deans and high-ranking administrators from various colleges. Haggerty chaired the committee (simultaneously heading the BER) and continued in this post until his death; Donald G. Paterson was a principal faculty member.

Research got under way almost immediately. There was much to do and there were many questions that needed to be answered:

> What standards . . . should now be set to govern admission of students? How should these differ for general and professional divisions of the University? Should instructional methods be altered to suit these larger, more heterogeneous groups, and if so, in what ways? How should student achievement be appraised? Should the University provide the personnel services, including closer supervision, of some of the nonacademic phases of student life?[23]

Ruth Eckert and Robert Keller both played crucial roles in the committee's life. Later, they recalled that its function had been to identify "the larger questions that required investigation, to evaluate the various research proposals submitted by faculty members, and then to recommend to the president those studies that the committee felt should be underwritten by University funds."[24] They also noted that "the committee was also expected to review critically the findings from such studies and to note their implications for University practice."[25]

Naturally, the University Committee on Educational Research did not reach its full stride overnight, regardless of its outstanding members. Not until 1930 would a central office and specialized staff be made available to it. At that time, a portion of the basement of Walter Library (which today houses the University Archives) was set aside for the use of the committee and the BER together, and Dorolese Wardwell was put in charge of the office, with Alvin Eurich and Palmer Johnson assisting Haggerty in determining what direction the committee's research would take. By 1938, the activities of the committee and the BER had increased to such an extent that more space was needed, and the two moved to Eddy Hall; in 1948, another move was necessary, this time to Burton Hall.

During the same year, the movement which had begun under Louis Wilson's instigation resulted in the formation of the BIR. By this time, the work of the Committee on Educational Research had grown to such an extent that a committee alone was insufficient to carry it out. A staff and a director were needed, in addition to other organizational trappings, and these formalized its efforts. The new BIR would provide the studies being carried out by the committee with a permanent place of residence and permanent facilities.

The University Committee on Educational Research and the BER had long been associates; they would now be peers. Under the expert management of Dorolese Wardwell, they would also be efficiently run. While the BER concentrated, as it had long done, on College of Education questions and concerns, the BIR continued the work which the Committee on Educational Research had started — namely, research into higher education and University self-examination. In a way, the establishment of the BIR signaled the beginning of a new era at the University of Minnesota. No longer would the direction of the University (and the College) be determined solely by strong personalities on its faculty and staff; an age of bureaucracy had begun, and it would have both its good points and its bad. Quite simply, the faculty could no longer do everything on its own; it needed assistance from a centralized system which could provide it with office help, a place where records on various research projects could be kept and made accessible, and a sense of permanence and organization.

Old Main, home of the Department of Pedagogy

David L. Kiehle

George F. James, as a young man
Dean, 1905–1915

Early faculty of the College of Education, 1910. *Top row: first and second from left*, Albert Rankin and Fletcher Swift; *second from right*, Edward Quigley. *Bottom row: first and second from left*, Christopher Hall, Henrietta Clopath; *to the right of* George James *(center)*, John Downey and John Hutchinson. *Others cannot be identified.*

Lotus D. Coffman
Dean, 1915–1920

Education Building, 1914 to 1926. Formerly the School of Mines, this building continued to house the University High School until 1952. Now part of the Institute of Child Development.

Burton Hall, home of the College of Education since 1926.

Melvin E. Haggerty
Dean, 1920–1937

Early carol sing. *Left to right:* Dean Haggerty, Ruth Merrill, Harold Benjamin,
Dora V. Smith, Archie Jones, Rudolph Goranson, Mrs. Haggerty

Wesley E. Peik
Acting Dean, 1937–1938
Dean, 1938–1951

Marcia Edwards
Acting Dean, 1952, 1963–1964

Later carol singers. *Left to right:* Dora V. Smith, Marcia Edwards, Lorraine Dahlstrom, Dean Peik

Peik Hall, under construction, 1952. Home of the University High School for twenty years

Early days at the Nursery School, Institute of Child Welfare

John Anderson with children at the Institute of Child Welfare

Walter W. Cook
Dean, 1952–1963

Robert J. Keller
Dean, 1964–1970

Jack C. Merwin
Dean, 1970–1976

William E. Gardner
Acting Dean, 1976–77
Dean

In the meantime, however, the original University Committee on Educational Research had undertaken a number of valuable studies. In conducting a historical review of its activities, John Stecklein, the final director of the BIR, reported:

> As might be expected from the origins of the Committee on Educational Research . . . emphasis during the first 15 years of the Committee was on studies of student personnel, student selection, testing, admissions, and retention. This is not to say that some studies of class size, methods of instruction, curriculum, and faculty characteristics, among others, were not also conducted, but the primary focus was on the students.[26]

Often, the committee's concerns were distributed among various subcommittees, including one on teaching problems in the social studies (chaired by A.C. Krey). Another was devoted to the concerns of parents and one on the reading problems of college students; Haggerty chaired both of these, while A.C. Krey and Eurich served as members of the latter. In addition, there were subcommittees devoted to the dissemination of research information (on which both Koos and Paterson served) and personnel records (chaired by Paterson and attended by Brueckner, among others). The efforts of the University Committee on Educational Research and its various subcommittees were evident from its large number of publications. At least three bore Palmer Johnson's name, either singly — as with *Curricular Problems in Science at the College Level*, published in 1930, and *Aspects of Land Grant College Education*, released during the same year — or in combination with A.C. Krey, with whom Johnson wrote *Differential Functions of Examinations*, published in 1934.

As Eckert and Keller recalled, the committee's reputation grew. "The plan," they stated, "met with notable success, so that within a few years this committee, which had become one of the most influential on the campus, had succeeded in interesting many of the departmental and college staffs in such research."[27] In the first of the president's biennial reports, which dealt with the years 1928-30, Haggerty was able to state that "approximately a hundred members of the faculty have been identified with one or more research projects," and he listed forty-four University departments that had been directly involved.[28] What Coffman had begun — and Haggerty extended — earned the College a central place in University self-study.

Coffman and Haggerty were followed by people like T.R.

McConnell, Ruth Eckert, Robert Keller, and John Stecklein. It became a common practice for the University to draw its administrative leadership from the ranks of the College's faculty. This contributed to the growth of University interest in the field of higher education, and a program was eventually devoted to its study. By 1940, the identity of instruction in higher education with the University Committee on Educational Research was complete and would remain strong thereafter. Ruth Eckert serves as an example of this relationship. When she came to the University shortly after Peik became dean of the College, she spent two years evaluating the General College, itself a unique experiment in higher education. Later, T.R. McConnell asked her to assume the responsibility for College courses he had been teaching in higher education. Eckert's efforts were rewarded in 1973, the year of her retirement, when she was named a Regents' Professor — the first College faculty member to be awarded this distinction.

While Eckert and others made sizeable contributions to the study of higher education, Coffman and Haggerty should be recognized as its forerunners. In 1930, when Raymond A. Kent edited *Higher Education in America,*[29] Haggerty contributed a chapter called "The Improvement of University Instruction through Educational Research." Coffman wrote the introduction to Kent's study, and took the opportunity to ask such rhetorical questions as: "Is it impossible . . . to define the aims or objectives of a college education and to organize programs for their attainment?" and "Are prerequisites based upon opinion or has their necessity been demonstrated in each instance?"[30] He posed a number of other questions at the time, including "Should methods of instruction in any of the subjects vary with types of ability or should all students be taught alike in a given subject? What is the optimum size of class for college work? What type of laboratory period produces the best result?"[31] In his chapter, Haggerty stressed — true to form — that "any thoroughgoing attempt at the improvement of college instruction must be founded upon a program of research."[32] Haggerty believed that research alone could answer certain questions relevant to higher education, such as "Is the lecture an effective method of instruction?" and "Are large classes inimical to student achievement?"[33]

Haggerty may have been opposed to the hiring of a University coordinator of higher education, but this did not prevent him from joining with Coffman to conduct a research-based approach to issues in higher education. In 1929, the North Central Association of Colleges and Schools, through its Commission on Institutions of Higher Education, appointed a committee, which Coffman chaired, on institutions of higher education. In 1937, the year in which Haggerty died, this committee published the first of several volumes of its research findings and recommendations. Between 1937 and 1939, seven volumes were published, two of them written by Haggerty. In *The Faculty*, for example, Haggerty drew inferences from data which had been collected from 4,000 college professors in fifty-seven institutions.[34] In the acknowledgments to this volume, Haggerty gave credit to his son, William James Haggerty, "who served with the Committee during the first two years of investigation and who has assisted the secretary of the Commission in putting the new accrediting policy into operation."[35] In another volume of the same series, he also acknowledged several of his colleagues:

> Counsel upon the involved problems of statistical procedure was provided by ... Dr. Palmer O. Johnson and Dr. Harl Douglass .... Four of the writer's colleagues at the University of Minnesota made special studies, the results of which have been used in this report. Professor James G. Umstattd explored and published literature on the objectives of higher education and compiled the data from the institutions. Professor Harold O. Soderquist examined the characters of higher institutions. Professor W.E. Peik made a comprehensive study of literature on the curriculum and prepared abstracts descriptive of new developments in the field. Harold R. Benjamin made a number of institutional case studies.[36]

The involvement of Coffman and Haggerty in the North Central Association of Colleges and Schools set a precedent for other University personnel, the College faculty in particular. When Charles Boardman retired from the University in 1954, for example, he became the executive secretary of the association and was succeeded by Robert Keller, who was named acting secretary in 1960.[37] After a year in this role, Keller then chaired the association's Publication and Information Services (later its editorial committee). It was not mere chance that College members were so eager to become involved in the North Central Association; the College itself had become well known for its work in the area of higher education, and its reputation was in no small measure due to the efforts of the BER.

Not even Haggerty's death would seriously affect the productivity of the University Committee on Educational Research and the BER, partially because of Dorolese Wardwell's steady administrative hand and T.R. McConnell's continuing vision. McConnell took over Haggerty's responsibilities on the committee, and it was fortunate that McConnell was as committed to research in higher education as Haggerty had been. He showed especially good judgment when he drew Ruth Eckert away from General College and into the College of Education when he himself became assistant dean of CSLA. The years 1924 to 1937, during which Haggerty had served on the educational research committee, had witnessed the completion of approximately seventy-four studies, some of "massive proportions," as were the studies of admission, class size, and examination procedures.[38] McConnell guided the committee for only seven years; yet, according to Ruth Eckert, several new studies were made during this time of "comprehensive faculty load [in addition] to curriculum studies undertaken just before the war, and a whole series of investigations made during the war years for the Senate Committee on Education, which was engaged in planning the University's program for the post-war period."[39] Two research-related volumes were published under McConnell's direction, both entitled *Studies in Higher Education* (one was concerned with the period 1937 to 1940, the other with 1940 to 1942), along with "a number of shorter bulletins summarizing research findings, before the war situation temporarily halted publication activities."[40]

The war years were more trying than this understatement suggests. Luckily, Eckert, who was then secretary to the University Committee on Educational Research (a position she held from 1940 to 1942) and later assistant director of the BER (from 1942 to 1946) was able to hold things together with help from Dorolese Wardwell. In 1947, the year which saw the beginning of another great period of both student and staff expansion, Eckert became the coordinator of the Office of Educational Research, which served as a home for both the Committee on Educational Research and the BER. After Robert Keller stepped in as associate director (a position held by Eckert immediately prior to her assuming the role of coordinator), these two leading scholars of higher education continued to work together. As coordinator, Ruth Eckert kept the BIR and the BER together; in only two years, the organization of both was streamlined and made quite responsive to the faculty.

When T.R. McConnell stepped down as director of the University Committee on Educational Research in 1947, he was replaced by Russell M. Cooper, assistant dean of CSLA and head of the General Studies Division. The committee then underwent a number of changes: it began to include more faculty members and it became directly responsible to the University Senate rather than the president. Not long afterward, the BIR was formalized as a visible unit distinct from, but coordinated with, the College of Education's BER. (The first was directed by Robert Keller, the second by Cyril Hoyt. Ruth Eckert worked closely with both men, much to the benefit of higher education.) The BER remained responsible for conducting research requested by the State Department of Education and by local school districts. Both organizations were housed in the College of Education, although the College made no more use of the BIR than did other units of the University, aside from providing its staff. (Since the two bureaus were so close together, it is especially interesting to note how little they actually had in common. For example, the BER might have supplemented the BIR by performing a self-study of the College of Education, which the BIR had done for the University. The structure and function of the College would not become subjects for BER inquiry, however; the BER would respond to what College faculty wanted to do by way of empirical research, or concentrate on the type of research that interested its director at the time, but unfortunately it initiated little or no collegiate self-examination.)

The post-World War II population explosion, the mass exodus to the suburbs, and other social changes generated pressures on the BER which led to the creation of another agency in 1948 called the Bureau of Field Studies and Surveys. Dean Peik was very proud of this new unit. Prior to its founding, he had written a long letter to Malcolm Willey, the academic vice president, in January of 1948 in which he expressed a strong belief in the necessity of balancing the BER's emphasis on problems of higher education (which Peik referred to as "Dean Haggerty's preoccupation") with research on field service to the schools and school districts of the state.[41] The Bureau of Field Studies and Surveys was designed to do just that, and it was an immediate success. In a letter addressed to President Morrill on February 1, 1951, Peik wrote of it with evident delight.[42] The bureau had been in existence only two years under the direction of M.G. Neale, a professor of educational administration, "but during its first 21 months of actual work," Peik stated, "thirteen survey projects have been completed and thirteen additional surveys are under way."

Although its directorship changed (over the years Neale was succeeded by Otto E. Domian, and Domian was followed by Charles Sederberg), the purpose of the bureau remained, until 1978, as Peik described it to President Morrill: "to serve the school districts of Minnesota by collecting factual information relating to specific problems which face the school boards and administrative offices."[43] This "factual information," Peik continued, "is studied and analyzed by the Bureau, and definite recommendations are made to the board of education and the citizens of the district."[44] Recently, however, the bureau has been replaced by the Center for Educational Policy Studies, an interdepartmental unit in the College which combines cooperative research in educational policy issues with "technical assistance to school districts, state agencies, and other educational organizations."[45] The emphasis of this new center on educational policy reflects in part the influence of large-scale social and economic changes in education since Peik's time. While the Bureau of Field Studies and Surveys met the needs of an expanding educational system, the Center for Educational Policy Studies addresses "larger questions of educational governance and policy" in an age of declining enrollment and its consequences for education.[46]

Nevertheless, in establishing the Bureau of Field Studies and Surveys, Peik guaranteed that the needs of elementary and secondary schools, along with the problems which plagued school district administrators, would not suffer from benign neglect. This focus, however, did not mean that Peik ignored the study of higher education typified by the research of the BIR. Had he done so, he may have met with opposition from President Morrill, who, while not hesitating to support the Bureau of Field Studies and Surveys, gave the BIR his wholehearted endorsement. The latter continued its habit of publishing with the University Press, which brought out several bulletins and a comprehensive volume, *Higher Education in Minnesota*. Although none of the essays in this 1950 publication are credited to Ruth Eckert or Robert Keller, many were in fact written by them.[47] In a later article coauthored by Gerald Erickson, Eckert mentioned a number of the research projects which she had formerly described in *Higher Education in Minnesota:*

> [They] were also initiated . . . to throw light upon other pressing questions the University was facing, as for example, the validity of foreign language requirements for graduate students, the place of the univer-

152

sity's sub-collegiate agricultural school programs, the quality of the later contributions Minnesota trained Ph.D.'s were making and the relation of these to their doctoral training.[48]

Eckert assumed her post as coordinator of the BIR and the BER just as graduate enrollment was reaching a new high in the University's history. It was to grow even more as veterans returned to the University for advanced and professional work, especially in the area of higher education. In his contribution to the 1948-50 *President's Report,* Dean Peik was able to comment:

> There has been much increase in the interest of graduate students throughout the University in special preparation for college teaching and professional service in the program of studies in higher education . . . . This department now offers fourteen courses and seminars in higher education.[49]

The famous sequence Ed. C.I. 250-251-252 (Higher Education in the United States, Curriculum Trends in American Colleges, and Effective College Teaching) assumed the character which so many graduate students have come to know.

The volume of research undertaken by the BIR and the BER, together with the lack of comprehensive records, makes it particularly difficult to realize what these two organizations achieved during their existence. The late 1940's and early 1950's proved especially seminal for the BIR, for example; fortunately, a report on its activities during this time is contained in *A University Looks at Its Program,* one of a series entitled "Minnesota Studies in Higher Education."[50] Reports on the founding and activities of the two bureaus are often vague or conflicting. In the midst of the resulting confusion, however, one fact remains clear: Ruth Eckert played a role whose importance can never be fully realized. When one considers that she was a principal figure in the College's program of studies in higher education while simultaneously coordinating the BER (with Hoyt as director) and the BIR (with Keller as director), she assumes truly remarkable stature. Of course, she did not have to do it all alone; the tradition of mutual help at Minnesota served her well, as did the College's associate dean, Marcia Edwards.

In time, it became impossible to maintain the BIR as a simple organization, and in 1956 the Administrative Research Unit was formed to carry out the BIR's traditional activities. This resulted in a less complicated organization, which, together with the BER, made a splendid training ground for graduate students. No historical record of either bureau should fail to emphasize this point. In a sense, what Cyril Hoyt did in the BER and what Keller (and later, Paul Torrance) did in the BIR can be summed up in this excerpt from John Stecklein's "The History and Development of the Bureau of Institutional Research at the University of Minnesota":

> For qualified individuals it is possible to begin with a half-time research assistantship and move up to a half-time or even a full-time research fellowship with the Bureau. Some feel that the provision of such experience for persons who are going into college and university work is, in itself, justification for the institutional research unit at Minnesota . . . . The list of prominent individuals who served an apprenticeship in this research unit can be quoted with pride. Included are such persons as: Alvin Eurich, vice-president of the Ford Foundation; Henry Harmon, President of Drake University; G. Lester Anderson, Vice-Chancellor for Educational Affairs, University of Buffalo [who continued to have an illustrious career in higher education]; C. Robert Pace, Chairman of the Department of Psychology at Syracuse University; John Dobbin, Director of the Cooperative Test Division of the Educational Testing Service [from which Mary Corcoran came to take her place as a graduate student and staff member of the BIR, later succeeding Ruth Eckert as head of the College's program in higher education]; Marcia Edwards, Associate Dean of the College of Education at Minnesota; and Marjorie Moore, a Division Head for the Vocational Rehabilitation Office of the U.S. Department of Health, Education, and Welfare, among many others.[51]

Unfortunately, the BIR and the BER were not destined to remain permanently in Burton Hall. In 1967, the BIR was moved off campus; according to Dorolese Wardwell, this signaled the beginning of the end not only for this unit but for the BER as well. No longer did the BIR staff have ready access to the faculty members or resources which it had long been accustomed to consulting, and nobody seemed to take any real responsibility for the BER once the two were separated.

The BIR formally ended on June 30, 1971. Prior to that time, its responsibilities had been gradually eroded or taken over by other University units. In 1956, the University's central administration established a small operation known as the Administrative Research Unit; this was intended to answer research needs that were ostensibly not being met by the BIR. The BIR was further handicapped by the fact that the Senate Committee on Institutional Research was not willing to see it enlarged or broadened to conform with the demands of the times. Today, the Administrative

Research Unit is known as the Office of Administration and Planning, and other former BIR responsibilities are carried out by the Measurement Services Center.

The BER, it seems, simply disappeared; more and more new faculty were able to perform complicated research on their own, and fewer graduate students were eager to perform internships with the BER. Paul Torrance, professor of educational psychology, served as its last director until he resigned in June 1966 to accept a position at the University of Georgia. The BER continued as an entry in the budget books under the jurisdiction of the dean of the College of Education until 1968, when its name was changed to the Office of Educational Research, Planning, and Development. It continued under this new title until 1973-74, when it became the Educational Research Office under the direction of Assistant Dean Wayne Welch. Then, in 1975-76, it fell under the jurisdiction of Associate Dean Darrell Lewis, who is responsible for promoting and supporting empirical research done by College faculty. It can be said, then, that while the BER no longer survives, the research tradition established long ago within the College is still alive. Nevertheless, the two organizations which proved so important to Lotus Coffman, Melvin Haggerty, Palmer Johnson, Ruth Eckert, and many others within both the College and the University are gone. Only time will tell whether or not the University's decision to disband them was a wise one.

Nine

Years of Growth
Years of Opportunity

THE END of the 1930's witnessed dramatic shifts in the direction of
the College. Both Haggerty and Coffman had worked hard to
build its reputation in empirical research, and a quickly maturing
program in higher education emerged whose central figures included Ruth Eckert, T.R. McConnell, Robert Keller, Alvin Eurich,
and Cyril Hoyt. But the deaths of Haggerty in 1937 and Coffman
in 1938 marked a turning point; when Wesley E. Peik succeeded
to the deanship and Guy Stanton Ford assumed the University
presidency, there were bound to be some changes made. In particular, it was clear from Peik's interests that there would be a
renewed emphasis on Minnesota's school systems and the professional preparation of teachers. Eventually, a concern with the
quality of elementary and secondary education throughout the
state replaced the College's preoccupation with higher education:
this was typified by Peik's enthusiasm for the Bureau of Field
Studies and Surveys.

Peik was not as dramatic a figure as Haggerty, and his ideas
about education and the College's role were quite different from
those of his predecessor; nevertheless, his appointment to the
deanship cannot be viewed as startling or unusual. Despite the
dissimilarities between the two men, Haggerty liked and supported Peik, as did A.C. Krey, one of Haggerty's closest friends.
Peik served as acting dean immediately following Haggerty's
death; when it came time to make a permanent appointment,
Krey's recommendation of Peik must have carried some weight
with President Ford, since both Krey and Ford were historians
with many interests and viewpoints in common. In addition, as
Marcia Edwards tells it, Krey's friend Edgar Wesley was also im-

pressed with Peik.[1] Earlier, Peik had addressed an annual conference on teacher education, and had shown such a command of the facts that he was able to speak entirely without notes. When Wesley discovered this, he threw his considerable influence with the College behind the acting dean; Peik's assistant, Marcia Edwards, also helped to marshal support from educators off-campus.

Coffman, on the other hand, did not display a similar confidence in Peik's abilities or qualifications. While Haggerty actively sponsored Peik's career in the College, Coffman was far more reluctant to do so; this is evident from at least five years of correspondence between the two. For example, in a letter from Coffman to Haggerty written in May 1929, Coffman wrote that he could not go along with Haggerty's recommendation that Peik's salary be increased $600; he would, however, approve Peik's promotion to assistant professor and a concomitant salary increase of $350.[2] In another letter written a few months earlier, Haggerty had praised Peik's doctoral thesis highly and had urged Coffman to find funds for its publication,[3] but Coffman's response indicated that he was not enthusiastic about the thesis. A few years later, in 1934, Coffman wrote Haggerty about an attractive offer Peik had received from Northwestern, and stated: "I wonder if the Northwestern offer really doesn't represent [Peik's] great chance. I also wonder why he hesitates."[4] Coffman went on to give his personal opinion of Peik:

> I regard him as a useful person; he is not brilliant in any way; an ordinary, if not poor writer; and in no sense a distinguished scientist and scholar. He does have good sense and managerial ability. He knows how to work with others so as to keep their confidence and respect. He is patient, faithful, and industrious.[5]

As events were later to prove, Haggerty's measure of Peik was more accurate than Coffman's.

When the new dean took office, he brought with him both a thorough training in the techniques of survey research and a strong social vision. His father had been a minister, and Peik's own career revealed a social conscience that made it easy for him to appreciate the values of educators like Wesley, Brameld, and Van Wagenen (whose promotion to associate professor he championed). His experience as a teacher in Scott County, Minnesota, had provided him with valuable insights into rural education; his managerial skills (which Coffman had somewhat grudgingly acknowledged) had led to superintendencies in the Minnesota communities of Blackduck, Tracy, and Faribault. What Wesley had learned by traveling the length and breadth of the state, Peik had absorbed long before commencing his doctoral studies under Haggerty's guidance.

Peik presented an attractive blend of the practical and the visionary. While he was most interested in the applications of educational practice, he also hoped that education in general would contribute to the strength of democracy. Nothing could have been more practical than his grasp of the fact that unless the College joined forces with accrediting agencies which were pressing for the upgrading of professional teacher preparation, the University was not going to get a sufficient number of well-schooled candidates for admission. In the *President's Report* for 1937-38, Peik noted that regional accrediting agencies and local school administrators were advocating a fifth year of college education for teachers; the University, he stated, had an "obligation" to supply such a fifth year.[6] This was not mere empire building; Peik knew the needs of school teachers. In the same report, he went on to point out that graduate requirements were too often established without knowledge of the actual conditions within the schools. In addition, he stated, graduate programs tended to be dominated by an interest in research instead of a concern with the problems of the schools.

The new dean may not have been as volatile as Haggerty, but this did not mean that he was hesitant to express his opinions. The message that was central to this first report was highly critical: in short, he asserted that too many marginal students were becoming teachers. Not many years later, Peik's name would be identified with a national drive by educational leaders to upgrade professional standards. First, however, he had to face two obstacles that confronted many American institutions of teacher preparation: the decline of both staff and enrollment during the war years (which made it difficult to think of setting higher standards), and the rise in student enrollment following the war. As the need for faculty members became especially acute, it was nearly impossible to convince educators to think about issues surrounding certification. Almost any graduate could be placed, and educators and administrators alike were more interested in sheer numbers of students than in ascertaining high professional competence. Peik had to curb his ambitions temporarily; in the meantime, however, he gave Minnesota's College of Education a great deal of attention.

Taking a realistic approach to the problems which existed during his deanship, Peik knew that staffing would make all the difference in the quality of the College. As a result, he invested a great deal of time and effort in recruitment, and went so far as to pay several personal visits to particularly interesting prospects. The way in which he sought new staff members is obvious from a letter he wrote to Guy Ford in 1937:

> I am quietly building up a file on available persons in secondary education who might succeed Dr. Douglass. I am looking up two types of persons — the first group, those who are well established but may yet be available to the University of Minnesota if we can pay them an appropriate salary . . . . The second group consists of young men who have won initial spurs and are either known to me and others or have been recommended.[7]

In response, Ford advised: "Look for brains and breadth of training. Let's avoid people who think that education is a cult to which you are admitted only by the rituals that they have observed."[8]

Peik's administrative style was also very different from Haggerty's; no one was ever kept waiting outside his office. Throughout his tenure, he invited the faculty to help develop College policy. Though no established formula for faculty participation ever evolved, Peik made it clear from the start that his associates' opinions were welcome.[9] He also advocated student involvement and went so far as to plan to add students to College committees in 1951. None of these efforts, however, diverted Peik's attention away from his first concern: the quality of future teachers. As though anticipating the rapid rise in enrollment that flooded the College with new students after World War II, he devoted a good portion of his 1944-46 report to the president to issues of student enrollment and student quality. Again, he emphasized the necessity of securing higher standards for certification. Before this goal could be realized, however, Peik knew that there would have to be statewide, regional, and national cooperation among educational institutions. They would have to work together in combating unselective admissions and low standards for graduation. He waged a constant campaign to see that these aims were accomplished, and his efforts produced immediately recognized and lasting results.

These changes could not take place all at once, of course; Peik realized this, and began devoting his efforts toward these ends early in his career. His 1930 publication *The Professional Educa-*

tion of High School Teachers[10] presaged later successes. This study delighted Haggerty, who saw it as embodying precisely the sort of survey research he considered to be the most fruitful. The word *education* in its title is revealing (Peik never ceased to bridle at the term "teacher training"; as he frequently asserted, "Training is a term to be used for dogs"). A general and liberal education, as he saw it, was the key to preparing good and competent teachers. His study was aimed at determining whether College graduates were indeed receiving this type of education. In conducting the study, he extracted 814 topics from courses which had been included in University certification requirements during the period 1923 to 1928 and asked graduates of the College to check those topics which they felt had been most useful. He also asked them to decide whether courses had overlapped or been redundant and to state whether they felt that what they had learned had proved worthwhile. As teachers, many of these graduates were engaged in field-testing the products of their own education. In carrying out his survey, Peik also indicated a willingness to cooperate with College alumni.

Cooperation with acting educators and administrators was also high on Peik's agenda when he assumed the deanship. In a letter he wrote to Acting President Ford in February 1938, he spoke of "promoting wholehearted cooperation with the State Department, the Minnesota Education Association, the Minnesota Council of School Executives, and the Twin City Schools, with all of whom the College of Education has important connections."[11] He went on to assure Ford that the College faculty was touching base with educators throughout the state, including "superintendents, teachers college presidents, former students, and teachers."[12] He then promised to emphasize not only "more specific service and leadership on education matters in the state which supports us" but also "representation on the [College's] staff of various points of view in educational and social matters, responsible academic freedom, and incorporation into the program of studies of a number of additional areas such as educational sociology [and] educational philosophy."[13]

Admittedly, these goals were somewhat lofty and abstract; in the meantime, however, Peik was also concerned with some eminently practical issues and did his best to see that they became realities. One of his most innovative ideas is now taken for granted: the curriculum laboratory (or, by extension, the contem-

160

porary instructional media center). Peik had enough foresight to recognize that future scientists were not the only students who needed laboratory experience; he believed that students in education also needed practical experience in observing teaching and having their own teaching observed by others. In addition, he felt that education students had to learn to appraise a variety of teaching materials — not only those which were obviously directed toward their own students but also those which were normally considered to be the property of various educational specialists.[14]

Peik's ambitions for the College were somewhat handicapped by the war. Even during these difficult times, however, it was clear that educational research could not be allowed to lose its direction or force. Fortunately, Peik's faculty was both supportive of its dean and sufficiently motivated to carry on the types of projects which would keep the College's reputation alive. One such project, the Laboratory of Physiological Hygiene, began operation at a modest level during the spring of 1938. The idea of doing research on the effects of exercise was characteristic of the spirit of inquiry that infused the College of Education; in addition, Coffman and Haggerty had seen to it that open lines of communication existed between College faculty and those in other disciplines. Thus, while the laboratory was not a part of the College itself, the College played a leading role in its founding.

Notes on the Laboratory of Physiological Hygiene written during 1945 provide information about its beginnings and goals: "The Laboratory . . . had its origin as a result of discussions between the late President Lotus D. Coffman, Dr. Harold S. Diehle [*sic*], Dean of the Medical School, Mr. Frank McCormack, Director of Athletics, and Dr. Maurice B. Visscher, Head of the Department of Physiology."[15] The purpose of the laboratory was "to establish a focus for research on the physiology of man as related to the conditions of his life and to provide better instruction in physiology for students of physical education."[16] Such research would be carried out via "the exact measurement of human function and the factors affecting human performance and behavior."[17]

Another enterprise in which the College was engaged during this time may have seemed minor at the outset, but it proved to be significant. During the last year of Haggerty's life, Gilbert Wrenn came to the University as assistant dean in the General College, which was then only four years old. Together with Willis Dugan, whose appointment began in 1942, Wrenn gave impetus to the high school and college guidance counseling programs within the College. Wrenn had been on the faculty only two years when the Student Personnel Department (later the Student Personnel Office and eventually the Education Career Development Office) was budgeted with Dugan as its director. Wrenn became a leader in postsecondary guidance counseling, while Dugan cultivated the secondary level. Both, of course, benefited from the ground-breaking done by Marcia Edwards. Wrenn held his position as assistant dean in the General College for two more years before Peik brought him into the College of Education, where he became world-famous as the architect of the College's program for preparing guidance counselors for colleges and universities.

A much more remote event which would have a significant impact during the Peik years was the passage of the George-Deen Act in 1936. While this was of singular importance to vocational education, no one could have foreseen that it would also underwrite business and distributive teacher education, which had its first stirrings in the College in 1940 before becoming a full-time program six years later. Warren Meyer's early introduction of this program at Minnesota gives some indication of the innovations that the College was making in professional preparation at that time. Meyer was so obviously a national leader that he was soon named president of the Council for Distributive Teacher Education. (Mary Klaurens, another College faculty member, was elected president of the council in 1975.)

Educators such as Meyer typify the sort of people whom Peik was able to attract to Minnesota despite the effects of the war. From the first year of his deanship, the quality of his faculty appointments was superior. In 1938, for example, Ruth Eckert was added to the staff, along with the man who succeeded Peik as dean, Walter Cook. G. Lester Anderson, who also built a distinguished professional career, was soon added to the faculty. In 1939, Theodore Brameld's appointment was recommended, and in 1940 Eloise Jaeger — who would later become the director of the College's School of Physical Education, Recreation, and School Health Education and subsequently an assistant dean — was hired as an instructor.

It is to the credit of both Peik and the College that people whose names would eventually be recognized nationally were brought to Minnesota during these years. Guy Bond and Emma Birkmaier were added to the staff in 1942, with Gordon Mork arriving in 1943 and Donovan Johnson in 1944. The year 1942 also witnessed Paul Oberg's initial appointment in music and music education.

Birkmaier's arrival at the University High School provides some indication of what a truly formidable training ground the high school was. When she first came to Minnesota as a teacher of German (the beginning of an outstanding program in modern foreign languages), G. Lester Anderson had been the high school's director for only a year. This was a full decade before Peik Hall was built in 1952 to house the school, and it was little short of remarkable that so much could still be accomplished in the old quarters of the Education Building. Unfortunately, Dean Peik died a year before the new building was named in his honor. No one had worked harder to see that a new building was provided for the high school; this must have been especially difficult for Peik to do, since the College itself was still inadequately housed. The faculty of the University High School returned the favor, however. When the legislature authorized a building for College use and the final decision was made on the basis of a faculty vote, the instructors of the University High School carried the day.

Pattee Hall housed the elementary school that Peik initiated in 1947, and its facilities were no better than those of the University High School prior to its move. One grade was added each year, and, because foreign language instruction at that time did not begin until the third grade, Emma Birkmaier had to wait three years before becoming involved in that endeavor. Once she began teaching there, she wasted no time in establishing a close relationship between the elementary and secondary training schools. In the meantime, though, she joined such luminaries as Dora V. Smith and Edgar Wesley by publishing a number of books in the field of education. Birkmaier's contribution to the *Modern School Practices* series, which came out between 1950 and 1964, reflected the practical emphasis on education which Peik had long advocated. During the same year in which the University High School moved into its new quarters, she edited *Illustrative Learning Experiences: University High School in Action*.[18] The faculties of both training schools — the elementary and the secondary — were very productive. As Birkmaier stated, the pamphlets in the *Illustrative Learning Experiences* series suggested that "one did not have to follow the whole routine of questions and answers, assignments and page after page after page, day after day after day, but could do different things."[19] She herself provided the stimulus which resulted in the University High School's being the first secondary school in the country to offer instruction in Russian. As her successor, Dale Lange, has remarked, "Birkmaier became a truly national leader in foreign language teaching."[20]

What lent strength to the work of educators such as Birkmaier and Lange was Minnesota's research tradition. Others benefited from it as well, including Guy Bond. Looking back at his College years, Bond recalled that the goals of that institution had been

> focused upon expanding the frontiers of education through research and developing students to assume national leadership, while still maintaining service to the community in training teachers, in-service training activities and working on national, state and local committees.[21]

Guy Bond's commitment to the study of reading reflected Haggerty's interest in the topic. Bond had been a graduate student of Arthur Gates at Teachers College, Columbia; Gates had studied with the famous James M. Cattell, a pioneer in constructing measurements of intelligence and conducting experimental studies in reading and other academic skills. Since Gates also worked closely with Thorndike, it was inevitable that Guy Bond would be influenced by him as well. Interestingly enough, the updated Thorndike tradition in which Bond studied was very much like that from which Van Wagenen had come; the two men were a generation apart, however, and did not engage in cooperative research.

It was typical of the College's attitude toward such matters that Bond was given leave to serve in the navy from 1942 to 1945. "At that time," he stated,

> I had the responsibility of developing a battery of tests for the Selection and Classification of enlisted and officer personnel in the U.S. Navy. These tests were used throughout the Navy and Marine Corps for the assignment of all the officer and enlisted personnel in all of the training programs under the jurisdiction of the U.S. Navy. In addition, we developed the advancement-in-rate tests which were used throughout the Navy. While these three years out somewhat impeded my professional goals, I felt fortunate that the College of Education allowed me to fulfill this obligation without losing my professional advancement.[22]

When Bond returned to the campus, he was joined by others who were either new to the scene or, like himself, back from the war. By that time, the academic world of Haggerty's day had undergone significant changes, the most obvious being a spectacular increase in enrollment and a pressing demand for teachers. As Bond points out, he and others were forced to succumb to these pressures:

> My one regret during the years that I taught in the College of Education, was that the demand for elementary teachers became so acute after World War II that the emphasis upon teacher training became dominant at the expense of research and professional leadership; and I, personally, as head of the department, had to devote too much time to administrative detail.[23]

Another more subtle demand of the time had to do with the rapidly increasing market for textbooks and teaching materials of all types. They were needed more quickly than they could be written — if they were to be written with an eye toward basic research. Unfortunately, many were not, and these must be considered mere diversions. Yet, regardless of the handicaps Bond felt, he was not so dissatisfied with the times that he could fail to say with hindsight: "Nonetheless, the success of my many graduate students in the academic world has somewhat eclipsed this regret."[24] A leading scholar inevitably attracts youthful colleagues of high caliber; in Bond's case, this description would certainly apply to Ted Clymer, who joined Bond's group in 1954 and similarly became a recognized leader in the field of reading.

Like many others who were recruited during Peik's deanship, Bond did not come to Minnesota with an established reputation. However, it was encouraged to develop there, and Bond eventually became one of the most highly respected reading specialists in the world. His reputation naturally reflects on two of the College's primary themes: empirical research and attention to individual differences. These were embodied in such publications as *The Diagnosis and Treatment of Learning Difficulties,* which he coauthored with Brueckner,[25] and the "companion" editions of his elementary school readers which were intended for those who found it difficult to learn to read.

Peik's own professional background in elementary school teaching made educators like Bond particularly attractive to him. The dean wanted the three R's — or at least reading and arithmetic — to be well represented in the College curriculum; with Bond and Van Wagenen in reading, and Brueckner in arithmetic, Peik felt secure in these areas and went on to make a series of appointments in secondary education and the vocational specialties. In the meantime, he took the three R's a step further by adding Gordon Mork to the faculty in 1943. Mork's credentials were well allied with the Coffman-Haggerty tradition. A respected learning theorist, he realized that graduate students would benefit greatly from practice teaching or "clinical experiences," and he assumed responsibility for coordinating a program with that as its aim. By the time the Education Career Development Office was ready to take over the administrative details of supervising such clinical experiences, Mork had provided it with a fully functioning plan of organization. With Peik's encouragement and blessings, he also served as the College's chief representative in the National Education Association and the Minnesota Education Association, as well as the State Department of Education.

Mork's involvement in these organizations was in keeping with the dean's determination to make communication between national and state educators a reality. This could not happen immediately, however, and Peik was careful to prepare the way by supporting faculty members who had already been hired and by making a series of astute appointments. G. Lester Anderson and Minard Stout (who would go on to the presidency of the University of Nevada) were made directors of the University High School, and Edgar Wesley and Dora V. Smith were given free rein in their respective fields of social studies and English language arts. The 1942 appointment of Emma Birkmaier resulted in an integrated sequence of modern language courses from the third grade through the secondary school, and Donovan Johnson gradually developed a similar series of mathematics courses for the high school years.[26]

Johnson's sequence was truly integrated and carefully monitored to avoid repetition and redundancy; it was also highly innovative. In 1956, when James Stochl joined Donovan Johnson and Robert Jackson (who had been named an instructor in 1955), an elementary school program of mathematics was in full swing and the high school program had undergone significant changes. Through Johnson's efforts, students at the University High School were introduced to a number of new topics taken from modern mathematics — such as statistics, number systems, sets and set theory, probability, and finite mathematics — and often reserved for college instruction. Tenth graders worked with both solid and analytical geometry, while seniors explored college algebra and calculus. Johnson's program had excellent results in at least two areas: not only did the high school students benefit, but student teachers were made to realize that the teaching of mathematics could be a stimulating and enjoyable endeavor. While the students themselves were encouraged to explore and study mathematics far more than was normally expected of them, their teachers began to see the possibilities inherent in new and exciting teacher aids. Johnson himself provided a number of these, including twelve pamphlets published as *Exploring Mathematics on Your Own.*[27] Over a million copies of these pamphlets were sold, and they continue to be marketed at the end of the 1970's.

In the exhilarating intellectual atmosphere provided by educators like Donovan Johnson, the mathematics teachers of the University of Minnesota developed more confidence in themselves, and many went on to become recognized leaders in the field. The list of graduate students includes such names as Richard Shumway of Ohio State University, Harry Hatfield of the University of Georgia at Athens, and Biggo Hansen of California State University at Northbridge.

In 1948, Clarence Boeck came to the University High School and did for chemistry what Donovan Johnson had done for mathematics. Like Johnson, Boeck was an innovator who initiated a number of changes in introductory courses. By 1958, he reported that "full year intensive science courses have been substituted [for what had previously been taught junior high school students] with the seventh grade students probing into the field of geology, the eighth grade students stressing astronomy and the ninth grade introducing meteorology."[28] In years to come, the University High School science staff was able to provide its students with challenging laboratory work in biology as well as in physics and chemistry, and all three fields of study would be brought into the students' programs far earlier than they were in the more conventional curriculum.

Despite Coffman's reservations about Peik, the College was in no danger of becoming mediocre under the dean's guidance. Its faculty also saw to this; they were willing to defend not only their own work but that of their students. Faculty in other colleges were willing to defend them, too. One of the College's faculty members recalls a situation which provides some idea of the flavor of the times. One day, he overheard a discussion between a senior member of the mathematics department and a junior colleague. The two were disputing the quality of students in the College of Education. The junior colleague, quoting from the *Minnesota Daily*, the University's student newspaper, mentioned something about Education's low overall grade point averages, while the senior professor argued that education students were among the very best he had had each quarter. Eventually, the senior colleague disappeared into an office insisting that something *"had* to be done" — not about students in the College but about the *Daily*.

Wesley Peik may have seemed like an unassuming man — any fair-minded person would have to admire him simply for daring to follow Haggerty's long performance — but his influence on the College was considerable. Not only were his wide-ranging interests reflected in faculty who were added under his direction, but his concerns also reached into the future and occasionally drew strength from the past. For instance, the attention Peik paid to vocational education was a further continuation of Kiehle's vision. For many years prior to Peik's tenure as dean, the industrial arts, home economics education, and agricultural education departments communicated with one another, but they were far from forming an identifiable unit. Conflict occurred within their ranks between those who saw their fields as belonging to *general* education and those who envisioned themselves as purely *vocational*. This "general-professional" categorization did not appeal to Peik, who preferred to think of the departments as forming a sensible blending of course offerings and emphases.[29] He also wanted to see more attention paid to the exploration of the vocational aspects of the secondary school. With these ends in mind, he characteristically set about recruiting qualified and capable faculty members. Industrial arts, business, agricultural, and home economics education were among the beneficiaries of his efforts. In 1945, for example, Howard Nelson was brought in as an instructor in industrial arts education; by the time he became a regular member of the faculty in 1948, he had been joined by William Kavanaugh. Nelson became chair of Industrial Arts Education and proved a fitting successor to Homer J. Smith, who had joined the staff in 1919 and chaired the department for over thirty years. With Kavanaugh's appointment, the history and philosophy of industrial arts came alive at Minnesota. In 1946, Warren Meyer opened the door for distributive education, and two years later Ray Price took command of business education. Milo Peterson and Gertrude Esteros joined the staff during the same year as Meyer. Peterson's contributions to the modern Department of Agricultural Education led to his being elected president of the American Vocational Association, and Esteros, together with Roxana Ford (who came to the University in 1947), helped to revitalize the program in home economics.

A close connection existed between the advances being made in the agricultural school and Peik's determination that the College would do something concrete for the citizens of Minnesota. Specifically, he supported the work of Milo Peterson and the Department of Agricultural Education in their efforts to help farmers and future farmers by devising a comprehensive farm record analysis which could be used to point out the strong and weak points of their business operations and thus increase their profits. Peik's own rural background undoubtedly contributed to his interest in this area. Just a year after his death in 1951, the Department of Agricultural Education received a grant from the Hill Family Foundation (later the Northwest Area Foundation) which allowed it to expand into adult education. Today's Farm Business Management Program is a direct result of what was begun early in Peik's deanship.

Throughout his career, Peik moved toward his favored objective of establishing professional standards for the preparation of school personnel.[30] Within a year after being named dean, he began to voice this concern. He corresponded with Malcolm Willey, a sociologist who was equally aware of society's need for adequately prepared professionals. In one letter, Peik wrote:

> Many of the standards [set for institutions preparing school personnel] are not valid measures of the worth and quality of an institution. Schedules set up for the return of information by single college institutions may have no validity as reports for institutions with complex organizations and with communities of numerous separate colleges which follow various procedures. I believe that there should be one accreditation for the universities ... as a whole and one accreditation of the professional colleges [normal schools or state teachers colleges]. All other accrediting agencies should respect that accreditation if its validity is established and its standards approved in some way about which I am not clear.[31]

The way would become clear to Peik in later years. In the meantime, however, he concluded this letter to Willey with the thought that "whether or not regional accreditation should step out of the picture for national accreditation I do not know....Personally I am not committed to the perpetuation of regional accreditation if a satisfactory set-up can be established otherwise."[32]

Peik's ambitions proved realistic; accreditation not only became a national issue but a national fact. Nine years later, he himself moved into a position of unquestioned national leadership in establishing high professional standards and ascertaining that only schools which were capable of offering sound teacher preparation would be accredited. He traveled throughout the country to further this goal, leaving the College to Marcia Edwards whenever it was necessary for him to be absent.

In a 1948 letter to President James Morrill, the dean reported that he would be off campus for two weeks. He had been invited to Atlantic City to deliver the keynote address at the opening session of the American Association of Teachers Colleges. "I have probably been asked to do this," he stated, "because ... of the merger of three organizations [into] a new over-all accrediting association [which] will probably take place at this meeting. I have sponsored this idea from the beginning and am very happy about the result."[33]

The merger did in fact take place, and the organizations — the American Association of Teachers Colleges, the National Association of Colleges and Departments of Education, and the National Association of Teacher Education Institutions in Metropolitan Districts — became a single organization representing 258 separate teacher training schools for the purpose of setting higher professional standards. In a front page article written the same year for the February 22 New York Times, Benjamin Fine reported the birth of the American Association of Colleges for Teacher Education. Peik's dream had become a reality.

Morrill applauded Peik's performance at the Atlantic City conference and congratulated him in a March 3 letter: "I note that the New York Times' stories gave you the principal credit for the merger of the three organizations . . . . Knowing something myself of the rigidity of organizations and their competitive attitudes, you must have been a skillful negotiator, indeed!"[34] Others would join in praising the College's dean both during and following his lifetime. On receiving word of Peik's death in 1951, Willard E. Givens, executive secretary of the National Education Association, may have said it best: "In Dean Peik's passing, American Education has lost a great leader. He has done more to unify and strengthen the organizations working in the field of teacher education than any other individual in our country."[35]

Ten

The Expanding Educational Horizon

THE DEATH of Wesley Peik on December 6, 1951, was a great loss to the College, but the momentum of well-established programs combined with the administrative skills of Marcia Edwards and the clerical proficiency of Jo Zimmar managed to keep matters stable until a new dean could be found. Thanks to Edwards, who stepped in as acting dean, and the staff in Burton Hall, the search for Peik's successor did not have to be a hurried affair. Both time and care could be taken to ensure that the person chosen to replace him would have the qualities necessary to make important administrative and policy decisions for the College during the coming years.

That Marcia Edwards was available to serve the College during the interim between deans was especially fortunate; no one knew better than she the extent of the College's problems and needs. These she aptly summed up in a letter written to President Morrill on March 19, 1952.[1] Accompanying the letter was a lengthy memorandum entitled "Comments on the College of Education." This was divided into five sections, each dealing with a different topic: the responsibilities of the College; staff problems and policy planning; the relationships of the College; budgetary problems; and problems of administrative organization. Even though the College was approaching its fiftieth anniversary, there was still a good deal of room for improvement, at least in her eyes, and she wanted to make sure that Morrill — and, by extension, the new dean — knew the full extent of the College's situation.

She began her "Comments" with a statement of responsibilities. Perhaps looking back at the College's early days, she substituted the term "mission" for "responsibility" and insisted that the

171

College's primary mission within a land-grant university was to maintain a superior staff. "This," she acknowledged, "we have done in high degree."[2] A good faculty did not guarantee a good college, however. As she pointed out, "for our students, we must provide the best possible training program for their future work in public education, and here we have a noticeable need . . . for further strengthening of our community and school practice facilities."[3] Finally, she stressed that it was time for the College to start paying more attention to Minnesota and less to furnishing "leadership for the general improvement of teacher education nationally."[4] While Peik had devoted a great deal of his time to ensuring higher standards for American teacher education and making sure these standards would be maintained through accreditation procedures, it would be best, in Edwards's opinion, if his successor stayed closer to home.

The acting dean then turned her attention to staff problems and policy planning. During the next three years, seven important staff members would retire: Boardman, Neale, Homer J. Smith, Brueckner, Van Wagenen, Jean Alexander, and Clara Brown Arny. Within a few more years, the retirement list would include Dora V. Smith, Louis Keller, Palmer Johnson, Nelson Bossing, Clifford Archer, and Gertrude Baker. Would these major figures be replaced by equally prominent faculty, or by young assistant professors? The latter seemed more likely, and Edwards warned that "insofar as we must replace these major graduate staff members at the assistant professor rank (which will be necessary budgetarily unless reserve funds are available for retirement coverage), the areas of our strength in graduate education and research will change."[5] It was, then, of the utmost importance that the "retirement picture . . . be in the front of the dean's thinking, in order that we may gain by planning and not lose by being caught in attempted one-to-one replacements."[6] Again and again she emphasized to Morrill that the new dean would have to devote much of his efforts to planning, especially in the area of staff utilization. In addition, she stressed that the College faculty was carrying far too heavy a load in student advising responsibilities, especially at the graduate level, and that this was having deleterious effects: "More than a third of our staff members reported chairmanships or memberships on advisory committees off-campus, and we stood lowest among the colleges in 'no writing' and 'no speeches.'"[7]

At this point in its history, Minnesota's College of Education had done more than its part to upgrade the teaching profession as a whole; it was now time to reexamine priorities. Under the third heading in her "Comments" to Morrill, "Relationships of the College," Edwards admitted that "state-wide, no one questions our in-service education responsibility"[8] but — she felt constrained to add — "our discharging of this responsibility [has] been uneven by fields and sporadic in terms of staff available, even though the total contribution is large . . . . At present, Minnesota is far behind several other states in the provision of consultative services to the public schools."[9] In conclusion, she stated that "the essential character of this work comes not just from a responsibility for the upgrading of teachers and administrators, but also from the necessity of keeping our undergraduate and graduate staff close to the crossroad problems of the schools of this State" — not for the sake of public relations but "to the end that our teaching itself may be improved."[10]

In the midst of these problems, others even more obvious had been caused by deficiencies in the College's budget; these were the focus of Edwards's next topic: "We find ourselves operating what we strongly believe to be a better program built on a broader base," she said, "but still with shoestring financing."[11] High enrollment would continue to pose a challenge for at least another decade. At the same time, professional requirements were being raised; Peik's ambitions were bearing fruit. Budget planning had always been nerve-wracking, and it did not look as though it would improve in the near future. Edwards explained this harsh reality to Morrill by leading him through some of the budget problems in field after field.

Administrative organization was no better off. It would be at least fifteen more years before the basic problems in organization were reasonably met; in the meantime, Edwards's memorandum did not attempt to gloss over existing difficulties:

> The Dean of the College of Education serves as head of two departments — Administration, with 27 budget items . . . and General Education, with 79 academic items of varying percentages . . . .This administrative organization places in the office of the dean all of the planning work for educational psychology, curriculum and instruction, planning budgets, making teaching schedules, preparing reports, processing appointments, finding staff, approving purchases, and so on.
>
> In these same areas, the administrative load for summer planning falls on the dean's office . . . .We have frequently discussed the desirability of more definite departmentalization of the College of Educa-

173

tion, but within the present budget limitations, it is impossible to consider so expensive a plan. Neither is it feasible, however, for the dean's office to continue carrying the work it has tried to handle in recent years. For example, in my own job as assistant dean, I have been unable to use my secretary for weeks at a time during spring because all of her work was needed on processing summer appointments, making arrangements for summer visitors (housing, office space, materials, booklists, etc.), handling special summer announcements and correspondence and preparing bulletins and schedules for the College. Actually I could not have dictated during the days anyway, because my day hours were needed for heavy coordination work with faculty committees, staff conferences on loads and schedules for the coming year, budget planning with Dean Peik, my own University committee schedule, conferences with present and prospective graduate students, and general administrative responsibilities. Since I am a typist, the fastest way for us to handle the pressure last spring was for me to serve evenings and weekends as a combination assistant dean and secretary, turning out about half of my correspondence in that way. If we had not had experienced and exceedingly competent young women as secretaries for the dean and assistant dean, I do not know how we could have come through the past year.

In the budget cut last spring, I lost my teaching assistant. But this was not important, because the relief needed in the dean's office is the kind possible only through additional continuing staff at a responsible administrative level.[12]

It was not until 1974 that the College was organized into seven departments; by then, this move was long overdue.

By the time Morrill finished reading Edwards's detailed memorandum, he must have had a good idea of the College's principal difficulties. He must also have been mindful of the source of this information. Marcia Edwards was no mere complainer; her vision of the College's responsibilities and role was secured by a faith in a philosophy of education that had long guided the College and its faculty. Nevertheless, Edwards felt it necessary to offer the president some reassurance: "Nothing in these comments about the College of Education," she stated, "should be construed as appointing a pessimistic future."[13] Though enrollments were increasing far beyond the College's budgetary capabilities, neither Edwards nor her colleagues were prepared to surrender to the pressure: "We well know that all divisions of the University must share in budget reductions, and we will carry our part, working around any special difficulties we may find. Heavy loads for faculty are involved, yes; but this is also true throughout the University, perhaps especially in its administrative offices."[14]

It was little wonder that after this communication President Morrill hoped that Edwards would undertake the deanship herself. He tried to persuade her, but she adamantly refused.[15] Though she foresaw no problems as a result of her accepting this position (either within the College or the University), she felt that educators throughout Minnesota and other states were not yet ready to see a woman appointed dean of a major college of education.[16] Edwards made this observation without bitterness, and Morrill was all the more impressed since it came from a person who was neither incapable of leadership nor indifferent to a career in administration.

Thus, a search committee composed of College faculty was established and charged with the responsibility of finding a new dean, preferably one with an extensive background in research. Not surprisingly, the committee did not have far to look. Walter Cook, a professor of educational psychology, had already made a name for himself in research (and would later be elected president of the American Educational Research Association). He had joined the College faculty in 1938 — the same year Ruth Eckert arrived — and, like Eckert, was well-respected by research-minded educators. In August 1952, four months after Edwards wrote her memorandum to Morrill, Cook was appointed dean.

An experienced researcher, Cook dedicated himself to empirical matters early in his career. His first major publication was a 1932 doctoral dissertation, *The Measurement of General Spelling Ability Involving Controlled Comparisons between Techniques.*[17] Everet Lindquist served as Cook's major adviser during the writing of his dissertation and remained a warm supporter. Two years earlier, Cook had served as a research assistant to the National Advisory Committee on Education in Washington, D.C. He also gathered administrative talents along the way during his superintendency at Hazleton, Iowa, between 1924 and 1929. In 1932, he succeeded Fiske Allen as head of the Eastern Illinois State Teachers College Training School. This latter post would prove similar to one he would accept twenty years later, when he agreed to head a combined Minnesota College of Education elementary and high school.

It was not long before Walter Cook was introduced to the national scene; during the same year in which he accepted the post at Eastern Illinois, he was named to a National Education Association committee which had been charged with drafting a comprehensive program of public education. He was not all that interested in formulating grand designs for the nation's schools, however. Instead, he was concerned with persuading educators of the "irreducible variability" of elementary school students and, by extension, of all students. Cook used the term "irreducible variability" to describe a phenomenon which he felt all teachers everywhere should be aware of — namely, that students are different. Through his own work, he meant to convince educators not only to accept students' individual differences but also to welcome them and to provide stimulation for each pupil. His enthusiasm about individual differences would win him support at Minnesota, whose faculty had become famous for voicing identical concerns.

Ten years after arriving at Minnesota, Cook summed up his theory of irreducible variability:

> When a random group of six-year-olds enters the first grade, two percent of them will be above the average eight-year-olds. Disregarding the extreme two percent at either end, there is a four-year range in general intelligence. By the time this group has reached the age of twelve (sixth grade level) the range will have increased to almost eight years. As long as all the children of all the people remain in school the range continues to increase, even through high school. When the educational achievement of a typical sixth-grade class is measured we find a range of approximately eight years in reading comprehension, vocabulary, arithmetic reasoning, arithmetic computation, the mechanics of English composition and other forms of achievement.[18]

His theory was sufficiently grounded in empirical data that he felt comfortable making generalizations based upon it. In particular, he was fond of asserting that almost any sixth-grade class would contain at least one student with second-grade reading ability and another with tenth-grade reading ability. In any grade above the primary level, then, students could be found who possessed the complete range of elementary-school abilities.[19] Cook's research was exactly suited to the objectives for which Dora V. Smith's *Individualization of Instruction* series had been started; his own monograph, *Grouping and Promotion in the Elementary Schools*,[20] was the paragon of that series.

Cook sympathized with his fellow educators who wanted answers to the problems they faced daily in their own classrooms, but he was eager to point out to them that the existing answers might not be identical to those which they sought. Namely, many teachers were concerned with bringing slow students "up to grade"; Cook stressed that slow learners and gifted ones — the extremes on any classroom continuum — could not (and should not) be homogenized. He made this point again and again, perhaps with greatest effect in an essay entitled "The Gifted and the Retarded in Historical Perspective."[21] There he argued his by-now familiar theme, "the extent of variability," turning almost at once to what he called "the acceleration fallacy." This fallacy, he believed, encompassed two equally erroneous notions: that bright pupils needed an accelerated course of study, and that slow pupils required failing grades and nonpromotion. "The bright pupil — the one who profits most from an educational environment — is eliminated from school first," he stated. "He spends less time there, while the slow pupil who can profit least from an educational environment spends the most time there."[22] Thus, the teacher's responsibility was to stimulate slow students rather than bore them. Bond, Brueckner, and others accepted this challenge and spent a good deal of time with remediation.

Above all, Cook avoided thinking in terms of "standards of achievement" at individual grade levels. Certainly, achievement tests were to be valued and used, but not for the purpose of holding students to standards. Instead, as Cook stressed, the purpose was "to enable the teacher to know more about the pupil, the books he can read, the type of problems he can solve, the amount of improvement that can be expected, in short, what he reasonably can be expected to do."[23] This did not mean that gifted students were to be ignored; on the contrary, Cook felt that every opportunity should be taken to make school equally significant for them, and that in high schools "there should be special honor classes for students who demonstrate unusual ability in the sciences, mathematics, or language."[24] Honors courses were a rather obvious way of recognizing outstanding abilities and interests, however. High grades or high I.Q. scores did not necessarily take into account other important characteristics like creativity. What was to be done for creative students whose talents might not be reflected in their classroom performance? While Cook did not extend his own research into this area, he was instrumental in appointing Paul Torrance to the directorship of the BER. Torrance served in this capacity from 1960 until 1966 where he became an unquestioned national leader in studies on creativity.

It was inevitable that Cook would also turn his attention to the attitudes of teachers; this interest culminated in the design of the

Minnesota Teacher Attitude Inventory (MTAI).[25] He felt that the needs of individual students could best be met by sympathetic and understanding teachers. Unfortunately, not all teachers fit this description; some, he wryly said, paraded "pharisaic virtues":[26]

> The teacher who scores low on the MTAI describes himself in his responses . . . as generally hostile towards others; he says that pupils are dishonest, insincere, untrustworthy, lazy, etc. His self-description also indicates that he: (a) adheres excessively to right standards of morality; (b) tends to dominate those below him and be subservient to those above him; and (c) prides himself on a thorough knowledge of his subject matter.[27]

Cook abhorred the ideals of what he termed the "schools of 1900" and saw the hostile or pharisaic teachers of his day as embodying many of these archaic and harmful ideals. His criticism of some of his contemporaries was subtle yet clear. As recorded in a newspaper article of July 1, 1950, his observations furnish a clue as to the type of teaching he hoped graduates of Minnesota's College of Education would never perpetuate:

> In the classroom [of 1900, but not only of 1900], potential mule-skinners, day laborers and janitors sat beside embryo research physicists, surgeons and business executives. They looked at the same texts, pursued the same educational goals and were marked on the same standards . . . . A docile personality and a good memory meant success in the rigid, tense, pin-dropping atmosphere of the classroom . . . . The commands, 'attention', 'position', 'sit', 'stand', 'wait for the order', 'march', controlled the packed pupils as they squirmed their way through the narrow aisles . . . .[And] in spelling, hours were spent learning such words as mordacity, perspicacity, triplicity, verticity, oleaginous, mucilaginous and vertiginous.[28]

Ironically, although he was appointed to the College deanship largely because of his experience as an empirical researcher, Cook found little time for his own research once he assumed the post. The hectic schedule he faced during his first several months as dean was forecast in the final sentences of Edwards's 1952 memorandum to President Morrill. There Edwards had reminded Morrill that the American Association of Colleges for Teacher Education would be coming to the College as part of its intervisitation program. The visit would require much preparation and planning on the part of the College: at the very least, a number of staff conferences would have to be held. In addition, all members of the faculty were asked to respond to a document requesting carefully thought-out opinions on the following three topics: (1) "problems of the College of Education toward whose solution the faculty and administration should work this year," (2) "the most urgent unsolved problems of the College of Education," and (3) "the greatest strengths of the College of Education."[29] Cook threw himself vigorously into planning for the association's visit, and Edwards must have been pleased about this. He soon found himself handicapped for want of sufficient data and funds, however.

No one who presumed to take the reins of the College could expect to have an easy job of it; the problems summarized in Edwards's "Comments" may have at times seemed like the mere tip of the iceberg. In our own era of diminishing student enrollments,[30] it is difficult to understand that the world Walter Cook faced was quite different from ours. In a paper which can be attributed to him,[31] Cook estimated that between 1945 and 1950 school enrollment in Minnesota had increased by 10,000 pupils per year. By 1952, this had doubled to 20,000 pupils per year, and Cook projected that this figure would represent the annual average increase in Minnesota student enrollment during subsequent years. Between 1952 and 1965, then, 10,000 new teachers would have to be added to the state's teacher corps. The shortage was already noticeable; it could only get worse.

Cook knew that the College's faculty had to be increased and that facilities had to be improved. Although the College already boasted a curriculum center, for example, Cook wanted it to have a full-fledged education library as well. He would have to bide his time until 1962 before seeing that dream realized; at that time, he wrote in a College of Education newsletter that "the best news of the year is that the College of Education is to have an adequate and up-to-date library," which had been one of its greatest needs "during the 57 years of its existence."[32] Walter Cook was a realistic man. He knew that the College would have to wait for its library and he also knew that his educational philosophy did not have a prayer of being translated into fact if teacher attitudes and curricula alike were not changed.[33] The direction of curriculum shift which Cook favored would be thought "progressive" even today; this is evident from the types of research which he undertook with Kenneth Hovet (a close associate of Nelson Bossing), who had been a superintendent of schools in Floodwood, and Nolan Kearney, superintendent of St. Paul schools, who specialized in the elementary school and was definitely not an educational conservative.[34]

179

Cook had a number of revolutionary ideas and a great deal of energy, but he never used his position as dean to his own advantage. The other faculty did not gravitate toward Cook's research either into pupil variability or teacher attitudes, and he would not have wanted them to. Rather than seeing himself as the director of the College, he preferred to think of himself as just another member of an already strong team. By nature a modest man, kept from pomposity by his sense of humor, he refrained from calling attention to his own work but never hesitated to brag about that of his colleagues. Not long before his death on September 9, 1964, he unblushingly admitted to Ed Haislet, the executive secretary of the Minnesota Alumni Association, that "truthfully I don't know of another college which ranks above us."[35] He went on to claim that Minnesota

> definitely ranks at the top in . . . educational psychology, research design and statistics, elementary education both at the undergraduate and graduate levels, secondary education both undergraduate and graduate (especially in languages, mathematics, science, social studies and English), educational administration, higher education, [and] vocational agriculture.[36]

Not wanting to appear overzealous, he did admit that the College had slipped in the area of the history and philosophy of education, stating that its efforts ranked "second to Teachers College."[37] In the same letter, Cook claimed that sixty-two percent of the College's professors (twenty-six out of forty-two) were listed in Who's Who.

Cook had been dean for three years when the University Short Course and Schoolmen's Week in March 1956 celebrated the golden anniversary of the College of Education. The theme of the week was "The Expanding Educational Horizon." In 1955, enrollment in the College had reached the highest point in its history, and it boasted 852 graduates: 588 with bachelor's degrees, 217 with master's degrees, and 47 with doctorates. President Morrill was scheduled to address a large audience of educators and administrators during that week, and it is likely that he drew upon the following letter from Dean Cook when preparing his remarks:

> Approximately 60 percent of the 405 superintendents in the State of Minnesota have received their master's degree from the University of Minnesota in educational administration with Dr. Neale. Seventy-five percent of the senior high school principals have earned their M.A. degree under Dr. Boardman's direction. One hundred and twenty-seven industrial education teachers of Minnesota have their master's degrees from the University of Minnesota.[38]

180

Cook closed this paragraph by assuring the president that "we feel certain that statistics in other areas of education would be equally impressive if they were available to us."[39]

Cook was justifiably satisfied with the College. Not only was its faculty consistently performing top-flight research, but it was fast becoming a central focus for the study of learning disabilities and the preparation of special education teachers. In 1950, the Institute of Child Welfare's Child Development Clinic merged with the Child Study Center to form the Psychoeducational Clinic;[40] its name was changed in 1968 to the Psychoeducational Center. The clinic was the idea of a study committee chaired by Guy Bond whose members included Marcia Edwards, Gilbert Wrenn, Willis Dugan, and Walter Cook. It developed an outstanding training program, graduating such people as Louis Smith of Washington University; Edgar Doll, a clinician and author of the *Vineland Social Maturity Scale*; and Bjorn Karlson, the major author of the *Stanford Diagnostic Tests*. The Psychoeducational Clinic offered possibilities for graduate students and faculty to do research while simultaneously serving as a major resource for the state. Its staff diagnosed sensory impairments and their causes, along with the causes of other handicaps, and studied their effects on the learning process. As many as 120 youngsters, many with reading problems, were diagnosed within any given year; most were boys of nine or ten. Staff members talked with parents, reviewed data from the schools, tested the children, and reported their findings back to the schools — often suggesting activities or teaching methods which might be used to solve particular problems. During the summers, as many as fifty school teachers at a time came to the clinic to observe thirty or more handicapped children. Following their visit, the teachers were able to return to their classrooms with new ideas, new experiences, and new materials.

Looking back at the early years of the Psychoeducational Clinic, Maynard Reynolds had very little doubt about its having been

> a very important mechanism for the training of teachers who were concerned with detailed clinical diagnosis of children with difficulties in basic skills. It linked very closely with Guy Bond's efforts in the field of remedial reading . . . [and] provided a large share of the remedial teachers who began to be employed in the schools in the 1950's and early 1960's.[41]

Although the clinic remained under the direction of the College of Education, faculty members from departments outside the College were welcome to join, too. Thus, its staff also included faculty from the Department of Psychology and the Medical School. The founders of the clinic never intended it to be strictly for the benefit of the College; instead, it was perceived as "an effort to build . . . a facility which would enable intercollege participation in the training of different professions that would be working with the schools in the care of children."[42]

Harold Delp came to Minnesota in 1948 from his post with the Psychological Clinic of Nebraska to serve as the first director of the College's Psychoeducational Clinic. Delp's assistant, Maynard Reynolds, was then a graduate student and would later become a national leader in special education. Before joining the staff of the clinic, Reynolds worked with Cyril Hoyt and Guy Bond in the BER; Donald Paterson of the psychology department was his adviser. Paterson was fundamental to the guidance counseling programs of the University, and it was from him that Reynolds learned to think in terms of tests and diagnoses aimed at constructing appropriate experiences for differing individuals who had to be guided along differing educational paths. Eventually Reynolds was to head the Department of Psychoeducational Studies, which incorporated counseling and student personnel psychology, school psychology, and special education. The joining of those programs made sense, and it was equally reasonable that Maynard Reynolds should become the first chair of such a combination. A substantial portion of Reynolds's time went to training teachers for special classes and special school work in programs for children who were mentally retarded, blind, deaf, crippled, and speech impaired. During those early years, however, the school psychology, special education, and remedial reading programs — in which Guy Bond was a prominent figure — were organized on an interdepartmental model, with many students gaining their clinical experience through the diagnostic and remedial programs of the Psychoeducational Clinic.

In 1951, Reynolds replaced Delp as the director of the clinic and served in this capacity until 1957, when he became chair of the Department of Special Education. Bruce Balow succeeded Reynolds as director until 1965, when he was replaced by Evelyn Deno. During these years, when the clinic was focusing its attention on learning handicaps, the University Elementary School, housed in the same building as the clinic, was concentrating on gifted and very bright children. The school offered "experience in observation for undergraduates who could see how a well-run school would function, and what very bright children look like."[43] Even with this school, the College did not do as much as it could have with (and for) these children; most of the faculty were more interested in research involving the learning handicapped. This, of course, was Reynolds's field, and he prospered in it. Mildred Thomson, author of *Prologue,* a book about the educational philosophies of mental retardation,[44] recognized the young assistant professor's potential and set about introducing him to people in the National Association for Retarded Children (now the National Association for Retarded Citizens) and to various institutions and programs of care for the handicapped. Unfortunately, these different associations and groups, while ostensibly having common goals, often interfered with one another, each exaggerating its own needs. The rivalry between them was substantially mitigated by the formation of the Minnesota Council for Special Education, which was abetted and supported by the College's faculty. Meanwhile, the parents of gifted children felt increasingly ignored and began removing themselves from College-related programs, and this further curtailed efforts aimed at the gifted.

The motives behind the formation of the Psychoeducational Clinic must have been similar to those which moved a visionary like David Kiehle to encourage the University to reach out to the citizens of the state by way of the Agricultural College. While the Agricultural College had benefited the state's farmers, the Psychoeducational Clinic gave invaluable assistance to the schools — and, through them, to the parents of affected children. Many of these parents responded in 1955 by acting through the Minnesota Council for Special Education to secure the creation of the Elmer L. Anderson Committee, which drafted legislation on special educational needs that passed the Minnesota legislature in 1957. One piece of this legislation resulted in the formation of an advisory committee chaired by Maynard Reynolds, who was appointed by Governor Orville Freeman; Reynolds served in this position from 1957 to 1961. To encourage research and training, the legislature appropriated $70,000 to the University to use for the preparation of teachers of the handicapped.

The latter years of Walter Cook's deanship saw the beginning of a rapid growth in the federal funding of research. "Soft money" (as distinguished from "hard money," which is generated by internal funds assigned to college and departmental budgets) flowed to many universities; Minnesota was no exception, and the College of Education in particular was a magnet since its reputation for research in many fields was well known to those who were most responsible for dispersing funds in support of research.[45] The special education department was only one of the programs which were amply supported by "block training grants," receiving between $300,000 and $400,000 annually — and it received yet another half million dollars in special training-related grants.[46] This generosity on the part of government institutions enabled Minnesota's special education department to rank in the top four or five across the nation. It also allowed many graduate students to gain a great deal of experience in research along with their professional training. The sudden influx of money was not universally applauded, however; there were many who felt that the College paid a heavy price for it. A significant amount of the research its faculty performed during this period was only distantly, if at all, related to the practical problems besetting the schools. Off-campus service was shunted to one side. Even teaching became secondary, according to some who look back on these years with a less-than-favorable opinion of them. Thus, a tension was created between those who advocated "pure" research — that is, research which is basic, theoretical, or unapplied — and proponents of actual teaching and service to the community.

Another familiar tension was felt during Cook's deanship, this one almost exclusively intellectual: it divided those who supported empirical research and those who felt that the arts and the humanities were of equal importance. Obviously, Haggerty had had faith both in research and in the significance of the arts; Cook's feelings on the matter were less evident. Those who knew Cook, however, claim that he was proud of the work done by Dora V. Smith and her colleagues, although documents in support of this position are not at hand. Additions to the College staff of persons concerned with literature and the arts do seem to indicate that Cook was not oblivious to these fields of study. Naomi Chase, an instructor in 1950, taught English language arts; she was a full faculty member by 1958, when she was joined by Norine Odland. Under Odland's direction, children's literature became more of a genuine program than it had been under Dora V. Smith, who had so much else on her crowded agenda. The appointments of Paul Oberg in music and Ayers Bagley in the history and philosophy of education can also be seen as indicating that Cook paid some heed to professional programs that were artistic and humanistic rather than merely empirical.

Nevertheless, the main focus of the College during Cook's deanship was on empirical study, especially psychological study. The existence of the Psychoeducational Clinic serves to substantiate this claim. Evelyn Deno, who directed the clinic for several years, was actually appointed to the Institute of Child Welfare, but her relationship with the College of Education could not have been closer. She was heavily involved in the Child to Adult Study, a follow-up of adults who as children had been in the Institute's nursery school during the period 1925 (when the Institute was founded) to 1935. Brueckner, Bond — and, indeed, anyone involved with skills development — became aware that Deno's areas of interest were integral to the College as well. Once that perception spread beyond a few faculty, it was predictable that the Institute of Child Welfare would join the College of Education. And, with Walter Cook as dean, it was assured a happy reception.

Although 1957 is the date of the official merger of the College of Education and the Institute of Child Welfare (renamed in 1960 the Institute of Child Development), the cooperative association of the two staffs had its roots in the Institute's earliest days. Subsequently, the years that surrounded its actual incorporation as a free-standing unit into the College of Education were crucial not only to institutional but also intellectual relations. Bridges between the two had long existed; it was not at all unusual for someone in the Institute to pursue a line of investigation similar to that being followed by a faculty member in the College. Although it was not essential from the standpoint of cooperative research or graduate training for the College and the Institute to join forces, it was nevertheless fortunate —if only for these reasons — that they did. A case in point is the professional career of Marian Hall. From 1943 to 1946, Hall was a teaching assistant for Joseph Warren Beach in the English department, after which she taught at Sheltering Arms, a school for the handicapped, for thirteen years. During her stay there, she became aware of learning disabilities and other forms of dysfunctional behavior among the young and was motivated to return to the study of child development. In 1959, she enrolled as a graduate student in the Institute. At home in Child Development, she was nevertheless pleased that the College could host a program in "school psychology." The relations between the Institute of Child Development and the College of

Education were good enough that the Institute did not feel cheated because this program was placed under the College's wing instead of its own. Eventually, Hall was appointed as the third director of the school psychology program, and she occupied that position until her retirement in 1977. When the College was departmentalized in 1974, the program became part of the Department of Psychoeducational Studies. This department, as stated, was headed by Maynard Reynolds, who knew the importance of school psychology and could help integrate the program with such natural affiliates as special education or counseling and student personnel psychology.

The point to be made here is that the College of Education maintained good relations with other parts of the University. At the same time, it satisfied a need of the school system by nourishing a program that the schools themselves had requested. Not only were the schools hungry for remedial teachers who had been exposed to the Psychoeducational Center as well as the teachings of such persons as Brueckner, Bond, Balow, and Dewey Force (who came to the staff of special education), but there was also a need for those who were able to undertake testing programs. Although the state of Minnesota boasted some first-rate school psychologists, including Virginia Hathaway and Sarah Holbrook, it had not had access to a well-conceived and developed program in school psychology prior to this time.

The program was made possible largely because of the close working relationship of Walter Cook and Dale Harris, the director of the Institute of Child Welfare. Their combined efforts — crystallized during discussions at a conference held in 1957 at the Thayer Hotel in West Point, New York — breathed life into the organization of a core program in school psychology. The effects of this conference spilled over into the College. Harris and Cook made sure that at least two faculty members, Willis Dugan and Maynard Reynolds, would be involved in the program.[47] Dugan represented educational psychology (as, of course, did Cook) and chaired that department; Reynolds, also a member of the educational psychology department, was about to become head of special education. Cook and Harris recognized, however, that the two men's interests and capabilities extended far beyond the bounds of their own departments. Dugan also represented psychology, while Reynolds symbolized the interrelationships which linked the College of Education, the Institute of Child Welfare, school psychology, guidance-counseling psychology, the Psychoeducational Clinic, and special education. Once the Thayer conference was over, Harris, Dugan, and Reynolds took major responsibility for forming a program in school psychology; Cook had other duties, but the three knew that they could count on the dean's support. When it became obvious that funding would not be available for getting a pilot program started, for example, Cook was happy to work with Harris in writing a proposal for a National Institute of Mental Health grant. When funds were in hand, a curriculum in school psychology took form, under the direction of Alan Hodges. Hodges had previously worked in the State Department of Welfare as a supervisor of all the psychologists employed by the state. When he left, Jan Duker took over and was in turn succeeded by Marian Hall.[48]

The cooperation between Dale Harris and Walter Cook signified more than an ephemeral gesture of goodwill — it translated into hard research. It is interesting to note that a November 29, 1957, application for a College training grant under the National Mental Health Act bears the signatures of both Cook and Harris. One section of the grant request, labeled "History of School Psychological Services in Minnesota," is particularly illuminating:

Psychology has served school children in Minnesota almost fifty years, since the days of Dr. Frederick Kuhlemann's revision of the Binet Test, and W.S. Miller's and Melvin Haggerty's work on group tests. This concern was greatly increased when the Institute of Child Welfare was established in 1925 by a substantial grant from the Laura Spelman Rockefeller Fund. The Institute has made fundamental scientific and practical contributions to psychological assessment, both psychometric and projective, of abilities and personal characteristics of children and adolescents.

Its consultation service for parents has existed since 1933. But school psychology and the training of personnel for school psychological services have lagged at this University, despite the fact that a substantial number of graduate students have trained in the departments of psychology, educational psychology, and child welfare and ultimately found their way into schools as psychologists.

In 1953 and 1954, Dr. Dale Harris of the Institute of Child Welfare served on the Planning Committee of the American Psychological Association, which established the Thayer Conference on School Psychology; he reviewed the literature and assembled a bibliography and working library of materials for the Conference. Dean Walter W. Cook of the College of Education attended the Thayer Conference in 1954. As one outcome of the Thayer Conference, Dr. Willis Dugan of the Educational Psychology staff of the College of Education in 1955, made an extensive survey resulting in the important title "Survey Report on Pupil Personnel and Psychological Service in Minnesota Public School Systems" . . . . Based on the findings of Dr. Dugan's survey in 1955, a two-year graduate program was instituted in the Graduate School to lead to a Psychological Certificate as Educational Specialist in School Psychological Services . . . .This certificate was designed to meet a need for trained people to do initial cases . . . . But an Educational Specialist in School Psychological Services differs from a School Psychologist in at least two ways: He is more likely to work in a direct remedial facet with children, and is less likely to supervise other psychological examiners or educational specialists.[49]

Although the Institute of Child Development has been a department of the College for more than two decades, this does not mean that College of Education students today regularly take courses offered by the Institute. There is no question, however, that faculty in both maintain several interests in common. The longstanding relationship between the two remains a credit to the efforts of Walter Cook; perhaps the most outstanding of the dean's administrative achievements occurred when he smoothed the way for their merger.[50] In retrospect, it seems more likely that the Institute of Child Development should have joined with the College of Liberal Arts (formerly CSLA), whose psychology faculty was — and is — well respected. No one was more pleased than Maynard Reynolds that the Institute instead chose the College of Education as its partner. Looking back, Reynolds commented:

> The institute was always a well balanced place. It did very good research, it had high level theoreticians, but it also kept itself carefully linked to the community. It appreciated the role of the family; it worked with parents. It had a lot of very practical kinds of connections to the people of the state.[51]

Just as the College was pleased with the Institute's reputation and performance, the Institute had no cause to be disappointed in its new host. The College was no longer merely a teacher training ground; it had expanded into special education, experimental design and statistics, remediation, the discrimination of and adaptation to individual difference theory, the practice of testing and measurement, and the study of learning and classroom interaction. Underlying all of these varied programs was, of course, educational psychology. This field had served as the backbone of the College for many years — from its beginnings in 1915. During that year, Haggerty had written Dean Coffman about the purposes and organization of a department of educational psychology and proposing a central core of work in general psychology, experimental psychology, genetic psychology, the psychology of learning, differential psychology, and mental testing.[52] A month earlier, Haggerty had informed Coffman of what he himself wanted to teach in that area.[53] In short, he intended to offer courses in educational psychology, mental testing (with a laboratory), the psychology of learning (again with a laboratory), the mental diagnosis of school children, and a seminar in educational psychology. That is, Haggerty intended to teach single-handedly five courses per term and prepare for five different classes six days a week while at the same time keeping up with his publications. The origins of educational psychology in the College were, in a word, formidable.

While College bulletins from 1924 to 1928 tell of a four-year curriculum for the preparation of school psychologists, it was not until 1938 that educational psychology became a program of graduate work. By the fall of 1954, a total of eighty-seven doctoral candidates in educational psychology had completed their dissertations. In the minutes of the College faculty for February 2, 1955, Willis Dugan, chair of the educational psychology department, reported that for the fall quarter of 1954 "a count of major adviser's [*sic*] records of currently active, part-time and summer only graduate students in educational psychology . . . revealed a total of 333 including 215 M.A. students and 118 doctoral students."[54]

A lengthy report on educational psychology published in 1955 did not allude to what might well have been on the minds of at least a few people at that time: the possible incorporation of the Institute of Child Welfare into the College of Education. It is highly probable that at least speculative discussion was under way by then. A scant year later, Section 7 of the *University of Minnesota Self-Survey Report on Physics, Mathematics, and Child Welfare*, entitled "The Institute of Child Welfare and the College of Education," made a case for the two joining forces: "We do not know what the wishes of the faculty of the College of Education may be," the argument opened, "but we believe they should welcome the opportunity to integrate the study of the teaching and development of children from infancy through age five with their own studies of the teaching and development of children from age six onward."[55] The report went on to "call attention to the fact that the College of Education is strongly research minded. It has also a faculty in Educational Psychology that has made excellent studies in the problems of learning, teaching, and testing."[56] The members of the educational psychology faculty at that time included Palmer Johnson, Gilbert Wrenn, Willis Dugan (chair), Gordon Mork, Maynard Reynolds, and Ned Flanders. (At that time Flanders was involved in research and training in the relatively new area of "group dynamics.")[57]

Having said something about the College, the *Self-Survey* went on to give a brief and cogent description of the Institute, saying that it was primarily concerned

> with children of below school age . . . and especially with their development from infancy up to school age. Development may be defined as the changes that take place in children in these years. Against a background of physical changes . . . research studies in the Institute concentrate upon the developments in children psychologically and educationally, in social and moral matters, in leadership, and in other factors that go to make up the total personality of the child.[58]

Multivariate, interaction analysis was altogether compatible with this approach. So also was the thinking associated with such a course as School and Society. The *Self-Survey* then stated that in order to study "a number of children over a period of time at first hand and under controlled conditions, the Institute conducts a Nursery School and Kindergarten."[59]

Section 8 of the *Self-Survey* carried a recommendation that the Institute merge with the College of Education rather than CSLA. Urging that the recommendation be reviewed at the end of three or five years (this proved unnecessary), the report concluded: "When all factors are balanced against each other, the committee's recommendation is to locate the Institute of Child Welfare in the College of Education with full status as a separate school or department within the College."[60] This recommendation came as no real surprise; according to informal faculty talk, the CSLA psychology faculty were worried that they would be overwhelmed by the sheer numbers of Child Development personnel should the two be merged. In return, Institute members thought of themselves as psychologists and were dismayed when their colleagues in CSLA rebuffed them. Interestingly, the College of Education had far fewer *educational* psychologists than CSLA had psychologists, and there was no sign that the College felt at all threatened. In the middle of May 1957, a memorandum was drawn up detailing the relocation of the Institute.[61]

In the Institute the College acquired a capable research partner. At the time of the *Self-Survey,* the Institute had already published some 750 research papers, monographs, and books; as one observer reported,

> some of the best known projects concerned the standardization of a widely used intelligence test for young children; studies of infant development, children's emotional development, and foster children's development; studies of children's thinking and language; the measurement of skin area and bodily dimensions in children; and investigations of children's sleeping, eating, temper, and adjustment problems.[62]

The Institute of Child Development has continued to thrive. Its annual report for 1974-75, compiled after fifty years of service, shows that it has added several programs during recent years. The Center for Early Education and Development was made operational in the fall of 1973; in June 1974, the Board of Regents gave provisional authorization for a University Child Care Center and lodged it in the Institute. Today, Child Development lists twenty-two faculty members and its statement of mission is not much different from that which appeared in the 1956 University *Self-Survey*: "Currently, the Institute of Child Development promotes research and trains students in child psychology. The research deals with basic issues in cognitive, motivational, and social development along with applications of developmental information to educational and therapeutic problems."[63] The Institute continues to draw a distinction between its own efforts and comparable programs at other universities: "The continued diversity of the faculty and student body distinguishes the Institute's programs from programs in developmental psychology at other universities. By bringing together most of its developmental psychologists in one unit, the University of Minnesota has fostered an unusually comprehensive and interactive program."[64] The 1974-75 annual report also contains a summary of the research being carried out by the Institute. These, it states,

> cover a wide range of projects which can be divided arbitrarily into four major groupings: studies of attention and perception; socialization and personality; learning and cognition; and language. Studies in attention-perception include work on the initiation, maintenance, and selectivity of attention; the development of perceptual capabilities; spatial orientation; and complex motor systems in infants, young children and adults. The socialization-personality program includes the development of greeting behavior; communication; cross-age interaction in children; role-taking; effects of self-evaluation and affect;

teaching strategies; and legal socialization of children. Work in learning and cognition involves problem-solving; memory processes; and individual differences in development of mental abilities. Work in language includes language and articulation development in normal children and psycholinguistics. Individual faculty members are also conducting research in behavior genetics and cross-cultural ethical concerns.[65]

The list of topics indicates how diligently Institute of Child Development faculty have been striving to work at the cutting edge of new ideas. To illustrate, John Anderson, the Institute's founder, invited Jean Piaget and some of his students to come to the Institute a full twenty years before Piaget became a distinguished name among developmental psychologists. Just as Haggerty would have held it unthinkable for a set of ideas — however imaginative and persuasive — to remain untested, Anderson and his students attempted to test Piaget's theories. Piaget's failure to systematically validate a great many of his own assertions was one of the points Anderson held against him.[66]

The current program of the Institute of Child Development bears little resemblance to that begun by John Anderson and his distinguished colleague, Florence L. Goodenough. Anderson originally intended to lead the Institute in two directions: he meant to establish a "knowledge base" about child development, and he planned to employ on the Institute staff a cadre of "parent educators" who would be available to go around the state lecturing or talking to groups and sharing research findings. This two-pronged approach became known as the "Anderson balance," and Anderson hoped that it would help to alleviate the tension between advocates of applied and unapplied knowledge. Unfortunately, the balance of the original plan became one-sided; before Harold Stevenson arrived to assume the directorship of the Institute, there was a period during which research actually languished. Stevenson not only stopped the program in parent education, but he insisted on a renewed emphasis on research.[67] Today, there is some question as to whether the Institute is doing enough to "spread the word" throughout the state. In response, many Institute supporters maintain that parental instruction is not the only valid way to effect change and improvement in the schools — and that the careful preparation of professional nursery, kindergarten, and elementary school teachers by developmental and school psychologists is an equally if not more promising approach.

One reason the Institute of Child Development is so strong today is largely financial; while initial funding amounted to about $50,000 per year for five years from the Laura Spelman Rockefeller Memorial,[68] the Institute's budget for 1974-75 was in excess of a million dollars. There has been a change in emphasis as well, reflected by the evolution of the Institute of Child *Welfare* to the Institute of Child *Development*, a focus which can be attributed to Harold Stevenson's direction. The underlying emphasis has changed little, however. This is made clear in an anecdote Anderson used to tell his graduate students. The Laura Spelman Rockefeller Memorial had offered money to any state that would match its grant with state-generated funds, he said, and an Iowa woman had therefore gone before the state legislature to plead for its assistance. She believed that the state university system had a responsibility to meet the needs of its citizens and that research into child welfare and development was an important aspect of this responsibility. After all, she argued, if she and her husband wanted to know anything about raising pigs, they could call their agricultural extension agent, who would come out to their farm, share the university's latest research with them, and help them to learn how to apply it to their particular situation. "Surely," she is supposed to have said, "children are just as important as pigs."

Eleven

The College
and the Counseling Tradition

WHEN the College of Education celebrated its golden anniversary in 1955, it could boast of having one of the finest guidance and counseling programs in the nation. This came as no surprise to anyone familiar with the College's history. The attention to individual differences which had long been a focus of the College — augmented by careful research, testing, and measurement — could only have resulted in a guidance program which served as a model for other colleges and universities throughout the nation. True, the program had changed over the years and continues to change. Originally, it had been a natural outgrowth of the College's work in educational psychology and especially the contributions of Haggerty, Palmer Johnson, and Walter Cook. Close association with the Department of Psychology and such influential leaders as Donald Paterson had added strength to the empirical aspects of the program; by 1955, under Willis Dugan's direction, the concentration on testing and measurement had been supplemented by an interest in individual qualities and characteristics which were not so easily measured. Dugan had come out of a tradition which differed from that of educators like Haggerty and Paterson; he and faculty members like Gilbert Wrenn gave the guidance and counseling program balance by adding to it an emphasis on humanitarianism.

Prior to assuming the chairmanship of educational psychology in 1950, Dugan had headed the College's Student Personnel Office and spent a great deal of time traveling throughout the state developing high school counseling programs. Unlike his predecessors, he did not serve a long apprenticeship in psychology; instead, he worked extensively with young people and found much personal satisfaction as a secondary school teacher and coach in the schools of rural Minnesota. During the Depression, being involved with young people often carried over into helping their families deal with financial problems. Dugan proved adept at such matters and eventually won a place on the staff of the Minnesota Youth Administration, where he remained as assistant director until 1938. It was probably during these years that he developed his somewhat radical view of student counseling, which involved the idea that it should be *systematic*. It was not enough to guide students in ways directly related to career choice or college entrance; it was also necessary to offer them assistance with personal and educational decisions. Dugan had his first real opportunity to develop a counseling and guidance program at the University High School, where he served as a counselor until 1942. Subsequently, he went to Washington, D.C., as assistant director of personnel for the American Red Cross. This experience taught him a great deal about the functioning of bureaucracies and served him well when he returned to the University of Minnesota. At that time, the College was faced with having to reorganize itself in order to meet the challenges of the post-war world, and Dugan's newly acquired organizational skills were especially valuable.

Student counseling in the College, however, had its beginnings many years before Willis Dugan arrived. A unit known as the Student Personnel Committee had been operational during the late 1920's, and as early as 1929 a monograph entitled *Student Counseling in the College of Education*[1] was widely used; Dora V. Smith, Homer J. Smith, and Wesley Peik were all contributors. In his study of the Student Personnel Office, William Edson emphasized that "throughout the monograph there is evidence of the central concern for the relationship between students and the academic program and for the development of individuals as they become teachers."[2] It included sections on counseling as well as College regulations, personnel procedures, and personnel services.

In 1939, the Student Personnel Committee recommended that a full-time counselor be hired to work with students who were preparing to teach. As a result of that recommendation, Dugan began his career with the University. He was appointed in 1942 as the first director of personnel in the College, but his wartime service with the Red Cross prevented him from assuming this role until 1945. Organizing the Student Personnel Office proved to be a demanding job, and matters were not helped by the fact that little money was available. Fortunately, Dugan was able to turn to three influential people for assistance and support: Edward Seldon, William Edson (who had been Dugan's teaching assistant in educational psychology), and Marcia Edwards (who in a very real sense had been responsible for opening the door to personnel psychology in the College). In time, Dugan's commitment to the preparation of high school counselors overshadowed his interest in student personnel work, and Edson replaced him as director of the personnel office.

During the period of change and reorganization, there were essentially two dimensions to student personnel services. The first dimension, counseling-personnel psychology, had several layers, one of which stressed theory and practice at the high school level. This was Dugan's particular interest. The other strata centered on college personnel work; chief figures in this area included Gilbert Wrenn, E.G. Williamson of the central administration (who began the statewide testing program that typed high school graduates in terms of suitable college programs), John Darley of psychology (who followed Williamson as head of the University Testing Bureau), and Donald Paterson of psychology. The second dimension involved the admission and subsequent guidance system of the University and the College.[3] Its most important architect of ideas and programs was Marcia Edwards, who outlined the concept of a guidance system and highlighted the responsibilities involved in its administration. She believed that the College should control the admission of students to teacher education programs in order to better regulate the quality of those who entered the teaching profession; her efforts paralleled those of Coffman and Haggerty, who had labored to see that all would-be school teachers were registered in the College of Education.

Edwards saw the College as playing a crucial role in the University, and partly due to her influence this role expanded over the years. Eventually it included determining criteria for recruitment and admission, evaluating students' performance in College courses, and supervising student teaching, placement, and follow-up. Throughout these varying but interrelated functions, assurance of quality was of primary importance. Very promising students were to be given excellent professional preparation, careful guidance along the way — because personal and academic problems were bound to occur — and thoughtful assistance with placement.

Out of these various elements, a sort of "system" evolved which consisted of intake criteria and periodic monitoring of the student's professional growth as he or she moved through the training program. Although this system may sound rigid, it was not; both Dugan and Edwards insisted that the student be given an important voice in determining the preparation he or she received. There was never any conflict between a "directive counseling" approach (a view associated with Williamson) or a "nondirective counseling" approach (supposedly typical of Chicago's Carl Rogers) simply because the College guidance program never adopted an either-or stance. The student was counseled, provided with alternatives, and then left alone to make essential decisions. Though courses were prescribed for this or that goal, no student was relieved of the responsibility of choosing. This did not mean that the students could do as they pleased, however; more than a few were placed on academic probation or counseled out of the College because it seemed all too likely that they would not be satisfactory teachers, counselors, or administrators. It was no accident that the College's reputation for turning out able graduates grew and that Arnold Woestehoff of the Bureau of Recommendations was able to report year after year that a high percentage of the College's graduates had been successfully placed. This emphasis on quality illustrated precisely the tradition begun by Coffman, who was dismayed by the low quality of the American teacher corps and worked for the establishment of a preparatory curriculum geared to graduating only superior teachers. Furthermore, Peik continued what Coffman had begun during his own battle on behalf of the accreditation of teacher preparation programs. Eventually, this tradition was institutionalized in the Education Career Development Office, which opened on July 1, 1973.

Today, under William Edson's leadership, this office provides a type of long-term guidance which is unique in this country. Originally a combination of the Bureau of Recommendations (established in 1925), the Student Personnel Office (1942), and the Department of Clinical Experiences (begun around 1951), the Education Career Development Office has expanded to embody a total counseling concept. Students are viewed both in terms of selection and preparation. They are closely supervised throughout their student teaching period and following their placement. Rather than providing a general sort of guidance program, the office focuses specifically on future teachers, school administrators,

197

counselors, and educators. In a sense, it successfully institutional-izes what Marcia Edwards began years ago: attention to the indi-vidual student and his or her needs, capabilities, and career — all with a special emphasis on directing students in such a way that they are able to realize their full individual potential.

Other forces were at work in the meantime. During the late summer of 1928, Haggerty assigned James Umstattd to direct the Bureau of Recommendations. Umstattd held this post for some eight years and during the 1930's was instrumental in creating the National Institutional Teacher Placement Association, which elected him its president in 1935. This association was an offshoot of the American Guidance Association, which had been neglecting the area of teacher placement. Since the two organizations had completely different focuses, guidance counseling was similarly divided into theory and practice. Reconciling the two into a work-able whole became one of the tasks which faced Edwards and Du-gan nearly a decade later.

Fortunately, the College already had a strong theoretical bent, chiefly in psychometrics, and Dugan and Edwards were able to direct their energies toward practical or institutional needs, using the Student Personnel Office as their primary vehicle. When Peik died in 1951 and Edwards became acting dean, she was able to write President Morrill that the Student Personnel Office could be counted on to give "inestimable help this year by taking on regis-tration and tallying students and the whole probation load of the College, as well as by removing from my office the first informa-tional interviews with prospective graduate students."[4] The work of the Student Personnel Office, she continued, has "in raising the quality of our teachers-in-training through selection . . . been of the utmost importance to the College directly, and to the whole Uni-versity indirectly."[5] This was made possible because of the fact that a year earlier the office had incorporated "the college registra-tion desk and the college information desk, and the director became responsible for the coordination of the registration pro-gram."[6] According to Edson, "this added a new kind of re-lationship with advisers and extended relationships with the other colleges and offices of the University. It permitted further integra-tion of the work of the counselors with the instructional program."[7]

The College not only aspired to excellence in its graduates, but it also ensured excellence with tools which had been developed by such leading educators as Palmer Johnson of the College's faculty and Donald Paterson in CSLA. The longstanding relationship between the College of Education and the Department of Psychology in CSLA continued to prove mutually beneficial. Graduate students in both colleges were free to go back and forth for courses they needed, and faculty in both were constantly exchanging ideas and research results. Throughout the 1930's and 1940's, College faculty members published both normative and predictive studies along with various recommendations for determining student selection. The normative studies included students' scores on the Miller Analogies Test, high school rankings, and other data. E.G. Williamson traveled the state on an annual basis to administer Paterson's scholastic test to high school seniors. These test scores, when combined with students' class standing and grades, served as the basis for admission decisions and were also seen as predicting subsequent college grades. Dugan used his firsthand knowledge of this testing program to create the College's program in secondary school guidance. He did not think that test scores alone were sufficient grounds for making judgments about students' abilities, however, and early in his career he made it a habit to compile "case histories" which combined test data with a good deal more. This is not to say that Dugan perceived the Miller Analogies and other tests as becoming less useful over the years; rather, he felt that they needed to be supplemented. Even the best of predictors failed to earmark all of the students who eventually were put on probation or had to have their curricular programs drastically modified. It gradually became evident that the College knew far too little about student personnel, and in 1957 the Student Personnel Office added a staff member to work full time on student personnel research.

By that time, Dugan had left the office to embark on his career of constructing a solid program for would-be secondary school counselors. His efforts did not go unrewarded. In May 1959, the *Minnesotan* reported that Dugan, one of the founders of the Student Personnel Association for Teacher Education, had been honored by the association "for outstanding service to the personnel and guidance profession."[8] Upon his retirement from the University in 1966, he was offered the post of executive director of the American Personnel and Guidance Association. In the meantime, he had been appointed head of the Association of Counselor Education in May 1961 and had also been asked to direct the National

Defense Counseling and Guidance Training Institute for secondary school teachers and counselors from a six-state area. In looking carefully at Dugan's record, one can see that his work branched into two different but interrelated directions. The first led from the Student Personnel Office; the second, which won him a national audience, came out of his experience in secondary school guidance counseling.

There are other names which come to mind during any discussion of Minnesota's guidance and counseling tradition, and chief among these are Gilbert Wrenn and E.G. Williamson. Although the two worked together, they were very different, and this seems to have resulted in some regrettable rivalry. The fact that Wrenn made a mark at all is noteworthy considering that his view of guidance often varied from that which was well established at Minnesota by the time of his arrival in 1936. If anything, Donald Paterson, E.G. Williamson, and John Darley had only strengthened the tradition of empirical research which had guided the College for so many years. While Wrenn acknowledged the importance of this tradition — and accepted some of its aspects — he was also drawn to the study of values and attitudes, neither of which can be readily measured. He envisioned counseling as encompassing a relationship with the entire person and not merely focusing on his or her training in specific skills or areas. He had little respect for what he termed "encapsulated counselors," those "who wall themselves off from the world around them . . . . They weave a little cocoon around themselves and are protected. They pretend that life inside the cocoon is the same as life outside the cocoon. And many counselors constantly do this . . . with the school environment as the cocoon."[9] He firmly believed that counselors had to learn to expand their fields of vision, as it were, in order to be truly effective. Those who insisted on following a "programmed text" for being a good counselor while neglecting the fact that each counseling client is an individual, were in essence

> missing the complete person . . . . You are missing the person that operates outside of the counseling office as well as in. The client comes to you as an accumulation of a lifetime of experiences in a certain order, in a certain period of time, in a certain ethnic background or cultural background. Unless you are aware of this, you aren't seeing a person, you are just seeing the outward verbal aspects of the person in the interview which isn't enough. The counselor must understand the matrix out of which the client has come, the background the client brings into the interview.[10]

Wrenn often found himself defending his position. When Dale Wachowiak interviewed him for the *Personnel and Guidance Journal*'s series "Pioneers in Guidance," Wachowiak remarked, "I'm impressed by the scope of your thinking, Dr. Wrenn. In your books, you are a sociologist one minute, then into philosophical concepts, then talking about the skills of the profession. Does this represent the kind of person that we should be turning out in counseling?"[11] Wrenn answered simply that "Ed Williamson and I disagreed on this back in the 1930's. Of course, he was at that time stressing diagnosis, and even in the 1930's I was more concerned with relationships and attitudes."[12] Although Wrenn was sympathetic with the psychoanalytic movement, here was yet another instance in which he chose to take his own stand by adopting — and adapting — only some of its concepts.

One aspect of guidance which Wrenn did support unquestioningly was the University's response to the large numbers of unemployed. Donald Paterson and John Darley had succeeded in adapting Paterson's particular form of vocational counseling for use in the Employment Stabilization Research Institute, which operated during the 1930's. Wrenn's background, primarily his specialization in vocational guidance, meshed well with the purposes and goals of the institute. It was in part because of this aspect of his background that Wrenn was invited to Minnesota to serve as assistant dean of the General College, which had always been conscious of and responsive to the world of work.

Wrenn received his Ph.D. at Stanford University, where he stayed on to serve as both a vocational counselor and an assistant professor of education until 1936. During that year, he came to Minnesota to become an associate professor of education and assistant director of the General College, a post he held for two years. It was not long before he was introduced to the work of Donald Paterson.[13] The General College was heir to fifteen years of thought and conversation; Paterson set down the essential history in his "Reminiscences Concerning the Development of Student Personnel Work at the University of Minnesota."[14] What Paterson did not relate in those "Reminiscences" was what he himself had brought to Minnesota upon his arrival in 1921 — specifically, a great deal of knowledge about the function, strengths, and weaknesses of the Army Alpha-Beta intelligence test.

One of Paterson's assistants, E.G. Williamson, went on to become even more outstanding than his tutor. In retrospect, it must be said that no one at the University has been as important to the College's guidance and personnel curriculum as Williamson. When the *Personnel and Guidance Journal* planned its series of reminiscences of outstanding contributors to the personnel-guidance field, Williamson was chosen as the first name in the series. He, in turn, chose to acknowledge Paterson's influence. Since the University had no research-based program in counseling during the 1920's, Paterson's work — as Williamson told *Journal* interviewer Dorlesa Ewing — was truly pioneering. "Donald Paterson," he stated, "had come here and established a whole program of research on student development and a program of counseling, including mental hygiene and social case study."[15] Paterson's first contribution, Williamson recalled, was to assist CSLA dean John Johnston "to identify students of low predicted grades and thus to increase the admission standards and scholastic performance of students enrolled in the University."[16] Johnston, who had been searching for a technique to determine which students would be "better in the sense of grade-getting" as prospects for the liberal arts college, used Paterson's "technology for measurement." Williamson, as Paterson's assistant, later tested students throughout the state for this purpose.[17] In sum, as Williamson expressed it in an introduction to his mentor's own reminiscences, Paterson brought the University "a newly evolved technology of identifying [objectivity] aptitudes and measured interests for occupations and for scholastic requirements of students."[18]

In his history of the University of Minnesota, James Gray embroidered a bit on what Williamson meant by students who would be "better in the sense of grade-getting." In a chapter entitled "Counseling: The Minnesota Point of View," Gray states that Johnston had "worked constantly at his studies of scholastic performance. His philosophy urged the recognition of four levels of educability. Applicants who stood lowest in entrance tests should, he suggested tactfully, be advised not [to seek entrance] to the university but be guided in vocational training elsewhere."[19] Guidance counselors in the public schools — such as Dugan — were to do the guiding. Gray went on to credit Johnston with being the first to formulate "the idea that those in a second group who showed [moderate ability] but [who are now doing poor work] be provided with a special course in the Arts College that would lead not to a baccalaureate degree but to a certificate given on completion of a shorter program."[20] It was this group of students with "moderate ability" that the General College was specifically designed to serve.

While Paterson himself was busy with the Committee on Educational Guidance,

> Dean Johnston was making his classic studies of student prediction and demonstrating that, while absolute grade averages from high school could not be relied upon, one could make surprisingly accurate predictions by converting such grades into ranks for each high school and averaging high school rank with a college ability test rank normatively based on liberal arts college freshmen. This immediately posed problems of what to do with the low ability students and how to maximize the performance of high ability students.[21]

Three actions were taken in an attempt to solve these problems: Paterson was asked to head a new committee on faculty counselors; Haggerty headed a committee on educational research; and, in 1928, a statewide testing program was set up "in cooperation with the Association of Minnesota Colleges as a means for providing better educational guidance to high school seniors in Minnesota. That committee was headed by Dean Johnston."[22] Meanwhile, the University Testing Bureau, which had been founded in 1923, was directed by the youthful Williamson, who had enrolled in the Department of Psychology as a graduate student and had served as Paterson's assistant while working on his doctorate.

Coffman was delighted with the testing bureau. It was, after all, a logical derivative of the "Magna Carta" of students' rights which had been issued in 1923 by his Committee on Educational Guidance. This document was important for a variety of reasons:

> Its recommendations took a searching view of the difficulties presented to a freshman by the new world of higher education into which he had come with a mixture of dewy-eyed expectation and sluggish self-doubt. It insisted that he be told more precisely what the University could do in preparing him for a profession or vocation and what, in stern reality, the possibilities of those life assignments were. It urged that he be given orientation courses to broaden his view of the possibilities of various fields of learning. It restated the right of the student to have an adviser of professional caliber capable of making and of interpreting a full personality profile. It insisted on the necessity of special vocational guidance for women, who had . . . notions of destination still more vague than had the young men. The importance of psychiatric help for the unstable was pointed out for the first time . . . . [The] Magna Carta also suggested pointedly that teachers needed not only to learn to teach better but also to be larger minded men and women in the discharge of their duties as counselors of youth.[23]

When Coffman wrote his "Educational Trends in a University" for the College's twenty-fifth anniversary volume,[24] he was obviously pleased with the testing bureau's accomplishments: "The superintendents, principals, and high school teachers of the state, in cooperation with the University of Minnesota and later with the Association of Minnesota Colleges, began testing high school seniors several years ago with a view to discovering those who possess college ability." Coffman boasted that "this movement is unique among the states of this union."[25]

Not everyone in the College of Education was equally enthusiastic about the University Testing Bureau. Harl Douglass certainly had reservations and expressed them in "Some Dangers of the Testing Movement,"[26] which E.G. Williamson answered in his article entitled "The Co-operative Guidance Movement."[27] As a rebuttal, Douglass wrote "Co-operative Testing and Straw Men,"[28] warning school people of the "seemingly inevitable stimulus such projects (as that represented by the University Testing Bureau) give to over-emphasis on outcomes measured by the written tests now available.[29] While Douglass admitted that there were "many items of merit in Professor Williamson's discussion," he nevertheless criticized it:

> [Williamson's] scientific disinterestedness could have been made more obvious had he mentioned, in addition to results which favor the use of co-operative testing for the purposes of guidance, results of studies by Professor C. W. Boardman, a colleague of ours, which show that high-school marks from certain Minneapolis high schools, where marking is on a superior basis, yield larger coefficients of correlation with college success than the multiple coefficients involving the Co-operative Tests reported by Professor Williamson.[30]

Finally, Douglass brought his remarks to a close by warning that too much testing might well result in too much concentration on abstract facts, as well as the discrediting of the measurement movement. And, in true Minnesota fashion, Douglass believed this movement to be "the most significant single contribution to education techniques."[31]

In a sense, this debate was resolved by the creation of the General College in 1936. Because it opened its doors to "poor college risks," it was considered vocational and illiberal, and its image gradually darkened until it was perceived as little more than a last chance for the academically incompetent or weak. Perhaps because the General College's reputation was declining, Gilbert

Wrenn soon left it to enter the College of Education in 1937, where he remained until 1964. At this point he was, to use his own phrase, a "measurement man." During the early 1930's, when Wrenn had studied at Stanford under Lewis Terman and Edward Strong, measurement had been considered an essential part of diagnosis, and diagnosis, in turn, was thought of as being necessary for remediation. After all, one could not solve a problem unless one first knew what it entailed and had a reasonable idea of its dimensions. No matter how sensible this argument sounded, however, it proved to have flaws; as Wrenn later recalled, "every major theory that has come into prominence over the years that I have been in the business has gone down the drain as a total theory."[32] It must be assumed that Wrenn's own flexibility, combined with his reluctance to accept any theory at face value, was what enabled him to survive in a volatile field. During his graduate studies, Wrenn had been influenced by Robert Ladd Thorndike, especially by Thorndike's "Law of Effect," and had worked with Strong on his famous Vocational Interest Blank, a diagnostic tool which ostensibly gave some clue as to the subject's vocational bent or aptitude. He was not bound to his past studies, though, and was able to move in directions of his own and eventually state: "Diagnosis in the 1930's was a great step forward, but it didn't take into account adequately the feelings or attitudes of the person."[33] Wrenn remembers that when he first came to Minnesota,

> I was already in some disagreement with what I thought was arbitrariness on the part of Williamson and Darley. [They proposed an] exact diagnosis, following through six steps, and if you did all of them you would have the key to an understanding of the client. I was already in disagreement with that, so I became a maverick at Minnesota right away.[34]

Though his stance did not lead to outright quarrels with persons like Williamson and Darley, Wrenn continued, "we didn't really have any agreements."[35]

During the early 1940's when World War II was drawing the Minnesota faculty to the armed forces, Wrenn, along with Guy Bond, enlisted in the navy. He returned after the war to find an even greater demand for personnel workers and guidance counselors: "During the war twenty million people went through some kind of personnel selection in industry and the military. So we came back and immediately began to experience a great demand for counselors, personnel workers and applied psychologists in general."[36] Wrenn was prepared to respond to this demand. Again, he was not limited to — or by — his background, but instead remained open to new ideas and new approaches. Constantly on the lookout for innovations, he seldom adopted an entire theory but preferred to develop an eclectic approach. This position gained him a great deal of professional respect in addition to winning him the presidencies of such groups as the National Vocational Guidance Association, the American College Personnel Association, and the Division of Counseling Psychologists of the American Psychological Association. In the meantime, he wrote hundreds of articles and books. Later, he would modestly tell Wachowiak, "I have written four or five hundred different items, and I suppose twenty-five or thirty of them are worth keeping."[37] Hesitant to praise himself, he was happy to praise his graduate students: "Out of eighty-some," he recalled, "I think sixty or seventy are pretty great."[38]

By the late 1950's, guidance counseling was an identifiable unit within the University, and in the late 1960's it was experimenting with any number of new ideas. L. Sunny Hansen, who had been on the counseling staff at the University High School, joined the College faculty during this time, and later developed Project BORN FREE, a career development training program aimed at reducing sex-role stereotyping in educational institutions.[39] This and other programs in guidance counseling (such as a recent group counseling and model training program for the development of the counselor-educator) reflect the vision and social conscience which have traditionally been part of the College and have consistently motivated its leaders.

Twelve

Reaching Out to State and Nation

THE COLLEGE first gained national recognition when the United States Bureau of Education issued a special bulletin encouraging other states to sponsor programs similar to the Superintendents' and Principals' Short Course held at the University of Minnesota in March of 1914.[1] This venture, which was a part of the spring meeting of the Minnesota Education Association, was a great success judging from the fact that 275 superintendents were enrolled in it. The State Department of Education, the Minnesota Education Association, and the College of Education had all cooperated in recruiting prominent educators (among them Lotus Coffman, then professor of education at the University of Illinois) to lecture on a variety of topics of interest to public school administrators. It quickly became obvious that the short course should be an annual affair, since total enrollment in 1915 doubled that of 1914. The superintendents responded enthusiastically by passing a resolution of appreciation endorsing the idea that the course be made a permanent feature of the spring meeting. In time, the course became known simply as Schoolmen's Week and earned a reputation for being the high point of the school year for Minnesota educators.

The program provided a rare opportunity for College faculty and state school personnel (primarily administrators) to meet and exchange ideas. As a result, it enabled the College of Education to have a significant impact upon the development of the schools. The College faculty was more than eager to participate. In one series of sectional meetings held in 1930 — the College's twenty-fifth anniversary — Melvin Haggerty spoke to the Minnesota Council of School Executives about cooperative efforts to improve education while Dora V. Smith addressed a concurrent session of the Minnesota Society for the Study of Education on the effects of class size on instruction in ninth-grade English. Fred Englehardt discussed the administration of personnel; F. H. Swift spoke on the financing of public schools in France; Harl Douglass gave an address entitled "Capital Report of Survey of Extra-Curricular Activities in Minnesota"; Homer J. Smith talked about industrial education; and Earl Hudelson spoke on class size and pupil achievement in the secondary school.

In 1931, the meetings provided a forum for the Minnesota Council of School Executives, the Minnesota Society for the Study of Education, the Fifteenth Annual High School Conference, the State Conference of County Superintendents of Schools, the Minnesota College Teachers of Education and Psychology, the Minnesota Chapter of the National Council of Administrative Women, and the Minnesota Deans of Women. In addition, the traditional Short Course for Superintendents and Principals was offered and the annual College of Education alumni-faculty-student banquet was held during the same week. The program had expanded to make room not only for public school superintendents of the state but also for college teachers. Topics were once again varied. At a dinner meeting of the Minnesota Society for the Study of Education, Palmer Johnson, then assistant professor of education, and Alvin C. Eurich, assistant professor of educational psychology, discussed research related to college students; on the following day, Leo Brueckner, professor of elementary education, addressed the group on recent developments in techniques of educational diagnosis, and Harl Douglass, professor of education, read a paper on the relation of certain factors to success in college courses.

These annual meetings provided an important avenue by means of which the College of Education could learn about and address the problems of the schools. It provided one of the few opportunities state educators had to get together and exchange ideas. Nevertheless, the program was discontinued after 1964 for reasons that remain unclear. It was with real regret that Vice President Stanley Wenberg wrote the College's dean, Robert Keller, in 1966 about the passing of Schoolmen's Week: "Now that Schoolmen's Week is gone, I think we've lost not only an invaluable tie with the people in education around the state, but I hear repeated comments from school administrators that they wish we would start the old type of Schoolmen's Week all over again."[2] Wenberg ended his letter by lamenting that junior college deans had not "had a meeting together since we ended Schoolmen's Week."[3] In conclusion, he wondered, "is there any chance we can resurrect the old program?"[4]

Wenberg was conscious of the value of maintaining relations with out-state professionals; his letter may have contributed to the establishment of Schoolmen's Day (renamed Educators' Day in 1972). While it was not an attempt to "resurrect the old program," Educators' Day addressed issues of interest to school administrators; the 1974 conference, for example, centered on the topic of how affirmative action requirements could be met (the proceedings were published in *Minnesota Education*).[5] The following year, the meeting was co-sponsored by the State Department of Education and combined with an Innovations Fair held in the spring of 1976. The program never aspired to the same goals that had motivated the old "short course" and Schoolmen's Week, and perhaps because of this it, too, has apparently been discontinued.

The original Schoolmen's Week had been based on the assumption that the College of Education was a source of innovative theory and practice which could be of real use to leaders of both public and private elementary and secondary education. As such, it worked well with the idea that a state university had a responsibility for relating to various public groups. It was also in keeping with the land-grant philosophy, which targeted teachers and school administrators for what might be termed "educational outreach." This sense of responsibility has been a driving force within the College since its earliest years. The original summer school, begun in 1881, had offered a series of courses for a small number of teachers (primarily those interested in botany, chemistry, geology, mineralogy, and zoology); after George James became dean in 1905, the summer program grew large and more inclusive. James, of course, had a longstanding interest in extending the professional resources of the College, and it can be assumed that he viewed the summer session as embodying this goal. In the *Sixteenth Biennial Report of the Board of Regents*, James expressed evident pleasure in reporting that

> the officers of this college have, from its first establishment, been in charge of the summer courses conducted at the university by the Department of Public Instruction. This school has enrolled between four and five hundred high school teachers each year and twice as many teachers from earlier grades.[6]

209

He did not look upon the summer courses as being sufficient in and of themselves, however, and in the same report to Northrop he wrote of an "insistent and increasing demand" for "vacation courses, to be selected from the various schools of the University and administered under the direction of the college."[7] James asked Northrop to set aside $7,500 for this purpose — almost twice what the summer program had been receiving.

Since its beginnings, the College of Education has been concerned with relating to educators and administrators throughout the state. While its programs and policies have at times seemed to center on more abstract, empirical matters, the fact remains that the College has always viewed itself as part of a statewide educational system. Anyone who doubts this assertion need only look at the history of the University High School, the BER, and the works of such College personnel as Dora V. Smith, G. Lester Anderson, Emma Birkmaier, Clarence Boeck, and Donovan Johnson — all of whom were staunch advocates of University outreach. Dean James was perhaps the first to implement this philosophy. The minutes of a Board of Regents meeting held toward the end of 1905 read in part:

> The Dean has prepared a course of study for the college and the same has been published in a bulletin for general information. Much interest in the new college has been taken by the leading teachers in all parts of the state and hearty cooperation with the college on the part of all the educational forces in the states is assured.[8]

The same report states that:

> the college is to have a large part in the work of training the teachers of the state in coming years. A. W. Rankin, who for several years has been a most efficient agent of the State High School Board in visiting graded schools, and who has had a large experience as teacher, superintendent, and lecturer, has been elected a professor in the College of Education, and it is believed that he will add much to the strength of the faculty.[9]

Extension was yet another aspect of the College's involvement with the state. In 1910, James wrote Northrop to acknowledge the receipt of $5,000 for extension work in 1908 and 1909, stating that the money had been used "to maintain one man in the field, who has brought the help of the university directly to more than ten thousand teachers, distributed through most of the counties of the state."[10] The dean added that "other instructors of the college have, under your direction and approval, been active participants in teachers' meetings throughout Minnesota, and have contributed to the health of the system of public instruction by frequent visitings of schools and consultations with school officers . . . .I respectfully urge, therefore, that the regents plan to continue this new activity of the college and make suitable estimates for it."[11]

As a result of James's prodding, the University inaugurated the "short course" for principals and superintendents four years later. In the meantime, Northrop approved James's request for a "continuance and increase in the traveling fund for purposes of enabling the staff to inspect schools and help graduates in service."[12] James reassured the president that the benefits of such a program would be mutual; this was the first written evidence of a growing recognition that the College could not only help the schools by bringing them the fruits of its study and research, but that it, too, stood to profit from knowing the realities and problems the schools were facing. When Vincent succeeded Northrop as University president, James continued his campaign and wrote Vincent in 1912 to once again request the $5,000 which the College had been receiving since 1907 "for supervision of graduates in the schools, inspection of secondary schools, and organization of meetings with teachers, parent groups, school officers, and general public gatherings to bring the University College of Education in closer contact with the state educational system and its needs."[13] Vincent's years in Chautauqua doubtless resulted in his looking upon James's efforts with favor.

While Vincent was enthusiastic about promulgating University extension — what historian James Gray has termed the "statewide university"[14] — his successor, Lotus Coffman, took a different approach to the topic. Coffman added a new dimension to the James-Vincent notion of extension — namely, the concept of *adult education*. He believed that the University should not "extend itself" per se, but rather offer adults every opportunity to pursue University work on the University campus at times convenient to them. He felt that it would be more advantageous if the University opened itself up to the people of Minnesota rather than attempting to spread its personnel and ideas throughout the state. In other words, he was convinced that the University's resources could best be used at the University. Thus, when Haggerty voiced his pleasure at the fact that Edgar Wesley was spending a great deal of time traveling to outstate schools throughout Minnesota, Coff-

211

man felt it necessary to voice his own opposing viewpoint. In his opinion, extension did not mean a "statewide university," but rather a system for campus-based adult education.

Coffman had a remarkable sense of the need adults have both to catch up with and to stay abreast of their fields after completing their formal education. In this respect (and in many others as well) he took his rightful place beside other College and University visionaries. In *The Changing Educational World,* he summarized his feelings on the subject of adult education:

> With a world changing almost overnight, with machinery being replaced every few years, with science venturing into unknown realms and revealing hidden secrets of vast importance, education must be continuous, even for adults, or they will soon lose step in the march of human progress. The desire to keep the road to promotion open, on the one hand, and to provide general training of a liberalizing character for everyone, regardless of age, was never so imperative as now — hence the movement for adult education. Minnesota is participating in the study of this movement. She has placed three members of her staff on part time and assigned to them the problem of studying the adult educational agencies of the state with the hope that there may eventuate a constructive program, statewide in scope and fundamental in importance. Can anyone really picture what would happen to a state if all of its various agencies were united in a great cooperative undertaking designed to promote the common welfare through the continuing education of all the people?
>
> Perhaps it may be said that this is too vast a picture for any one vision; we may even be accused of being visionary and utopian in suggesting it. But it is my settled conviction that democracy is nothing but a process of continuous education. To halt the process will mean the disintegration of democracy. Not only is it necessary if the institutions of democracy are to survive, but it is necessary also if unemployment and dependent old age are not to become greater and greater burdens. As a practical matter, therefore, the University owes to the society that gives it sustenance and strength to return to it through the processes of education, leading into every corner and section of the commonwealth, types of training that will insure continued employment, greater wealth, greater security, more health, longer lives, and more abundant living.[15]

This position, which was restated in the 1932-34 *Biennial Report,* resulted in a concrete proposal for the Center for Continuation Study (later renamed the Nolte Center after Dean Julius Nolte).[16] This center has often been described as a self-contained residential school aimed at bringing professional and vocational groups together, with the aid of University staff, for the purpose of conducting graduate study on common problems and new developments.

Coffman's hopes for the future were shared by a least one other educator in the College of Education — the relatively new assistant dean, Harold Benjamin. When the center was still in its planning stages, Benjamin proposed that the College offer a new course to its students entitled Adult Education.[17] The following year, he added another related course, Problems in Adult Education. No one was surprised when Coffman appointed Benjamin to direct the new center. Appropriately, the 1934-36 *Biennial Report* carried not Coffman's but Benjamin's statement of the center's purpose: "The University of Minnesota has established the Center for Continuation Study as a means of extending and improving its services to those citizens who feel a desire and need for continuing their education beyond the formal limits of their secondary, college or professional schooling."[18] More explicitly, Benjamin described the center as "designed primarily for the use of men and women who wish to spend relatively short periods of time in serious and intensive study of problems related to their professional, civic or cultural interests."[19] The center was not to supplant evening classes, extension offerings, correspondence study, or other educational efforts; rather, it was to serve a function all its own. Benjamin brought his remarks to a close by stressing the implications of the center's name. It would truly be a *center* in that it would have residential facilities for its students, who could thus live and work together "under one roof during their period of residence on campus."[20] Its primary goal was to provide its participants with ample opportunity for *study* that would reach beyond traditional modes. And, in particular, it was to be a "place for definite study rather than for conventions or social gatherings."[21] The Center for Continuation Study was dedicated on November 13, 1936. As the Nolte Center, it has continued to meet the objectives and needs it was established to address nearly a half century ago.

Benjamin left the University in 1937, and he seemed to carry with him some of the enthusiasm the College had felt for adult education. Other factors were at work during that period; with World War II at an end, a teacher shortage and a baby boom generated much more interest in childhood education than in programs aimed at adults. Some critics of the College feel that it responded too hastily to immediate pressures and did not adequately plan for the future; at any rate, it was not until the mid-1960's that adult education reemerged as a genuine concern, prompted by a State Department of Education request that the

College renew its program in adult education. While Marcia Edwards was characteristically at the forefront of this effort, Harlan Copeland and Reynold Willie gave it its modern structure and found warm support in the College of General Extension (renamed the College of Continuing Education and Extension in 1972). The program was funded by the U.S. Department of Health, Education, and Welfare. At long last, the nation was beginning to recognize — and acknowledge — the fact that a number of adults lacked sufficient schooling in basic knowledge and skills. This awareness came about in large part because of the efforts of civil rights activists and advocates of minorities, the poor, and the disadvantaged. Other groups were concerned with special education and well-being of the handicapped, and they, too, were gaining an audience.

The pioneering spirit present during the 1960's was forecast in many ways by the 1930's. Other colleges and universities imitated Minnesota's venture into adult education, and even with the demise of Schoolmen's Week during Cook's tenure the impetus for outreach continued — especially where teachers were concerned. In 1954, when President Morrill was invited to address the final Schoolmen's Week program, Dean Cook wrote a lengthy letter to him in which he attempted "to summarize some of the facts which dramatize our relations and assistance to the schools of the state."[22] Echoing James's earlier report to Northrop, Cook hastened to state that outreach was a two-way street and that the University in turn benefited from the endeavor. Specifically referring to practice teaching, the dean wrote: "There will also be some situations . . . in which the schools of the state serve us very effectively in the preparation of teachers." Later he added: "Each year, over 600 students are given assignments in approximately 125 different schools of the state."[23]

Cook went on to remark that "almost 6,000 present and prospective teachers in the State of Minnesota are students or participate in conferences at the University of Minnesota during parts of each year."[24] Moreover, "in addition to the regularly enrolled students on the campus, the College of Education reaches approximately 1,000 teachers each year through the Extension Division."[25] As if these figures were not sufficiently impressive, Cook continued by stressing that "during the past seven years [1947 to 1954] the College has offered a total of 234 extension classes in the state. This is an average of 33 classes each year. During these seven years a total of 135 instructors have taught a total of 6,355 in-service teachers."[26] It was clear to the dean that the College was playing an active role in shaping the schooling of Minnesota, if only because so many of its graduates had gone on to positions within the state schools. Again, he cited figures: "Sixty percent of the 405 superintendents in the State of Minnesota have received their master's degree from the University of Minnesota in educational administration with Dr. Neale, [and] seventy-five percent of the senior high school principals of Minnesota have earned their M.A. degree under Dr. Boardman's direction."[27] In addition, 127 state industrial education teachers had received their master's degree from the University. "We feel certain," Cook added, "that statistics in other areas of education would be equally impressive if they were available to us." Finally, Cook pointed out to Morrill that the College was serving the state in other ways as well — namely, through the Bureau of Recommendations, the Bureau of Field Studies and Surveys, the BER, the Psychoeducational Clinic, and the University's model elementary and high schools.[28]

There were those who were not quite as enthusiastic about University outreach as Dean Cook. They preferred to see more of the College's energies spent on research, and in fact believed that the College had an obligation to make a significant contribution in that area. Unfortunately, those who conducted the most sophisticated research were not always able to report their results in an understandable and meaningful fashion to anyone but their professional peers. As a result, teachers and administrators in the field frequently questioned the validity of such research. Wouldn't it be better, they wondered, if students spent less time on abstract, theoretical research and more on practice teaching? This tension between research and service has never been completely resolved, either within or outside of the College. The College itself sometimes seemed to be of two minds in the matter; while undergraduates, for example, have been expected to know a great deal about research in reading, mathematics, and child development, they have also been encouraged to engage in practice teaching as soon as possible. This set of conflicting expectations has proved confusing at times. Which really benefited the students and the state more: research experience or teaching experience?

The changing times have, in effect, made questions like these moot. There have simply been fewer young people to educate in recent years, and this has resulted in a decreased demand for teachers. Thus, those enrolled in teacher preparation programs have been freer to continue on with more extensive graduate studies, primarily in research-related areas. And the College in turn has become more of a graduate school enterprise in which research is a primary focus. This is borne out by data provided by the Education Planning and Development Office (see Appendix):

> Considering fall quarter headcounts, the total number of students in education programs has ranged from 897 in 1945 (because of World War II) to 4,408 in 1970. In the last four decades, enrollments have typically been in a range from about 2,000 to 4,000. Prior to 1957, enrollments were less than 3,000; since that time, most enrollments have been between 3,000 and 4,000. The years 1968 through 1970, with enrollments of over 4,000, exhibited unusual support for education. Following this period of national and student unrest, enrollments stabilized between about 3,400 and 3,700.
>
> Some indications of difficulties ahead appeared in about 1969, when campuses experienced a period of instability. During this time, the College began serious discussions of planned growth with the possibility of curtailing teacher certification program enrollments. Simultaneously, students became increasingly interested in continuing education and the M.Ed. degree. The proportion of Graduate School enrollment has thus steadily increased, as well as the proportion of other postbaccalaureate students. Postbaccalaureate programs involved 37 percent of students in the College in 1969, while in 1976 such students accounted for 57 percent. At the same time, the percentage of students seeking B.S. degrees dropped from 63 percent of the total in 1969 to 43 percent in 1976. The three decades since 1959 show an even greater reversal in the objective of the majority of students from teacher certification programs to postbaccalaureate degrees.[29]

In the meantime, however, land-grant tradition has mandated that the College and the University also engage in service, or outreach. Not long after Ruth Eckert reminded her colleagues of the necessity of maintaining research as a high priority within the College, Dean Cook appointed a committee on College of Education policy on the role of service. Willard Lane of educational administration chaired this committee, and its members included Willis Dugan and Gordon Mork, as well as E. Paul Torrance, who was very much concerned with research. The majority of the committee, however, came from the land-grant areas of home economics, agricultural education, and industrial education. On May 1, 1959, the Lane committee filed a report entitled "Service Activities of College of Education Staff Members." This report used as its basis a questionnaire compiled by the committee which covered a five-year period. Fifty-one persons responded to questions regarding services they had provided to the College, the University, the state, public and private schools, other colleges, professional organizations, parents, and others.[30]

In summarizing their findings on services provided to the state, the Lane committee noted a "relatively high response" — measurably higher than that for services provided to the College and the University: "Almost one-half of the respondents consulted with a staff member of the State Department of Education during 1958. Most respondents see these activities as a legitimate part of their role as College of Education staff members."[31] In the "service to public schools" category, Lane reported that "almost half of the respondents conducted workshops or other in-service training; over half spoke to the faculty or staff groups of a public school; almost half addressed a PTA; and an equal number consulted with a school group concerning some problem."[32] In the area of "off-campus teaching," the committee noted that the "faculty participate only moderately in extension teaching and only one-third see this as a part of their job expectations."[33] On the other hand, results of the survey showed that "a majority of the respondents see participation in conferences and special events as a part of their jobs."[34] The committee concluded that "the most highly valued present service activities appear to be: (1) leadership and consultation, (2) the discovery and dissemination of new information about education problems, and (3) in-service workshops and other in-service training activities."[35] All three, of course, reflected an active concern for outreach, and the second seemed to imply that there was not as great a separation between research and service as had previously been believed.

The shock of *Sputnik* in 1957 prompted an upsurge in research activities and curriculum development during the next ten years, sometimes at the expense of service. Within a year of this monumental event, the National Science Foundation and other groups were financing large research projects, and the idea of outreach assumed a secondary role, at least for the time being. In an apparently immediate response to the Soviet educational challenge, the College faculty joined together with representatives from area school districts to form the Metropolitan School Study Council, which in 1963 became the Educational Research and Development Council (ERDC) of the Twin Cities Metropolitan Area, a consortium of school districts designed to improve education through research, the development of instructional programs, and

the training of school personnel. In a surprisingly short time, the
ERDC proved to be not only productive but influential. The Cooperative School Rehabilitation Center, which began operation in
July 1965 at Glen Lake Sanitarium, was conceived by the ERDC
and was so successful that it was taken over in July 1970 by the
Hennepin County Joint Board, which recognized the value of its
program for developing services for retarded adolescents.

Another achievement of the ERDC was the Social Studies Service Center, which opened in July 1971 after three years of planning by social studies educators. The College contributed a great
deal of thought to its design, and the center became nationally
recognized by 1975. Its collection of social studies curriculum materials is judged by many to be the most complete anywhere.
While the mere existence of the ERDC was evidence of the College's concern for service, it alone could not entirely resolve the
tension between service and research. The creation of the Minnesota Research Coordinating Unit for Vocational Education was
still another attempt to integrate these two aspects of the College's
mission. It opened on June 1, 1965, with funding from the U.S.
Office of Education. The State Department of Education, the State
College Board, and the State Junior College Board all cooperated
with the College of Education in this endeavor. Jerome Moss, a
College faculty member whose research record in the domain of
industrial arts education had proved attractive to Dean Cook, was
invited to serve as its director and remained in this position until
1974, when he became chair of the Department of Vocational and
Technical Education. In the intervening decade, he managed to
demonstrate that industrial arts, business and distributive education, home economics, and agricultural education could all be
joined in a single academic province that combined research and
service. Moss's successor, Brandon Smith, carried on what Moss
had begun.

The fact that the Research Coordinating Unit was located at
the University allowed administrators of other agencies offering
secondary and postsecondary vocational programs to coordinate
their efforts. This arrangement culminated in what was termed a
"Cooperative Agreement" which the Research Coordinating Unit
entered into with the Minnesota State Board for Vocational Education and University Board of Regents in 1968. There were four
explicit reasons for making this agreement: (1) to stimulate, facilitate, and coordinate research and development, (2) to increase the

number and improve the skills of producers and consumers of career and vocational educational research, (3) to assist and disseminate research, and (4) to create knowledge and procedures with promise of long-range and general qualitative improvements in vocational or career education programs.[36] Each of these objectives was aimed at serving either the schools or the community. The "Agreement" — and the College — were both in keeping with the times. During the same year, the Vocational Education Act was amended in such a way that funds were earmarked for cooperative vocational education extension to serve more people and to cover a broader range of occupations.[37] The nation was becoming aware of the fact that ethnic and minority groups in particular were in special need of vocational preparation.

The establishment — and the successes — of the ERDC and the Research Coordinating Unit seemed to indicate that the College could do quality research without ignoring what lay beyond the walls of the campus. Both Dean Cook and his successor, Robert Keller, worked to achieve a balance between service and research. Keller's experience, particularly with the BIR, the North Central Association of Colleges and Schools (now North Central Association of Colleges and Secondary Schools), and the fields of secondary and higher education, made him aware of and responsive to the needs of both. During his tenure as dean, for example, the long tradition of research in physical education for men and women resulted in the establishment of the Human Performance Laboratory. Its staff worked closely with that of the Laboratory of Physiological Hygiene while conducting research aimed at practical and useful results. With John Alexander as its leader, the Human Performance Laboratory ran a variety of tests involving participants' strength and psychomotor response and made anthropometric measurements of respiratory functions and cardiovascular changes during and following exercise.

When Dean Keller wrote his report on the College's progress between 1964 and 1966, he was able to cite any number of research projects — few of which failed to have some service application.[38] Three pages of his report were taken up with a statement of services listing enterprises which had been itemized in the Lane committee's 1959 questionnaire. This report and others set the stage for the establishment of the Leadership Training Institute in 1969 with funds from the Bureau of Educational Professional Development. During the mid- and late-1960's, the federal government funded several programs through the Educational Professional Development Act, many of which focused on the training and retraining of educational personnel to better educate handicapped children. The Leadership Training Institute was charged with assisting other development act project directors and potential directors by identifying national resource personnel and conducting leadership training activities and program evaluations.

Projects like the Research Coordinating Unit, the Human Performance Laboratory, and the Leadership Training Institute found homes at the University precisely because it had proved its strength in the two equally important but occasionally conflicting areas of service and research. And the College had, of course, consistently led the way in its efforts to provide both. This tradition was summaized and highlighted in the "Robb Report" of 1967-68, *A Survey of Cooperative Programs of Educational Research, Curriculum Development, and Preparation of School Personnel between the University of Minnesota College of Education and the Elementary and Secondary Schools.*[39] The report did not include descriptions of "regular College programs such as the student teaching program or the normal in-service graduate coursework being taken by elementary and secondary school personnel.... [or] the extensive participation of the College of Education faculty in planning and advisory councils or committees related to elementary and secondary school systems."[40] Almost all of the College faculty participated in one or more of these advisory activities, and it was more or less taken for granted that they would continue to do so. Nor did the Robb Report list the many individual research projects involving the faculty and the schools. Instead, "those listed are genuinely cooperative efforts in which local educational agencies and the College of Education have *planned, developed,* and *implemented* programs aimed at *exploration* or *solution* of educational problems."[41] Some of these — such as the ERDC and the Cooperative School Rehabilitation Center — were already well known by that time. Others, however, were new and worthy of mention; these included the Minnesota School Districts Data Processing Joint Board, which had been planned by the ERDC, and the Minnesota Center for Curriculum Studies (MCCS). While the first proved to be short-lived, the MCCS went on to perform a vital coordinating function not unlike that played by Ruth Eckert when she simultaneously supervised both the BIR and the BER.

So much research and service activity was taking place at the

University during the mid-1960's that some attempt at coordinating them was clearly needed; as a result, the Board of Regents created the MCCS in July 1965. Many of the curriculum development projects had simply outgrown the College of Education. Such large-scale programs as Project English, Project Social Studies, and those developed through the Minnesota School Mathematics Center (Minnemast) were interdisciplinary and required more input and supervision than any one college could provide. The MCCS was temporarily directed by Stanley Kegler and later by James Werntz, a professor of physics, and supervised by an administrative committee consisting of the deans of the colleges of Biological Sciences, Education, Liberal Arts, the Graduate School, the Institute of Technology, and the Office of the Vice President for Academic Administration. With the dean of the College of Education as its chair, the MCCS was reminiscent of the BER, which, under Coffman and Haggerty, had reached University-wide proportions. Of course, the objective of the MCCS differed from that of its predecessor. While Coffman intended the BER to perform research on University-related issues, the MCCS served the five-state region of Iowa, Minnesota, North Dakota, South Dakota, and Wisconsin — its chief rationale being that "curriculum development for elementary and secondary schools, as well as higher education, demands close liaison and cooperative efforts between subject matter specialists, teacher education personnel, and classroom teachers in the schools."[42]

A close look at the MCCS can help to clarify that period of the College's history which followed the nationwide reaction to *Sputnik*. That reaction was characterized by a sense of anxiety and a desire to perform as many innovative studies as possible within the shortest period of time. The MCCS took over as a guiding force after the furor had somewhat diminished but while educational specialists and their academic colleagues were still recognizing the necessity of revising curricula which had long remained fundamentally unchanged. A large number of these revisions were directed at mathematics and the sciences, and this resulted in the formation of the Minnemast project. The persistence of mathematician Paul Rosenbloom was primarily responsible for bringing Minnemast into being in 1964. It was funded by the National Science Foundation and attracted such College personnel as Alan Humphreys, Robert Jackson, James Stochl, and the powerful group of educators associated with Donovan Johnson.

221

Minnemast encompassed four affiliated projects: the Minnesota National Laboratory, the Programmed Algebra and Geometry Project, the Geometry Film Project, and the Minnesota Math and Science Teaching Project. Related endeavors found homes in other colleges and universities throughout the country where college of education faculties and their colleagues in the sciences voiced an interest in cooperation.[43]

If Minnemast represented a collegiate concern with mathematics, the Minnesota Project English Center, founded in 1962, was its counterpart in the literary humanities. It was natural that the English language arts would become a Minnesota specialty; after all, the College had hosted such scholars as Dora V. Smith, who made a name for herself in that field. The center was directed by Stanley Kegler, Donald K. Smith of the Department of Speech Communications, and Harold Allen of the Department of English. Like Minnemast, Project English was not funded by state appropriations but by federal monies. In this case, the Cooperative Research Program of the U.S. Office of Education offered its support to the development of "language-centered" curriculum materials for grades seven to twelve. Project English originated from a simple assumption: that instruction in and about language was absent from most secondary school English courses. Given this assumption, the project directors identified five major topics which they felt belonged in any fully developed English language arts curriculum: culture, structure, esthetics, communication, and learning. To realize this goal, materials were written which emphasized the interrelatedness of language with these five concepts.

The social studies was another academic area in which the College was particularly strong. Edgar Wesley had already given this field an excellent reputation at Minnesota; he was followed by his young colleague, Edith West, who liked to describe herself as a "shirt-tail relative" of Alice Mott, the first principal of the University High School. West herself served as the head of social studies education in the high school and also acted as the director of the Minnesota Social Studies Curriculum Center, which grew out of a grant from the U.S. Office of Education. The aim of Project Social Studies was summarized by the title of its final report, *Preparation and Evaluation of Social Studies Curriculum Guides and Materials for Grades K to 14.*[44] The center's research director, William Gardner, was also on the social studies staff of the University High School. College faculty members, including Vincent

Rogers, Fred Johnson, and Everett Keach, joined with liberal arts faculty from geography and each of the social sciences to implement Project Social Studies. No other curriculum program in the College could rival it in the number of contributors who participated in developing new curriculum materials. The success of this project, incidentally, is evidence of the good relations which existed between the members of the social studies department and the social scientists of the University.

One member of the team, Darrell Lewis (who would later become associate dean of the College), was especially concerned that Project Social Studies was not doing justice to the field of economics.[45] Largely as a result of his influence, the Center for Economic Education, which opened at the University in 1961 (along with the Minnesota State Council on Economic Education) collaborated with the Project Social Studies staff to conduct workshops. Lewis found it easy to work with such faculty members as Ray Price in business education and Edith West, the director of Project Social Studies, to bring economic ideas to bear on the development of curricular materials in social studies and business education. This was no small accomplishment during the early 1960's, when the shadow of McCarthyism was making the discussion of economics in the schools a dangerous topic. Fortunately, Minnesota could count on the support of a number of unusually open-minded and visionary people in both the University and the community. Business leaders like George Dayton, academicians like Richard Kozelka, dean of the College of Business Administration, and organizations like the AFL-CIO all supported the notion of helping students to become increasingly knowledgeable about basic economic forces.

In looking back at efforts like Project English, Project Social Studies, and Minnemast, one readily sees how they managed to combine both research and service. The reasons behind their successes should be obvious. Only research can produce excellent teaching materials, and only dissemination, communication, and assistance in using these materials — all service functions — can make research worth supporting. The sheer number of activities carried out by the Minnesota State Council on Economic Education and other organizations noted in the Robb Report provides testimony that the College was able to give service of a high order precisely because it had a strong research capability. Even during those times when research seemed to be getting an inordinate amount of attention, the willingness to serve the state and the community never faded away completely. The twenty-one programs for "the preparation of school personnel" cited in the Robb Report give validity to this assertion.[46] It has also been supported by persons outside the College's walls. In November 1974, the National Council for the Accreditation of Teacher Education sent a team of observers to Minnesota's College of Education. Upon leaving, they remarked that the College showed evident strength in the relationships it had built with practicing school people.[47] The service tradition which was established during the College's earliest years by David Kiehle and carried on by his successors remains active to this day.

Thirteen

Putting the House in Order

IN REVIEWING the history of the College of Education at the University of Minnesota, it is easy to focus on its many fine activities and programs — teacher preparation, research, outreach, extension, and guidance and counseling (to name the most obvious) — and equally easy to concentrate on its exemplary faculty and students and their careers. Often ignored, however, is another aspect of the College: its management. In the midst of all of the changes that took place over the years, who was minding the store? And how efficiently? How is the College being run today, and what determined its organizational structure?

Though it has rarely been apparent, at least on the outside, the College for many decades was a dense and thorny thicket of managerial complexity. Outwardly, its organization seemed to be a rather simple bureaucracy: nearly all decision-making power was centralized in the Office of the Dean, and often in the person of the dean alone. This may have looked like a sensible arrangement, but it led to a weak departmental organization and a somewhat disorganized faculty. It was not until 1932 that the College had an assistant dean, and it would be another forty years before the dean's office would begin to assume an up-to-date bureaucratic structure. In the meantime, power and responsibility were unequally divided among faculty and administration, resulting in frustration for both camps. In spite of this, however, there was never a "struggle for power" per se, and whatever tensions were left over subsided with the onset of bureaucratic rationalization — or departmentalization — during the 1960's and 1970's.

In recent years, departmentalization has resulted in the dean and a handful of prominent faculty having less power overall. The old "elite" system especially has given way to more teamwork, more direction from individual departments, and more structure and procedure. But while this division of responsibilities has had good effects, it has also entailed heavy costs. Search committees, affirmative action, accountability, and innumerable regulations have brought benefits, but they have also tied the hands of deans and more enterprising faculty members. An emphasis on more careful planning has resulted in more paperwork and reporting and fewer creative, high-risk ventures. In general, smoothing out the College's organization has sometimes been an expensive endeavor in terms of output and innovation.

Marcia Edwards was one of the first to recognize clearly the problems inherent in the College's organizational structure. In the noteworthy memorandum she sent to President Morrill on March 19, 1952, "Comments on the College of Education," she pointed out that the dean of the College was responsible for twenty-seven budget items in Administration and seventy-nine academic items in General Education, in addition to eighteen cross-charges. She went on to explain:

> The size of this departmental administrative responsibility is shown by the fact that ten of our departments having their own administrative set-ups account for about $155,000 in our budget this year; University High accounts for roughly $126,000; and departments administered by the dean account for approximately $375,000 expenditure. This administrative organization places in the office of the dean all of the planning work for educational psychology, curriculum and instruction, educational administration, and others, involving bulletin preparation, planning budgets, making teaching schedules, preparing reports, processing appointments, finding staff, approving purchases, and so on.[1]

During his deanship Peik had been known to start his workday by five in the morning. With the installation of Walter Cook as dean, Edwards warned Morrill that "it would be unrealistic and most short-sighted to consider the new dean's time without realizing that any change in national responsibility must be more than met in his schedule by the need for much more careful planning of the college's program and state services."[2]

Marcia Edwards was not the only person to recognize the fact that the College's structure necessitated a major overhaul; on December 4, 1954, Willis Dugan wrote a letter to Dean Cook on the analysis of college administrative structure. In it, he stated:

Our College of Education administrative structure, lines of relationship and responsibility often must seem to you as perplexing and
unclear as they do to some of us on the general faculty level. Often
committees, departments, and faculty groups appear to overlap in
functions and responsibilities in ways that are completely confusing.[3]

Dugan went on to propose that "this analysis might serve as an
interesting topic for an informal administrative council to consider
under your leadership."[4]

Either Cook was unable to come to grips with the issues of
organization or he felt that it was not necessary to do so. At any
rate, his eye was on research in the College — his own included — which he probably thought to be of higher priority than mere
organization. Even though Dugan warned Cook that some thirty-
six people in the College would be reporting directly to him, Cook
did not seem to be bothered by that fact.

Even Marcia Edwards seemed reluctant to suggest that the
College move in the general direction of departmentalization (although this proved inevitable); as she informed Morrill in 1952,
"we have frequently discussed the desirability of more definite
departmentalization in the College of Education, but within the
present budget limitations, it is impossible to consider so expensive a plan."[5] Nearly a quarter century later, despite severe budgetary restrictions, departmentalization was to become a reality.
Edwards knew that the staff of the dean's office could not continue carrying on the work it had tried to handle in recent years
but did not consider departmentalization to be a feasible alternative. Neither, apparently, did Cook, who left the issue to his successor, Robert Keller.

Although the situation within the College at times resembled a
logjam, it was not without some advantages. While there were far
too many items which fell under the umbrella of budget number
3003 — the General Education budget — and these translated into
far too many people reporting to the dean, there were benefits that
partially offset the costs. The sheer number of items included
within that budget resulted in the dean's having considerable lati-
tude and flexibility. For example, when someone who was budgeted by General Education went on leave, his or her salary could
be used to underwrite urgently needed teaching assistantships.
Funds could be shifted around with a minimum of difficulty — which would not be the case if budgets were lodged
firmly within individual departments. When reorganization did
occur, this flexibility was lost for a time.

After a year as dean, Cook had learned how burdensome it was to handle the many responsibilities of the deanship in addition to chairing the Department of General Education, the largest in the College. At a faculty meeting held on February 2, 1955, he let the faculty know how difficult it was to handle that department, which comprised educational administration, educational psychology, curriculum and instruction, higher education, the history and philosophy of education, and business and distributive education.[6] General Education was not only the largest department in the College but one of the largest in the University system; it encompassed most undergraduate professional education as well as the majority of related graduate work. True, various "group" committees existed within General Education, and each had its own chair, but this had not resulted in a marked lessening of the dean's responsibilities. At a November 16, 1955, faculty meeting, Cook heard reports from several of these chairpeople: Guy Bond (elementary education), Robert Keller (secondary education), Willis Dugan (educational psychology), Clifford Archer (rural education), Ruth Eckert (higher education), Otto Domian (educational administration), and Paul Grim (undergraduate theory and practice of teaching, which included the coordination of supervised student teaching).[7] Even with this large representation, not all elements of General Education were heard from; no one spoke for curriculum and instruction nor for the history and philosophy of education.

The General Education budget was long overdue for some major revamping; in fact, the 1964-65 budget shows that by that time it had been pared down to include only business and distributive education, higher education, the history and philosophy of education, and secondary education. Conspicuously absent were educational administration and educational psychology, both of which had been made separate departments during the previous year. In the academic year 1965-66, budget number 3003 designated a new "foundations of education" department which encompassed both higher education and the history and philosophy of education. Finally, in 1974, the Department of Social, Psychological, and Philosophical Foundations of Education was formed to pick up any loose ends. For all intents and purposes, then, General Education, as it had long been known, came to an end in 1964-65. At that point, it was thirty-seven years old — a venerable age for any department. It was not the oldest of the College's departments, however; the departments of Educational Psychology and School

Administration jointly held that distinction. Both had been named in 1915 and were subsequently absorbed into General Education. In 1964, the two reemerged and once again became individual departments.

In its early years, the College had been divided into eight separate departments. According to the regents' report for 1916-17, these were the departments of Art Education, Educational Administration and Supervision (formerly "school administration"), Educational Psychology, History and Philosophy of Education, Theory and Practice of Education, Trade and Industrial Education, Agricultural Education, and Home Economics Education. Two years later, the Minneapolis Handicraft Guild was taken into the University under the name of the Department of Art Education and became the College's ninth department. There is no clear explanation of the initial appearance of the Department of General Education in the 1927-28 budget (as item 2603) other than in terms of Haggerty's professional ambitions; the formation of this large department in essence stripped the smaller departments of their budgets and made the dean responsible for the entire operation. Instead of letting the faculty manage the smaller, more viable departments which had originally existed, Haggerty created a sort of Frankenstein monster, a department that would remain out of hand for a number of years.

During a meeting on September 22, 1914, the College faculty was divided into two factions: the "general" and the "executive."[8] This may have been an attempt on Haggerty's part to divide up some of his own responsibilities; it did not have that result, however. The executive faculty took over the areas of new student admissions, program planning, graduate placement, and the selection of furnishings and supplies, but it never really participated in the formulation of basic policy. Haggerty continued to hold the reins.

Perhaps Haggerty recognized that General Education was not an entirely satisfactory answer to the College's organizational problems. At any rate, in an essay entitled "The College of Education as Related to Other Divisions of the University," written to commemorate the College's twenty-fifth anniversary in 1930,[9] he avoided mention of General Education altogether. He did, however, stress that "no defense is here offered for this particular type of internal organization" and admitted that "equally cogent reasons can be offered for other arrangements of courses and personnel, and it is an open question whether the professional interests of the College might not be better served if . . . departmental lines were all eliminated."[10] He went on to voice his opinion that "highly organized departments tend to become academic rather than professional in character, to emphasize knowledge rather than workers to be trained."[11] His logic was dubious at best; Haggerty wished to retain control over the College, and he knew that remaining in charge of the budgets of most departments (in other words, maintaining General Education) was a useful means to that end.

After many years of centralized decision-making and clogged management, the College moved toward rationalization and departmentalization in a relatively short time under Keller's leadership. This is not so surprising when one remembers that Edwards and Dugan had voiced their impatience with the existing structure over a decade earlier. And three events which occurred in 1957 made it even more clear that things had to be changed. Until then, the Department of Physical Education for Women was a separate department whose director reported directly to the University president. In the budget year 1957-58, this department was placed under the College of Education, with the director reporting to its dean.[12] In the same year, the Institute of Child Welfare was also brought into the College. While its director did not report to Cook, it nevertheless became necessary to create a "department" of special education within the Department of General Education. The field grew so rapidly that it was eventually decided to make special education a free-standing department; this took place in 1961.

The third event of 1957 which had long-term effects on the College caused a great deal of anxiety not only at Minnesota but nationwide. On October 4, when the U.S.S.R. launched the first artificial satellite, educators everywhere were concerned about the quality of American education vis-a-vis Russian. All across the nation, men like Arthur Bestor (who had spoken at the 1936 inauguration of Minnesota's Center for Continuation Study) called for more subject matter in the preparation of teachers. The eminent physicist Alfred O. C. Nier reported to a 1958 industrial education conference that a Minnesota Board of Education advisory committee, which he headed, felt that "the subject matter requirements insofar as they affect prospective science teachers are low and should be strengthened."[13] In December 1958, Guy Bond testified on the requirements for science teachers at a public hearing before the Board of Education;[14] he argued that CSLA students who were forced to take additional required subjects would end up having to prolong their University studies. This led to the suggestion that some students register both in the College of Education and CSLA. The matter was discussed at length by the faculties of both colleges, and in the CSLA faculty bulletin for February 19, 1959, it was reported that "by a vote of 177 to 7, the SLA faculty endorsed the proposal for a program of joint registration with the College of Education leading to the BA and BS degrees."[15] (Interestingly, Coffman had suggested precisely this arrangement during his tenure as dean.)

Three years prior to Cook's death in 1963, Jack Merwin came to the University as professor of educational psychology and assistant director of the Student Counseling Bureau. Ten years later, in 1970, he was to become dean of the College of Education. During his administration, the College would be radically reorganized into the seven departments which exist today. His predecessor, Robert Keller, did much of the necessary preliminary work for him. Before examining the careers of these two men, however, it is necessary to look back at the year 1963, which proved important for a number of reasons.

During November of that year, the Committee on Structure and Function (sometimes irreverently referred to as the "Committee on Stricture and Friction") began the task of streamlining the organization of the College. This committee had an elected membership of seven, including Robert Beck, Ruth Eckert, William Edson, Robert Keller, Gordon Mork, and Maynard Reynolds; Gilbert Wrenn served as its chair. Marcia Edwards, who was then serving as acting dean for the second time, gave the effort her official blessing. As a result of the committee's recommendations, the dean's office was given two assistant deans: one would be responsible for undergraduate and fifth-year programs, the other for managing the dean's office in the areas of research and graduate preparation. In addition, the Structure and Function Committee suggested that the catch-all Department of General Education be done away with altogether and proposed a structure of "related departments" grouped into divisions. In the hope of minimizing redundancy and increasing efficiency, it also recommended the streamlining of College committees. Two other recommendations made by the committee would prove to be especially significant: one suggested the formation of a policy and planning committee, and the other proposed that a statement of the College's mission be drafted.[16]

Both recommendations were accepted. In January 1964, the Policy and Planning Committee was elected; in 1965, a statement entitled "The Mission of the College of Education at the University of Minnesota" spelled out the "triadic function of the college": (1) responsibilities for scholarly and creative study, (2) responsibilities for teaching and related student services, and (3) responsibilities for consultant and other types of services.[17]

The Structure and Function Committee set a pace which Robert Keller was all too happy to follow when he was named dean in 1964. He had had experience with various forms of organization and was able to rely heavily on Marcia Edwards's expertise in the field. In the same year, educational administration and educational psychology left the Department of General Education to become units in their own right. General Education's days were numbered; there were few regrets when Dean Keller did away with it in 1965.

That was not his only accomplishment, however — far from it. He also encouraged the Department of Secondary Education to expand and embrace audiovisual education as well as business and distributive education. In the meantime, he gave credit to the Policy and Planning Committee for their tireless efforts. In his "College of Education: 1964-1966," he wrote:

> Most active during the 1964-1966 biennium have been the members of the standing faculty Committee on Policy and Planning which had just been elected and organized during spring quarter, 1964 [with Maynard Reynolds as its chair]. This committee was able to build upon the reports and recommendations of its predecessor, the Committee on Structure and Function, which had completed its work in December, 1963. Both the number and size of existing college committees were reduced and efforts were made to equalize committee assignments. The establishment of the Policy and Planning Committee helped to provide a vehicle through which the faculty could become officially involved in immediate and long-range planning and policy formulation for the College.[18]

He went on to draw attention to three documents which had proved crucial:

> This committee itself assumed responsibility for drafting and recommending three policy statements which were subsequently adopted by the faculty as follows: Constitution and By-Laws of the College of Education (adopted February 5, 1965), the Mission of the College of Education (adopted May 14, 1965), and A Report on College Organization (adopted December 14, 1965).[19]

232

William Gardner chaired one Policy and Planning subcommittee on a College constitution and by-laws; Clifford Hooker, chair of the re-created Department of Educational Administration, headed another having to do with the organization of the College. The Hooker subcommittee proved pivotal. Reporting at a June 9, 1965, College faculty meeting, the subcommittee recommended that the College adopt a "flat" or "horizontal" type of departmental organization.[20] This would minimize the hierarchical structure in administrative bureaucracy. The rationale for this type of configuration was that it was in keeping with College traditions of decentralization and widespread faculty participation in decision making. Eight "divisions" were recommended which included the divisions of Educational Psychology, Secondary Education, Social Foundations and Higher Education, and Vocational Education; the School of Physical Education; the Institute of Child Development; the Department of Educational Administration; and the Department of Elementary Education. In addition, it was suggested that the Department of General Education be dropped. By December 1965, the implementation of the Policy and Planning Committee's recommendations had begun.

Not long afterward, Stanley Kegler joined Marcia Edwards as a second associate dean. A year earlier, Kegler had played a key role in another part of the College's organization — the elementary and high schools. Upon entering the dean's office, he chaired the College program development committee on University laboratory schools. That committee had been appointed in the fall of 1964 and was instructed to implement a new University policy — namely "controlled growth." Key recommendations were made and action taken in the spring of 1965. President O. Meredith Wilson, who had asked Dean Keller for a report on the laboratory schools, was not convinced that they were worth the expense of maintaining them.[21] On February 5, 1965, Keller received a memorandum from Kegler stating that the elementary school was not fulfilling its mission and ought to be phased out.[22] Keller concluded that this should be begun during the academic year; the fifth grade, on the other hand, was to be carried forward for one additional year and the sixth grade for two. This decision was announced by Dean Keller at a March 12, 1965, faculty meeting.[23] The University High School was not to meet a similar fate; Kegler's committee judged that it had fulfilled its mission, and therefore it was recommended that the high school not only be continued but expanded. Three years later, the University High School was joined with Marshall Junior-Senior High School. No changes were made in the Institute of Child Development's Nursery School; Dean Keller took that stand on the basis of an assessment made by Harold Stevenson, the Institute's director.

The thoroughness with which Keller and Edwards blocked out the areas of the College which would benefit from reorganization is nothing short of astonishing. Keller's biennial report for 1964-66 tells of two other hard-working committees. The first was the most important; it is doubtful whether the second really had all that much effect. Both, however, suggested the extent to which faculty were becoming involved in policy setting:

> Two . . . policy statements were developed by . . . standing committees of the college faculty. The first of these, which originated with the Research Committee, was adopted by the faculty on December 14, 1965. Entitled "Policies for Research in the College of Education," this statement sought to clarify faculty responsibility for research, preserve free inquiry, and to promote effective use of college resources for research. The second statement, adopted June 7, 1966, was proposed by the Faculty Personnel Committee. Entitled "The Policy for Faculty Recruitment," this statement sought to highlight the importance of attracting quality professorial staff to the college faculty and established some procedures which should be helpful in recruitment of new faculty.[24]

Incidentally, the minutes of a December 14, 1965, faculty meeting report that when a proposed College constitution was first discussed there were those who wished to include a provision for consultation with College faculty on the appointment of a dean.[25] However, this was considered by the Gardner committee to exceed the normal and proper function of the faculty.[26] The day had not yet come when faculty search committees would rank names of prospective deans before submitting them to the University president.

Five years later, a new dean, Jack Merwin, would be able to look back at this new organization and structure in attempting to provide a forum for faculty and student participation in College policy making. In 1965, though, there was no talk of a College senate or assembly; this philosophy of governance was simply too abstract and too remote at a time when the basic structure of the College and the shape of the dean's office held the spotlight. It took long enough to get at those essentials; in fact, it was not until 1968 that the recommendations of the Policy and Planning Committee were realized. At that time, six divisions were recognized: these were the divisions of Educational Administration, Educational Psychology, Elementary Education, and Vocational-Technical Education; the Institute of Child Development; and the School of Physical Education. The administrative heads of these divisions made up the Administrative Council. In the meantime, a ragbag of other programs (i.e., secondary education, art and music education, higher and teacher education, history and philosophy of education, and psychological foundations) were also represented on the council, and it became obvious that something would have to be done with these remnants as well.

As it became more manageable in size, the dean's office took on a more definable shape. Otto Domian, a professor of educational administration who was about to retire, was brought in as associate dean for the academic year 1968-69. His knowledge of organization and administration was badly needed. In the next year, William Gardner, Jack Merwin, and Frank Wilderson were added to the bureaucracy of the dean's office — Gardner being made associate dean, and Wilderson and Merwin being appointed assistant deans.

Wilderson, who would go on to become vice president for student affairs, was a particularly significant addition. He was one of the first appointees to the dean's office to recognize the special needs of minority students. He exemplified a new sensitivity — first to minority groups and later to women — which directed attention in part to the growing percentage of women enrolled in graduate programs in education (see Appendix).[27] Similar data on minority students is unavailable due to legislation which made it illegal to inquire about an applicant's race on forms used for enrolling in colleges or universities.

The years 1967 and 1968 saw the addition of a number of faculty members who had special interest in and knowledge of minority groups and women. In 1967, Arthur Harkins held a joint appointment in the Center for Regional and Urban Affairs and the College of Education. Harkins was intensely interested in educational futures, particularly as they affected minorities. Shirley Clark joined the staff the following year; as a sociologist of education, she brought to the College both a profound knowledge of the adolescent and a commitment to the support of equality for women in higher education. She also possessed organizational abilities and eventually was invited to fill the post of assistant academic vice president. The later emergence of Project BORN FREE under L. Sunny Hansen's leadership would reflect many of Shirley Clark's earlier concerns.

Jack Merwin was hardly settled in as assistant dean before Robert Keller was prompted to resign the deanship due to illness. Merwin took over the post for the next six years, which witnessed the final stages of reorganization within the College. Among his first actions as dean was the organization of a systematic approach to collegiate planning. The research tradition of the College proved helpful in this matter; it ensured the availability of a great deal of data which might have been lacking under different circumstances. Merwin also received valuable assistance from Mary Corcoran, who was named the first director of the Education Planning Office following Marcia Edwards's retirement in 1970.

The early 1970's saw the beginning of a new era in more ways than one; financial retrenchment was mandated for all units of the University and the wise allocation of scarce dollars became of the utmost importance. Merwin knew that College budgets could not simply be slashed; it was essential that priorities be set, and planning was to be a key element in the thinking that went into the setting of those priorities.[28] Mary Corcoran had had years of experience in the BIR as a graduate student in the College and had earlier been a member of the staff of the Educational Testing Service in Princeton, New Jersey; Merwin himself had had a good deal of practice with the design of data collection and alternative methods of interpretation. Both came to recognize that before effective data could be collected, it would first be necessary to organize a data base which would describe the accomplishments and plans of each faculty member. Not only would this be of use in College reports, but it would also be worthwhile in departmental planning and counseling.

Corcoran fashioned the Education Planning Office and made it possible to supplement its planning function with the concept of development. When the College was departmentalized in 1974, this planning office was renamed the Education Planning and Development Office. According to its "Report of Activity," the addition of the development function allowed it to assume "responsibilities associated with improving internal and external communication and with facilitating faculty research," much of which "had been handled through the research and development activities of the Office of the Dean."[29] After Ted Kellogg took over as director of the Education Planning and Development Office in September 1974, Mary Corcoran was invited to revitalize the program in higher education which had languished with the retirement of Ruth Eckert in 1973.

When Dean Merwin addressed the College of Education Assembly on June 4, 1974, he made special mention of Corcoran's stewardship:

> It was in the fall of 1970 that Mary was good enough to honor my request that she help establish a Planning Office for the College. Thus, by June of 1976 she will have given five years to this effort which has put us ahead of the planning operations of other units in the University and made us a leader in this area among colleges of education in the nation.[30]

When Jack Merwin spoke of the value of planning, he knew what he was talking about. His own administration was characterized by the thoughtful design of the several responsibilities lodged in the dean's office, the increase in responsibilities of the College's seven departments, and the wise use of resources diminished by the retrenchment mandated by central administration. He knew that the College's bureaucracy, whether in his office or at the departmental level, would need to be orderly if it were to function well. He may have been the first dean who was completely oriented toward the administrative responsibilities of that office; he regarded his primary task as leadership in the formulation of fundamental College policy combined with communication with other deans and central administration.

Looking back on that early period of retrenchment, which blanketed most of his term as dean, Merwin felt that his major accomplishment was that of persuading central administration to think in terms of the retrenchment of *programs* rather than of vacant budget line offerings. In other words, he convinced central administration to think in terms of whole areas of course offerings or research instead of focusing solely on particular positions. Merwin's work was complicated by a turnover in central administration, but he was able to return to his professorial duties in the field of measurement and evaluation in 1976 without feeling as if he had left a disorganized set of chores for his successor.

There was also a certain amount of turnover in the dean's office itself. By the budgetary year 1972-73, Associate Dean William Gardner and two assistant deans, Wayne Welch and Frank Wilderson, had joined Dean Merwin.[31] Wilderson left the dean's office in

1974 to become the vice president for student affairs, and his responsibilities were picked up by Eloise Jaeger. She had shown her administrative skills both in directing Physical Education for Women — one of the oldest and most distinguished programs in the College — and in heading the new School of Physical Education, Recreation, and School Health Education, one of the seven departments created in 1974.

The movement of personnel into and out of the dean's office simply meant that its staff had to be more than ordinarily flexible. Frank Wilderson, the first black administrator in the College of Education, not only empathized with black students and the black community but also with the handicapped. Jaeger carried on his commitment to affirmative action. As the only assistant dean at that time, she also became responsible for "special projects" (e.g., a human relations training program which is closely associated with the philosophic rationale for affirmative action) and the summer session; in addition, she inherited "special services," a disbursement of support funds that helped many graduate students and faculty members. Besides all of these duties, she was charged with maintaining a relationship between the dean's office and Continuing Education and Extension. Thus, she sat with program coordinators and representatives of all departments of the College that had programs involving professional preparation.

Associate Dean Darrell Lewis's primary responsibility was planning, and the planning and development office reported directly to him. He was also allotted graduate education and liaison between the Graduate School and the College. His own concern with research led to an increase in the numbers of externally sponsored research and training programs.[32] The third portion of Lewis's responsibilities was faculty personnel, the most sensitive part of which involved the budget and its particulars — salaries, appointments, and promotions.

Balancing Darrell Lewis's obligations to graduate programs was the undergraduate teacher education curriculum; this was the chief part of William Gardner's responsibilities as an associate dean. Once again, careful planning had gone into the apportionment of his duties; consequently there was no danger that the undergraduate program would be underestimated or overlooked. Undergraduate affairs — somewhat parallel to the faculty and staff personnel policies overseen by Lewis — fell within the realm of Gardner's duties; thus, it made sense for William Edson, the director of the Education Career Development Office, to report to

Gardner. In addition, Gardner was intimately involved with the development of the undergraduate curriculum. His secretary, Lee Wesson, was integral to the mechanism of the College curriculum committee while simultaneously assisting Eloise Jaeger with the summer program. And, while Jaeger was active in outreach to intercollegiate professional programs, Gardner devoted some of his time to liaison with extramural professional groups.

The organization of the dean's office went hand in hand with the reconstruction of the governance of the College, which resulted in a new constitution in 1965 and the creation of a senate and an assembly in 1971. The "powers" of the faculty were spelled out in Article III, Section 2 of that constitution:

> The faculty shall establish the internal policies of the College, such as those relating to entrance requirements, curricula, instruction, examinations, grading, degrees, disciplinary matters, and the general organization of the College, except as these fall within the jurisdiction of all-University Committees.[33]

Unfortunately, the reorganization of the College overlooked one very important point: the spirit of community felt by so many faculty and administrators. In the late 1960's and early 1970's the voices of college students were loud and angry — first in Europe and then in the United States. Students insisted on taking part in the governance of their colleges and universities. Fortunately, there was never a perceived need for anything approaching violence in the College of Education at Minnesota, largely because the students had an advocate in William Gardner. He chaired a task force on student involvement set up by the Policy and Planning Committee during the 1968-69 academic year which developed the organizational plan for the Education Student Assembly and proposed legislative changes in the College's constitution.

On June 3, 1969, the task force reported to the faculty, and its recommendations for the establishment of the student assembly were unanimously accepted "in principle."[34] But a major question still remained unanswered: should student members be included in the College assembly or not? At a December 1, 1970, faculty meeting, a draft was submitted for the rewording of Article III, Section 3 of the Constitution entitled "Composition of the College Assembly." The draft included these radical words: "The student members of the Assembly shall be those elected according to provisions of the By-laws. Student representatives to the College Assembly shall be designated collectively as the Education Student Assembly."[35]

This occasioned considerable debate. Finally, at a faculty meeting of March 15, 1971,

> Richard Hill, vice-chairman of the Policy and Planning Committee, outlined the proposed changes in the Constitution and By-laws as recommended by the Policy and Planning Committee. He stated that the purposes of the proposed changes were to move toward a goal of community governance which would include students and to make [policy and planning] more rapid-moving and accountable .... Changes included the addition of students to a body to be called the College Assembly.[36]

The proposals Hill made were passed and "the Constitution and By-laws were adopted as amended."[37]

Such people as William Gardner welcomed the participation of students in College policy making. There were others who followed suit by welcoming yet another group — civil service employees — into the "community" that made up the College of Education. Those with long memories were able to recall Dorolese Wardwell's contributions to the BER and BIR; she had come to the University not long after Haggerty had been named dean and made it possible for the two bureaus to function effectively. Marcia Edwards had also begun her College career with secretarial experience. A heightened awareness of the importance of the civil service staff resulted in another amendment to the constitution on December 4, 1973, which provided for official civil service representation in the College of Education Senate in the form of a chairperson selected by the College of Education Staff Association.[38]

In matters of record keeping, the preparation and maintenance of budgets, and so much else, the civil service staff has been vital to the well-being of the College. Prior to departmentalization, many of the faculty's secretarial duties were carried out by the Office of Faculty Secretarial Services, directed from its inception by Jo Zimmar. In later years, her headquarters moved to 105 Burton. Across the hall, the dean's office staff was managed by such able personnel as Dorothy Mitchell, secretary to the dean, and Lee Wesson, who at first served as secretary to Marcia Edwards and then to Associate Dean William Gardner. Wesson eventually took over the management of various details associated with the summer session, College bulletins, and the College curriculum committee. Following departmentalization, the responsibility of civil service staff members in the several departments greatly increased. The fact that the individual departments have flourished is due in no small part to the expertise of their civil service employees.

In late 1971, Dean Merwin and his staff decided that it was time to conduct a major study of the basic divisional and departmental structures within the College. A three-person team was hired to conduct that study, and on June 21, 1972, three off-campus consultants in organizational design — J. Victor Baldridge (who specialized in organizational policy making in higher education), Myron Atkins (whose field was science education), and Robert Howsam (in educational administration) submitted their landmark report, *A Program for Increased Organizational Effectiveness for the University of Minnesota College of Education.*[39] It would be two more years before the College unveiled its new plan for departmentalization.

The year 1974 proved crucial, for it was then — and in the year following — that the College was effectively reorganized from the inside out. Personnel needs of the faculty were brought into order, and as part of a campus-wide push for a faculty grievance review process, the College evolved its grievance review procedure, including the institutionalization of a College appeals committee and a grievance review officer. Affirmative action, the adjudication of grievances, curriculum, the annual review of priorities, personnel matters such as promotion and tenure — all were assigned to particular members of the dean's staff, while the seven departments formed committees of their own which oversaw these several provinces. This mixture of centralized and decentralized responsibilities fit well into the "flat" organizational model suggested by Clifford Hooker in 1965.

Before the College Senate adopted the policy manual prepared by its personnel committee in 1975, the issue of departmentalization overshadowed everything else. Ironically, the first inkling of organizational renewal had come almost midway between Marcia Edwards's noted memorandum to President Morrill in 1952 and the denouement of the departmentalization furor in 1974. The turning point, in fact, had come in 1963. During that year, when Edwards was serving as acting dean, she received a letter dated March 14, 1963, from Malcolm Willey, the vice president for academic administration. Willey had been a sociologist and was very interested in organizational structure. In the letter — which he described as "semi-formal" — Willey broached the issue of departmentalization in the College of Education. He had had a discussion with a person whose anonymity he wished to protect concerning the College's strengths and weaknesses. After summing up the strengths, which included "a strong guidance program with Professor Dugan and a strong special education program with Professor Reynolds," he moved on to describe the weaknesses:

> It was then suggested that in the area of educational psychology and, particularly, in the segment relating to measurement in educational psychology, we have lost ground and do not enjoy the status that once we held nationally. Our former strength related to such people as Palmer Johnson and Dean Cook, himself. It was the feeling of our colleague that with the death of Palmer Johnson and the shift to administration of Walter Cook, there had not been replacement that enabled us to maintain our former level of excellence. Indeed, it was suggested that Professor Hoyt is the only full-time measurement person that is left. This led into a general discussion of how this had come about, and it was suggested that the problem reflects the fact that there is not departmentalization in the College of Education and, accordingly, certain areas get lost from sight because there is no one who professionally in terms of departmental affiliation is interested in or responsible for pushing developments in given areas.[40]

Seven departments and two offices comprise the basic organization of the College. These are the Department of Curriculum and Instruction, chaired by Robert Dykstra; the Department of Social, Psychological, and Philosophical Foundations of Education, chaired by Clyde A. Parker; the Department of Psychoeducational Studies, chaired by Robert Bruininks; the Institute of Child Development, directed by Willard Hartup; the Department of Vocational and Technical Education, chaired by Jerome Moss, Jr.; the School of Physical Education, Recreation, and School Health Education, directed by G. Alan Stull; and the Department of Educational Administration, chaired by Van Mueller. In addition to these departmental units, two offices which contribute to collegiate planning and administration report to the Office of the Dean. These are the Education Planning and Development Office, directed by Theodore Kellogg, and the Education Career Development Office, directed by William Edson. Department chairs, office directors, and deans make up the College's Administrative Council.

The governance structures for faculty and students — whose delicate balance of separate interests and powers were combined with the spirit of community — complement the more visible organization. The Education Student Board parallels the faculty assembly, and the College Assembly and College Senate both have faculty and student representation. The Committee on Personnel Policy and the Committee on Educational Policy are standing committees of the College Senate. The first published the *Regular Faculty Policy and Procedure Manual* which was adopted by the College faculty in the fall of 1975;[41] the second devoted its efforts to the development of a document entitled "Contexts and Priorities for College of Education Planning."[42] The Educational Policy Committee's publication was an attempt to juxtapose the College's statement of context and priority with separate statements for individual departments, and it has proved very worthwhile.

Other organizational elements appear in the present College structure as well. Although conveniently allied with the Department of Educational Administration, the Center for Educational Policy Studies, directed by Charles Sederberg, encourages faculty from all departments of the College to work with state educational agencies in research on educational policy or to provide technical assistance, such as data analysis, to citizens' groups or local educational organizations.

In the Department of Curriculum and Instruction, two other units similarly exemplify the entire spectrum of research and service as these functions relate to teaching and learning in the schools. First, the Teacher Center, directed by Frederick Hayen, has two somewhat separate missions: to reach out to public and private schools, and to function as one of three similar agencies that are "state facilitators" in a "national diffusion network" sponsored by the U.S. Office of Education. The main purpose of the network is to ensure that new theories and practices in education are made available to the schools as rapidly as possible. Second, the Instructional Systems Laboratory, directed by Robert Tennyson, uses new technology in designing "instructional systems"; that is, it updates conventional "methods" courses. It stands ready to help faculty exploit a variety of teaching methods and conducts (and disseminates) research while developing prototype instructional systems.

The division of the College of Education into various departments and subdepartments has made it possible to integrate research, program, and personnel development, and to evaluate new methods in a way that was simply not possible before. The Department of Psychoeducational Studies, for example, organizationally houses the Institute for Research on Learning Disabilities, directed by James Ysseldyke. The Institute of Child Development's Center for Early Education and Development, directed by Shirley G. Moore, is another example of combined emphases. Under Brandon Smith's direction, the Minnesota Research and Development Center of the Department of Vocational and Technical Education not only coordinates research but, like other units, centers, and laboratories within the College, is also concerned with utilizing and evaluating that research.

In recent years, College faculty have been welcomed into research and development units that are not part of the College structure, such as the Center for Research in Human Learning (part of the Department of Psychology in the College of Liberal Arts), the Measurement Services Center (which is attached to the Office of the Vice President for Academic Affairs), and the Consulting Group on Instructional Design (which, prior to 1972-73, was known as the Programmed Learning Center). Directed by Russell Burris, a member of the faculty in the Department of Social, Psychological, and Philosophical Foundations of Education, the Consulting Group on Instructional Design is an "all-university development unit with responsibilities for providing leadership and support for systematic improvement of the educational process at all levels,"[43] and as such has close ties with the College.

The organization of the College appears almost deceptively simple (see Appendix), but no illustration accurately depicts the years of effort that went into the new departmentalization of the College which has so far proved successful. Happily, the College has been comfortable with the new arrangement, which has allowed its traditional mission to be carried out in an orderly fashion. Teaching and research have become coequals, and the several tasks involved in the development of methods and curricular materials and the preparation of professional teaching and administrative personnel have not gotten in one another's way. At its inception, most College faculty and staff regarded the new scheme with optimism, though nobody expected miracles; nevertheless, in 1976, Dean Merwin was able to return to full-time teaching, research, and service with a feeling that he had presided over a process which Marcia Edwards had called for over two decades earlier.

At long last, the College of Education had been trimmed and readied. With William Gardner as dean, it could move forward into relatively unknown waters while relying on its traditions for strength. Appropriations would not be adequate; they never had been. Scarce resources would have to be spent wisely and well — but the College had learned to plan. The dual sense of vision and mission which has moved the College since its earliest days has continued to provide a driving force, but this has been tempered by wisdom garnered through the careful research which has become the College's hallmark.

Alfred North Whitehead coined a term which may be used to describe the College of Education: an "adventure of ideas." Thanks to the men and women who have moved through the College's history — as educators, administrators, researchers, students, and staff — the field of education at the University of Minnesota remains an adventure full of excitement and promise.

Appendix

TABLE 1

STUDENT HEADCOUNT ENROLLMENT

(Selected Years, 1940-1975)

Year	Undergraduate and Continuing Education	Graduate School	Total
1940	1,562	263	1,825
1945	897	179	1,076
1950	2,350	466	2,816
1955	2,456	517	2,982
1960	2,738	579	3,317
1965	2,916	902	3,818
1970	3,298	1,110	4,408
1975	2,401	1,110	3,511

SOURCE: Education Planning and Development Office.

NOTE: Beginning in fall quarter 1962, the Graduate School required continuous registration by doctoral degree candidates; these registrations are therefore included in the total Graduate School count.

TABLE 2

DISTRIBUTION OF EDUCATION STUDENTS BY DEGREE OBJECTIVE
(Selected Years, 1950-1975)

Fall Quarter	Collegiate Programs					Graduate Programs					All Programs		
	BS in Education N	MED and Adult Special %	N	Collegiate Total %	N	MA, Spec. Cert., EdD and PhD %	N	Postbaccalaureate MEd., Adult Special & Graduate Programs %	N	%	N	%
1950	1,943	71	321	12	2,264	83	466	17	787	29	2,730	100
1955	2,162	73	301	10	2,463	83	517	17	818	27	2,980	100
1960	2,524	73	331	10	2,855	83	600	17	931	27	3,455	100
1965	2,657	67	344	9	3,001	76	949	24	1,293	33	3,950	100
1970	2,862	63	486	11	3,348	74	1,186	26	1,672	37	4,534	100
1971	2,675	62	448	11	3,123	73	1,160	27	1,608	38	4,283	100
1972	2,284	60	460	12	2,744	72	1,045	28	1,505	40	3,789	100
1973	1,869	53	641	18	2,510	71	1,042	29	1,683	47	3,552	100
1974	1,663	48	786	22	2,449	70	1,040	30	1,826	52	3,489	100
1975	1,627	45	852	24	2,479	69	1,110	31	1,962	55	3,589	100

SOURCE: Education Planning and Development Office.

TABLE 3

WOMEN IN EDUCATION PROGRAMS

(Percentage of Total Graduates Registered)

	1949-50	1959-60	1964-65	1968-69	1974-75
M.A.	21.1	19.4	27.9	30.9	30.3
Ph.D.	2.2	3.2	4.4	7.0	14.3
All	29.5	26.7	34.8	41.3	48.3

SOURCE: Education Planning and Development Office.

NOTE: Data on graduate registration of men and women in education programs prior to 1949-50 is not complete. However, there has been a general trend toward greater numbers of women since that date. During the same period, total registrations have fluctuated somewhat from the lowest figure of 1,633 in 1949-50 to a high of 2,867 in 1968-69. The figure for 1974-75 declined to 2,055.

TABLE 4

WOMEN WITH GRADUATE SCHOOL DEGREES IN EDUCATION FIELDS

(Percentage of Total Degrees)

	1949-50	1959-60	1964-65	1968-69	1974-75
All Degrees	33.8	24.4	29.5	35.7	49.5
Ph.D. Degrees	18.2	13.8	15.3	14.9	21.7

SOURCE: Education Planning and Development Office.

College of Education Departmental Organization

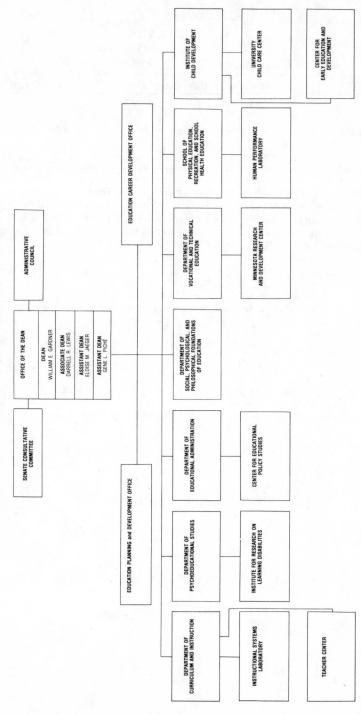

Notes

Since most materials cited in the following notes are available in the University of Minnesota Archives, entries which do not show facts of publication may normally be considered part of this extensive University collection. As an additional aid, however, parenthetical information other than facts of publication has been included to indicate box, folder, or file locations within the archives. In a few cases, catalog numbers have been added for books and monographs which are difficult to locate outside the University library system.

CHAPTER 1: *First Fruits*

1. James Gray, *The University of Minnesota, 1851-1951* (Minneapolis: University of Minnesota Press, 1951), p. 67.

2. E. Bird Johnson, ed., *Forty Years of the University of Minnesota* (Minneapolis: The General Alumni Association, 1910), p. 303.

3. Jean H. Alexander, "Chronological Outline of the Development of Public Education in Minnesota," in Alvin C. Eurich, ed., *The Changing Educational World 1905-1930: Papers Read on the Occasion of the Twenty-fifth Anniversary of the College of Education, University of Minnesota* (Minneapolis: University of Minnesota Press, 1931), p. 246.

4. In 1826, according to a College historian, Edgar Wesley, there were 103 state, 22 city, and more than 100 private normal schools. Edgar B. Wesley, *NEA: The First Hundred Years* (New York: Harper and Brothers, 1957), p. 83.

5. The high schools of the preparatory department are not to be thought of as precursors of the University High School. Had there been an adequate number of acceptable, quality secondary schools in Minnesota, it is highly unlikely that the University would have incorporated a preparatory department. In any case, its sole function was to supply students for the University. If it were a "model" high school, so much the better, for it was neither expected to be nor advertised as such.

6. *Minnesota Alumni Weekly* 13 (November 10, 1913), p. 120.

7. Ibid.

8. Alexander, "Chronological Outline," in Eurich, ed., *The Changing Educational World*, p. 248.

9. *Minnesota Alumni Weekly* 13 (November 10, 1913), p. 148.

10. Johnson, ed., *Forty Years*, p. 33.

11. University of Minnesota, *Second Biennial Report of the Board of Regents of the University of Minnesota to the Governor (1881-1882)*, p. 61.

12. Willis M. West, "The University of Minnesota," in John N. Greer, ed., *The History of Education in Minnesota*, United States Bureau of Education, Circular of Information No. 2, Contributions to American Educational History No. 31 (Washington, D.C.: Government Printing Office, 1902), pp. 94-132.

13. Ibid., pp. 95-96.

14. Ibid., p. 99.

15. *Minnesota Alumni Weekly* 13 (November 10, 1913), p. 14.

16. Ibid.

17. University of Minnesota, *Sixteenth Biennial Report for the Fiscal Years Ending July 31, 1909, 1910*, pp. 18-19.

18. Harold E. PaDelford, "A Historical Study of Vocational Education in Minnesota with Special Reference to the Minnesota Vocational Association" (M.A. thesis, University of Minnesota, 1967), p. 24.

19. For some fifteen years after the College of Education was made a unit of the University in 1905, a teacher's certificate could be granted to graduates of the College if they had "maintained a good average of scholarship through four years of college work." ("Good" was not defined.) By 1915, the executive faculty of the College of Education had established a twelve-credit combination of the following courses for the junior year: History of Education, Principles of Teaching, the High School Pupil, and Special Methods. A course in psychology was prerequisite for any of the professional education courses. In the fourth year only six credits were required, three in a course entitled The High School as a Social Institution and three in practice teaching, mandated the year before by the State Department of Education. Prior to 1921, graduates of the College of Science, Literature, and the Arts could be certified under the following conditions: "First, they must have maintained a good average of scholarship through four years of college work. Second, they must have the recommendation of at least one department concerned with high school studies. Third, they must have completed a semester course in psychology and twelve credits in education, or a year course in psychology and nine credits in education. Including the class of 1913, 2172 such certificates have been granted." *Minnesota Alumni Weekly* 13 (November 10, 1913), p. 179.

20. College of Education general faculty meeting minutes, June 16, 1919. Miscellaneous Minutes and Reports, 1914-1923.

21. University of Minnesota, *Seventh Biennial Report for the Fiscal Years Ending July 31, 1891, 1892*, p. 32.

22. Ibid.

23. University of Minnesota, *Catalogue, 1891-1892*, p. 62.

24. I am indebted to Berneil Nelson, library assistant at the Kiehle Library, University of Minnesota—Crookston, for her assistance in verifying these facts.

CHAPTER 2: *David L. Kiehle and the Department of Pedagogy*

1. Eurich, ed., *The Changing Educational World.*

2. George Aiton, "Beginnings of Secondary Education in Minnesota," in Eurich, ed., *The Changing Educational World*, p. 224.

3. Ibid.

4. Ibid.

5. Ibid., pp. 224-25.

6. Ibid., p. 225.

7. Ibid.

8. Ibid.

9. David L. Kiehle, *Education in Minnesota*, Part I (Minneapolis: The H.W. Wilson Co., 1903), p. 7.

10. Ibid., pp. 8-9.

11. *Ariel* 15 (April 23, 1892), p. 320.

12. Kiehle, *Education in Minnesota*, I, pp. 28-29.

13. Livingston C. Lord, "The Schools of Minnesota in the Last Quarter of the Nineteenth Century," in Eurich, ed., *The Changing Educational World*, p. 324.

14. Ibid.

15. Alexander, "Chronological Outline" in Eurich, ed., *The Changing Educational World*, p. 252.

16. Ibid.

17. This is well detailed in Sanford Niles's "The Common Schools," in Greer,

252

ed., *The History of Education in Minnesota.*

18. David L. Kiehle, "The Obligation of the University to the Profession of Teaching," an address delivered before the Minnesota Education Association in St. Paul on December 26, 1900, p. 5.

19. Horace Coon, *Columbia: Colossus on the Hudson* (New York: E.P. Dutton and Company, Inc., 1947), p. 217.

20. As an example of the national coverage which this received, see the *New York Times*, February 22, 1948, p. 34.

21. In 1893, the year when Kiehle became a lecturer in pedagogics, Teachers College became formally associated with Columbia University. See PaDelford, "Historical Study," p. 10.

22. Charles A. Bennett, *History of Manual and Industrial Education, 1870 to 1917* (Peoria, Illinois: Chas. A. Bennett Co., Inc. Publishers, 1937).

23. Kiehle, *Education in Minnesota*, I, p. 76.

24. Ibid.

25. David Kiehle to Cyrus Northrop; undated but probably written in 1902, judging from the evidence given in the first line (p. 10): "The following report is submitted after nine years of experimental service in the department of pedagogy" (Comptroller Papers: Education, 1900-1919).

26. Kiehle, *Education in Minnesota*, I, pp. 62-64.

27. "An Act donating Public Lands to the several States and Territories which may provide Colleges for the Benefit of Agriculture and the Mechanic Arts," July 2, 1862, *U.S. Statutes at Large*, chap. 130, vol. 12, p. 503.

28. Quoted in Kiehle, *Education in Minnesota*, I, p. 63.

29. Ibid., pp. 73-74.

30. Ibid., p. 74.

31. "Reply of Hon. D. L. Kiehle, State Superintendent of Public Instruction and Secretary of the Board of Regents of the University of Minnesota to the Address of Hon. E. H. Atwood, President of the State Farmers' Alliance, Relating to the State Agricultural School." This four-page document is not dated or otherwise identified.

32. Ibid., p. 2.

33. Ibid.

34. Ibid.

35. When E. Bird Johnson wrote his *Forty Years of the University of Minnesota*, Kiehle's part in the dramatic background of the School of Agriculture received official acknowledgment in the following passage (p. 56): "Dr. David L. Kiehle, who was at that time superintendent of public instruction and a member of the board of regents, gave the subject much careful study and investigation and after visiting many manual training schools and agricultural colleges, both east and west, gave a communication to the public press in February 1888. This was the first formal plan to be submitted along lines substantially similar to those afterward to be worked out in the Minnesota school of agriculture." See also Ralph E. Miller, *The History of the School of Agriculture: 1851-1960* (University of Minnesota: Institute of Agriculture, Forestry, and Home Economics, 1979), p. 5.

After the school opened, young women soon became as important to its curriculum as young male future farmers. The roots of home economics and home economics education were in the School of Agriculture. "Domestic science" courses were offered, but it was some time before a student earned a four-year degree in the subject; in 1904, Mary Matthews was graduated in what had come to be called home economics. Later, she would be dean of home economics at Purdue University; even before this time, home economics at the University of Minnesota would be nationally visible. This would come about after 1913, when Josephine Berry was named professor of nutrition and head of the home economics education department. (In 1916, she was called to Washington to organize and administer home economics nationally under the new Smith-Hughes law.) Thus, in just a few years the school Kiehle had done so much to found would produce a home economics program considered to be in the first rank.

36. Wesley, *NEA: The First Hundred Years*, p. 56.
37. David Kiehle to Cyrus Northrop, undated letter [1902], p. 11.
38. Ibid.
39. Ibid., pp. 12-22.
40. Ibid., p. 6.
41. Ibid.
42. David L. Kiehle, "A Special Report of the Department of Pedagogy to the President of the University of Minnesota," May 1, 1900, p. 5.

This report takes the form of a letter, and includes two other letters, one from President Eliot of Harvard University, and the second, in Kiehle's words, from "doubtless the best known representative of the normal schools at home and abroad, ex-president Irwin Shepard, Secretary of the National Education Association" (p. 10). President Eliot championed the idea of having those who had been thoroughly schooled in the subject they would teach go on to learn what a department of pedagogy could teach them about teaching. Shepard was aware of the move to do away with Kiehle's department and came directly to the point:

I regret that a movement has been inaugurated to abolish Pedagogy from the State University. I cannot believe that the Board of Regents will take such action. It would be a backward step which would seriously injure the standing of the University at home and abroad.

To urge that action on the ground that the Normal Schools' interests oppose the maintenance of such a department is misleading and unjust for the Normal Schools . . . .

In view of the tendency to demand a college or university diploma as qualification for Superintendents of Schools and principals and teachers of high schools, it becomes of the utmost importance that the department of Pedagogy be maintained in the University, and it should be strengthened and supported by adding the requirement that graduates who intend to teach in the high schools of the state take its course.

This letter, found on page 11 of Kiehle's "Special Report," is signed by Irwin Shepard and dated April 7, 1900.

43. Ibid. The first professorship for college instruction in professional education courses was funded by New York University in 1832. In 1850, Brown University established a chair of education, and a few years later Horace Mann, president of Antioch College, persuaded his trustees to underwrite a similar chair. A professorship including the teaching of didactics was budgeted at the University of Iowa in 1873. Kiehle could have cited earlier precedents than the professorship of the science and art of teaching which the University of Michigan started in 1879.

45. Kiehle, "Special Report," p. 5.
46. Ibid., pp. 5-6.
47. Ibid., p. 5.
48. Coon, *Columbia*, p. 81.
49. Samuel Eliot Morison, *The Development of Harvard University Since the Inauguration of President Eliot, 1869-1929* (Cambridge, Mass.: Harvard University Press, 1930), pp. 519, 522.
50. William James, *Talks to Teachers on Psychology and to Students on Life's Ideals* (New York: Henry Holt and Company, 1919).

51. S. Willis Rudy, *The College of the City of New York: A History, 1847-1947* (New York: The City College Press, 1949), pp. 229-30.

52. Henry C. Johnson, Jr., and Erwin V. Johanningmeier, *Teachers for the Prairie: The University of Illinois and the Schools, 1868-1945* (Urbana, Ill.: University of Illinois Press, 1972), p. 67.

53. It is doubtful whether Kiehle realized the assistance given teacher education by politicians and others influential in legislative halls. Had he been in a position to examine and comprehend national developments, he would have been impressed with the fact — or, rather, with what seemed to be the fact — that in many states the real "push" for professional teacher training came as a result of legislative action which was intended to make the profession more accessible. Usually this legislation proposed that the requirements for obtaining a teaching license be changed and that a state teachers' examination be substituted for the traditional prescribed course of study.

Clifford S. Griffin's history of the School of Education at the University of Kansas will prove instructive: "The events leading to the School of Education began in 1893 when the legislature passed an act regulating the certification of public-school teachers. Henceforth the State Board of Education could exempt from examinations in academic subjects graduates who had taken them in an institution that had as 'efficient' a course of study as the Emporia Normal School." Academic eyebrows must have been raised at that; nevertheless, as Griffin continues, "this left only examinations in the professional subjects: the history and philosophy of education, teaching methods, school laws, and school management." Clifford S. Griffin, *The University of Kansas: A History* (Lawrence, Kansas: University of Kansas Press, 1974), p. 273.

By 1901 — a year before Kiehle wrote his second letter to Northrop — the University of Kansas had created its own Department of Education.

54. *Ariel* 22, Summer School Edition No. 4 (August 25, 1899), p. 27.

55. David Kiehle to Cyrus Northrop, undated later [1902], p. 1.

56. Ibid., p. 2.

57. Students of David Kiehle to Cyrus Northrop, May 21, 1902, p. 1 (Comptroller Papers: Education, 1900-1919).

58. David Kiehle to Cyrus Northrop, undated letter [1902], p. 7.

59. James Wyman and Thomas Wilson to the Board of Regents, April 14, 1902 (Comptroller Papers: Education, 1900-1919).

60. James Wyman and Stephen Mahoney to the Board of Regents, May 22, 1902 (Comptroller Papers: Education, 1900-1919).

61. Ibid.

62. J. W. Olsen to the Board of Regents, [May] 1902 (Comptroller Papers: Education, 1900-1919).

63. Ibid.

64. Mary Folwell, "Reminiscences of Faculty" (Folwell Family Papers).

65. Ibid.

CHAPTER 3: *From Pedagogy to Education: 1905-1915*

1. The Ohio State University, for example, established its College of Education in 1907 (two years after Minnesota), and the University of Kansas took a similar step in 1909, followed a decade later by Indiana University. Harvard organized its Graduate School of Education even later, in 1920, five years after Coffman had come to Minnesota.

2. Johnson and Johanningmeier, *Teachers for the Prairie*, pp. 142-44.

3. Ibid., pp. 121, 137-38.

4. Ibid., p. 149.

5. Ibid., pp. 79-80.

6. Ibid., p. 82.

7. Gray, *The University of Minnesota*, p. 208.

8. Ibid. Gray goes on to say: "Vincent's immediate predecessor as principal had been Dr. William Rainey Harper, later to become president of the University of Chicago. The result of this intimate association was that in 1892 when the university opened and Dr. Harper began making raids on educational institutions to find its most brilliant young men, he immediately caught up George Edgar Vincent and launched him on a career as teacher of sociology."

9. Ibid., p. 341.

10. Ibid., p. 208.

11. *Ariel* 9 (October 3, 1885), p. 6.

12. *Ariel* 9 (March 15, 1886), p. 91.

13. *Ariel* 13 (January 15, 1890), p. 57.

14. Harry P. Judson, "An Unknown Quantity and One Possible Value," in George F. James, ed., *Handbook of University Extension* (Philadelphia: American Society for the Extension of University Teaching, 1893), pp. 330-31. Reprinted from *University Extension* 1 (1892) pp. 327-31.

15. According to this 1891 report, the University played no official part in extension until, "at the annual meeting of the Board at St. Paul, on December 22 [1890], it was voted to undertake the experiment of conducting Extension work in the State for the current academic year . . . . Of course, the expense must still be borne by local centres." Report of Harry P. Judson to the National Conference on University Extension, *The Proceedings of the First Annual Meeting of the National Conference on University Extension,* compiled by George F. James (Philadelphia: J. B. Lippincott Company, 1892), p. 203. This subject is more fully treated by James Stuart in "The Origin of University Extension," *University Extension* 3 (July 1893), pp. 1-8. This publication was the official organ of the society.

16. James, comp., *Proceedings*, p. 201.

17. Ibid., p. 204.

18. John H. Vincent, "Chautauqua and University Extension," in James, comp., *Proceedings*, pp. 32-37.

19. Ibid., pp. 34-35.

20. Ibid., p. 35.

21. George E. Vincent, "The Chautauqua Extension Printed Lectures," *University Extension* 3 (July 1893), p. 220.

22. Wesley, *NEA: The First Hundred Years*, p. 87.

23. George F. James, *Syllabus of a Course of Six Lectures on Prose Fiction in America*, University Extension Lectures, Series A, No. 24 (Philadelphia: American Society for the Extension of University Teaching, n.d. [c. 1893]).

24. John H. Vincent, "Chautauqua and University Extension," in James, comp., *Proceedings*, pp. 35-36.

25. *Minneapolis Tribune*, January 7, 1950.

26. Johnson and Johanningmeier, *Teachers for the Prairie*, p. 136. See also *Who Was Who in America*, Vol. 1 (Chicago: The A.N. Marquis Co., 1960).

27. Johnson and Johanningmeier, *Teachers for the Prairie*, p. 75.

28. George F. James, "The Basic Philosophy of Froebel," in *Proceedings of the National Education Association* (Ann Arbor: National Education Association, 1912), pp. 621-24.

29. Gray, *The University of Minnesota*, p. 209.

30. Ibid.

31. Ibid.

32. State of Minnesota, *General Laws of Minnesota for 1905*, chapter 120.

33. University of Minnesota, *Fifteenth Biennial Report of the Board of Regents for the Fiscal Years Ending July 31, 1907, 1908.*

34. Ibid.

35. Copies of the *Minnesota Alumni Weekly* are on file in the University Archives.

36. *Minnesota Alumni Weekly* 13 (November 1913), p. 149.

37. Robert H. Beck, "American Progressive Education: 1875-1930" (Ph.D. dissertation, Yale University, 1942), chap. 3.

38. *Minnesota Alumni Weekly* 13 (November 1913), p. 150.

39. *Bulletin of the University of Minnesota* 12 (July 10, 1909), p. 26.

40. Fletcher H. Swift, *A History of Public Permanent Common School Funds in the United States, 1795-1905* (New York: H. Holt and Company, 1911).

41. Fletcher H. Swift, "Social Aspects of German Student Life." There is no proof of this having been published separately as a book. It may have been published by Swift himself at Lancaster, Pennsylvania. It originally appeared in a series of articles in *School and Society* 4 (July 8, 1916), pp. 49-53; 4 (August 12, 1916), pp. 242-48; and 4 (August 26, 1916), pp. 313-18.

42. Fletcher H. Swift, *Studies in Public School Finance*, 4 vols. (Minneapolis: University of Minnesota Press, 1922-1925).

43. University of Minnesota, *Sixteenth Biennial Report of the Board of Regents*, p. 38.

44. University of Minnesota, *Fifteenth Biennial Report of the Board of Regents*, p. 9.

45. University of Minnesota, *Sixteenth Biennial Report of the Board of Regents*, p. 38.

46. In fact, according to a newspaper account of the time, Dean Downey "designed the arrangement of the interior and the entire furnishings" of Folwell Hall. Undated clipping entitled "Folwell Hall Campus Model" (Folwell File).

47. University of Minnesota, *President's Report, 1912-1913*, p. 87.

48. University of Minnesota, *President's Report, 1911-1912*, p. 147.

49. Ibid., pp. 60-61.

50. Ibid., p. 61.

51. Ibid.

52. University of Minnesota, *President's Report, 1913-1914*, p. 120.

53. Ibid., p. 122.

54. Clifford S. Griffin, *The University of Kansas: A History* (Lawrence, Kansas: University of Kansas Press, 1974), pp. 429, 440, 484.

55. See Johnson and Johanningmeier, *Teachers for the Prairie*.

56. Mary Folwell, "Reminiscences of Faculty" (Folwell Family Papers).

57. "Memorandum Concerning the College of Education Deanship" (Fred Snyder Papers: Correspondence, 1907-1921).

58. *Who Was Who in America*, Vol. 1.

CHAPTER 4: *A New Emphasis on Professionalism*

1. Guy Ford to Frederick Miesnest, March 12, 1915 (Graduate School: Education, 1914-1916).

2. Guy Ford to B.F. Shambaugh, March 12, 1915 (Graduate School: Education, 1914-1916).

3. Guy Ford to C. P. Colgrave, March 12, 1915 (Graduate School: Education, 1914-1916).

4. College of Education executive faculty meeting minutes, April 26, 1915.

Miscellaneous Minutes and Reports, 1914-1923.

5. Fred Snyder Papers: Correspondence, 1907-1921.

6. Ibid.

7. Ibid.

8. Johnson and Johanningmeier, *Teachers for the Prairie*, pp. 142-49.

9. L[otus] D. Coffman, *The Social Composition of the Teaching Population*, Contributions to Education, Number 41 (New York: Teachers College, Columbia University, 1911).

10. *Report of a Survey of the School System of St. Paul, Minnesota* (St. Paul, Minnesota, 1917). The survey commission was composed of G. D. Strayer. L. D. Coffman, and C. A. Prosser.

11. Walter W. Cook, "Organization for Research of the College of Education at the University of Minnesota," *Scientia Paedagogica* 9 (1963), p. 9.

12. Johnson and Johanningmeier, *Teachers for the Prairie*, p. 158-65.

13. Ibid., p. 158.

14. George Counts, *The Selective Character of American Secondary Education* (Chicago: University of Chicago Press, 1922).

15. George Counts, *The Social Composition of Boards of Education: A Study in the Social Control of Public Education* (Chicago: University of Chicago Press, 1927).

16. George Counts, *A Call to the Teachers of the Nation* (New York: The John Day Company, 1932).

17. Lawrence Cremin, David Shannon, and Mary Townsend, *A History of Teachers College, Columbia University* (New York: Columbia University Press, 1954), p. 48.

18. Quoted in Ralph H. Gabriel, *The Course of American Democratic Thought* (New York: The Ronald Press, 1940), p. 297.

19. Ibid., p. 298.

20. Ross Finney, *Personal Religion and the Social Awakening* (New York: Eaton and Mains, 1913).

21. Ibid., p. 16.

22. James L. Wattenbarger, "Leonard V. Koos: Leader of Pioneers," *Community and Junior College Journal* 47 (October 1976), p. 50.

23. Ibid.

24. James Umstattd, *The Odyssey of Jim Umstattd* (Austin, Texas: The Whitley Company, 1977), p. 116.

25. Lotus Coffman to Marion Burton, October 24, 1917 (President's Papers: College of Education, 1945-1960: Joint Registration in SLA and College of Education).

26. Gray, *The University of Minnesota*, p. 225.

27. Ibid.

28. Ibid., p. 53.

29. College of Education executive faculty meeting minutes, November 16, 1914. Miscellaneous Minutes and Reports, 1914-1923.

30. College of Education executive faculty meeting minutes, November 23, 1914. Miscellaneous Minutes and Reports, 1914-1923.

31. Gray, *The University of Minnesota*, p. 223.

32. College of Education executive faculty meeting minutes, February 1, 1915. Miscellaneous Minutes and Reports, 1914-1923.

33. College of Education executive faculty meeting minutes, March 25, 1918. Miscellaneous Minutes and Reports, 1914-1923.

34. College of Education executive faculty meeting minutes, December 9, 1919. Miscellaneous Minutes and Reports, 1914-1923.

35. Emily L. Veblen, "Fifty-three Years: A Record of Growth," p. 14.

36. Ibid.

37. Ibid.

38. Ibid.

39. Ibid., p. 15.

40. University of Minnesota, Board of Regents, *Minutes* 4 (1914-1917), p. 118.

41. Ibid.

42. Ibid.

43. Ibid.

44. College of Education general faculty meeting minutes, November 21, 1916. Miscellaneous Minutes and Reports, 1914-1923.

45. Minutes of the Joint Meeting of the Executive Faculty of the College of Education and the Advisory Committee of the College of Science, Literature, and the Arts, April 2, 1917. Miscellaneous Minutes and Reports, 1914-1923.

46. Ibid.

47. Ibid.

48. Ibid.

49. Ibid.

50. Minutes of the Joint Meeting of the Executive Faculty of the College of Education and the Advisory Committee of the College of Science, Literature, and the Arts, April 23, 1917. Miscellaneous Minutes and Reports, 1914-1923.

51. Lotus Coffman to Marion Burton, October 24, 1917 (President's Papers: College of Education, 1945-1960: Joint Registration in SLA and College of Education).

52. Marion Burton to Lotus Coffman, September 26, 1917 (President's Papers: College of Education, 1945-1960: Joint Registration in SLA and College of Education).

53. College of Education executive faculty meeting minutes, November 5, 1919. Miscellaneous Minutes and Reports, 1914-1923.

CHAPTER 5: *The Haggerty Years and the Maturing of the College*

1. A. C. Krey, "In Memoriam: Melvin E. Haggerty, 1875-1937" (College of Education Papers: Haggerty Biographical Materials).

2. Ibid., p. 1.

3. Ibid., p. 2. Haggerty gathered the data for his doctoral work in the Harvard Psychological Laboratory while working on determining the abilities of monkeys to learn by imitation. The assumption was that animal behavior provided clues to the more complex operations of humans. Haggerty began his work in 1907 with three Cebus monkeys and published his "Imitation in Monkeys" in *The Journal of Comparative Neurology and Psychology* 19 (July 1909), pp. 337-455. In this article, Haggerty cited as his primary studies Edward Lee Thorndike's "The Mental Life of Monkeys" (*Psychological Review*, Monograph Supplement, 3 [May 1901]) and John B. Watson's "Imitation in Monkeys" (*Psychological Bulletin* 5 [June 15, 1908], pp. 169-78). These two citations characterize Haggerty's early work as having been in the tradition of behaviorism.

4. Krey, "In Memoriam," p. 2.

5. Melvin E. Haggerty, "Arithmetic: A Cooperative Study in Educational Measurements," *Indiana University Studies* 19 (1915), pp. 385-507.

6. Virginia Education Commission, *Virginia Public Schools* (New York: World Book Company, 1921).

7. Krey, "In Memoriam," p. 3.

8. Ibid., p. 3. Specifically, the volumes to which Krey referred are entitled *The Evaluation of Higher Institutions.* Volume 1: *Principles of Higher Institutions* (co-

authored with George F. Zook [Chicago: University of Chicago Press, 1936]); Volume 2: *The Faculty* (Chicago: University of Chicago Press, 1937); and Volume 3: *The Educational Program* (Chicago: University of Chicago Press, 1937).

9. Melvin Haggerty to A. C. Krey, September 21, 1934 (President's Papers: College of Education, 1934-1937).

10. Melvin E. Haggerty, "The Low Visibility of Educational Issues," *School and Society* 41 (March 2, 1935), pp. 273-83.

11. Krey, "In Memoriam," p. 4.

12. See, for example, the letters of May 31, June 2, and June 28, 1915 (Coffman Papers: Correspondence, 1912-1929).

13. Lotus Coffman to George Vincent, July 1, 1915 (President's Papers: Correspondence, 1912-1929).

14. Melvin Haggerty to Lotus Coffman, August 27, 1926 (President's Papers: College of Education, 1919-1926).

15. Ibid.

16. Ibid.

17. Ibid.

18. Ibid.

19. Guy Ford to Lotus Coffman, November 19, 1926 (President's Papers: College of Education, 1919-1926).

20. Melvin Haggerty to Lotus Coffman, May 23, 1928 (President's Papers: College of Education, 1927-1928).

21. Ibid.

22. Lotus Coffman to Melvin Haggerty, June 12, 1928 (President's Papers: College of Education, 1927-1928).

23. Ibid.

24. Ibid.

25. See, for example, a March 22, 1928, letter from Melvin Haggerty to Lotus Coffman (College of Education Papers: President's Office Correspondence, 1928-1931).

26. Melvin Haggerty and Dora V. Smith, *Reading and Literature* (Yonkers-on-Hudson: World Book Company, 1927). The final edition of this study was published in 1937, the year of Haggerty's death.

27. Project Social Studies was officially entitled *Preparation and Evaluation of Social Studies Curriculum Guides and Materials for Grades K to 14.*

28. Melvin Haggerty to Lotus Coffman, November 28, 1927 (President's Papers: College of Education, 1927-1928).

29. Ibid.

30. Ibid.

31. Ibid.

32. Ibid.

33. Ibid.

34. Ibid.

35. Marvin Van Wagenen to Lotus Coffman, May 26, 1928 (President's Papers: College of Education, 1927-1928).

36. Melvin Haggerty to Lotus Coffman, October 14, 1926 (President's Papers: College of Education, 1919-1926).

37. Lotus Coffman to Melvin Haggerty, October 19, 1926 (President's Papers: College of Education, 1919-1926).

38. Melvin Haggerty to Lotus Coffman, October 14, 1926 (President's Papers: College of Education, 1919-1926).

39. Ibid.

40. Ibid.

41. Lotus Coffman to Melvin Haggerty, August 16, 1926 (College of Education Papers: President's Office Correspondence, 1916-1927).

42. Edgar Wesley to Robert Beck, June 20, 1977 (Robert Beck Papers).

43. Melvin Haggerty to Lotus Coffman, undated letter from the summer of 1937 (President's Papers: Personal Correspondence, 1937).

44. Melvin Haggerty to "Miss Gopher," November 19, 1926 (College of Education Papers: Melvin Haggerty Biographical Materials).

45. Melvin E. Haggerty, untitled typescript dated Christmas, 1932. Later mimeographed under the title "Who Made the Book? The Story of the College of Education Carol Sings" (Robert Beck Papers).

46. Ibid.

47. Ibid.

48. Alvin C. Eurich, ed., *The Changing Educational World.*

49. Melvin Haggerty to Lotus Coffman, August 6, 1937 (College of Education: President's Office Correspondence, 1937).

50. Melvin E. Haggerty, *Children of the Depression* (Minneapolis: University of Minnesota Press, 1933).

51. James Umstattd, *Odyssey*, p. 128.

52. Ibid.

53. Melvin E. Haggerty, *Enrichment of the Common Life* (Minneapolis: University of Minnesota Press, 1938), p. 18.

54. Gray, *The University of Minnesota*, pp. 455-56.

55. Ibid., p. 456.

56. Melvin Haggerty to Lotus Coffman, March 29, 1926 (College of Education Papers: President's Office Correspondence, 1916-1927).

57. Melvin Haggerty to Lotus Coffman, February 7, 1936 (College of Education Papers: President's Office Correspondence, 1936).

58. Melvin E. Haggerty, *Art, A Way of Life* (Minneapolis: University of Minnesota Press, 1935).

59. Frederick P. Keppel, whose son became dean of education at Harvard, was then president of the Carnegie Corporation.

60. Melvin E. Haggerty, *Enrichment of the Common Life*, p. 24.

61. University of Minnesota, *President's Report, 1932-1934*, p. 258.

62. Haggerty, *Enrichment of the Common Life*, p. 26.

63. University of Minnesota, *President's Report, 1932-1934*, p. 259.

64. Haggerty, *Enrichment of the Common Life*, p. 25.

65. Haggerty, *Art, A Way of Life*, p. 11.

66. Ibid.

67. Edwin Ziegfeld to David Wetzel, September 6, 1977 (Robert Beck Papers).

68. Ibid.

69. See, for example, Ruth Raymond, *A Letter from Living*, Guild Studies Number 3 (Middletown, California: Guild for Psychological Studies, 1963).

70. Melvin Haggerty to Lotus Coffman, February 7, 1936 (College of Education Papers: President's Office Correspondence, 1936).

71. Ibid.

72. Lotus Coffman to Melvin Haggerty, February 13, 1936 (College of Education Papers: President's Office Correspondence, 1936).

73. Ibid.

74. "Department History: Art Education Program" (Robert Beck Papers).

75. Ibid., p. 2.

76. Ibid.

CHAPTER 6: *The Haggerty Faculty*

1. Wesley, *NEA: The First Hundred Years,* p. 91.

2. Leo Brueckner, *Scales for the Rating of Teaching Skill* (Minneapolis: University of Minnesota Press, 1929); Leo Brueckner and E. O. Melby, *Diagnostic and Remedial Teaching* (Boston: Houghton Mifflin, 1931).

3. Lotus Coffman to Melvin Haggerty, July 9, 1931 (President's Papers: College of Education, 1929-1933).

4. Leo Brueckner, *Adapting Instruction in Arithmetic to Individual Differences* (Minneapolis: University of Minnesota Press, 1941); Leo Brueckner and Guy Bond, *Diagnosis and Treatment of Learning Difficulties* (New York: Appleton-Century-Crofts, 1955).

5. See Leo Brueckner's report, "Administrative Status from 1923 to the Present" (President's Papers: College of Education, 1919-1928).

6. Brueckner's procedures in *Scales for the Rating of Teaching Skill* were quite convincing. He had 150 supervisors discuss four teaching methods and then rate teachers using these four methods. The supervisors each had their favorite methods, and the ratings differed a great deal. It was difficult to devise reliable scales but, with Van Wagenen's help on statistics, Brueckner felt he had succeeded.

7. Leo Brueckner, *The Changing Elementary School: Report of the Regents Inquiry into the Character and Cost of Public Education in New York* (New York: Inor Publishing Company, 1939).

8. Much of the information on Van Wagenen has resulted from an interview with Van Wagenen's daughter, Helen Swalin, May 26, 1977, and subsequent conversations (Robert Beck Papers).

9. See, for example, Oscar K. Buros, ed., *The Mental Measurements Yearbook* (Highland Park, N.J., 1938, 1940, and 1941). The reviews in the *Yearbook* are representative.

10. Guy Bond to Robert Beck, March 19, 1978 (Robert Beck Papers).

11. Guy Bond and Eva Bond Wagner, *Teaching the Child to Read* (New York: Macmillan Company, 1943).

12. Guy Bond, *The Auditory and Speech Characteristics of Poor Readers,* Contributions to Education Number 657 (New York: Teachers College, Columbia University, 1935).

13. Guy Bond and Miles Tinker, *Reading Difficulties: Their Diagnosis and Correction* (New York: Appleton-Century-Crofts, 1957).

14. Guy Bond and Bertha Handlan, *Adapting Instruction to Individual Differences in Reading* (Minneapolis: University of Minnesota Press, 1948).

15. Oscar K. Buros, *Tests in Print II* (Highland Park, New Jersey, 1974), p. 505.

16. A. C. Krey and Palmer Johnson, "Differential Functions of Examinations," *Bulletin of the University of Minnesota* 36 (January 25, 1933).

17. Dora V. Smith, *Class Size in High School English: Methods and Results* (Minneapolis: University of Minnesota Press, 1931).

18. Dora V. Smith, *Instruction in English,* U.S. Office of Education Bulletin 1932, Number 17 (Washington, D.C.: Government Printing Office, 1933).

19. Melvin E. Haggerty and Dora V. Smith, *Reading and Literature,* 3 vols. (Yonkers-on-Hudson: World Book Company, 1927-1928).

20. Dora V. Smith, *Evaluating Instruction in Secondary School English* (Chicago: National Council of Teachers of English, 1941).

21. National Council of Teachers of English, Commission on the English Curriculum, *N.C.T.E. Curriculum Series* (New York: Appleton-Century-Crofts). Individual titles are: Volume 1, *English Language Arts* (1952); Volume 2, *Language*

Arts for Today's Children (1954); Volume 3, *The English Language Arts in the Secondary School* (1956); Volume 4, *The College Teaching of English* (1965); and Volume 5, *The Education of Teachers of English for American Schools and Colleges* (1963).

22. See, for example, Dora V. Smith, "Ventures in Education around the World — Their Significance for American Education," *University of Kansas Bulletin of Education* 11 (November 1956), pp. 15-25.

23. These observations on Book Week were made by Professor Norine Odland of the College of Education. Professor Odland has been closely connected with the planning that has made Book Week a success; she has also done a great deal of the work necessary to build a College collection of children's literature.

24. Edgar Wesley to Robert Beck, June 20, 1977 (Robert Beck Papers).

25. George D. Heiss, "Edgar Bruce Wesley and the Social Studies" (Ed.D. thesis, Rutgers University, 1967), p. 36. Wesley has approved Heiss's study and wrote to Robert Beck, June 22, 1973, that "everything I did in my field is faithfully recorded in George Heiss." (Robert Beck Papers).

26. Ibid., p. 75.

27. Edgar Wesley to Robert Beck, June 20, 1977 (Robert Beck Papers).

28. Ibid.

29. Heiss, "Edgar Bruce Wesley," p. 47.

30. Edgar Wesley to George Heiss, July 8, 1966. Quoted in Heiss, "Edgar Bruce Wesley," p. 49.

31. Edgar Wesley to Robert Beck, June 20, 1977 (Robert Beck Papers).

32. Ibid.

33. Ibid.

34. Lotus Coffman to Melvin Haggerty, July 9, 1931 (President's Papers: College of Education, 1929-1933).

35. Heiss, "Edgar Bruce Wesley," p. 107.

36. Grove Dow, *Social Problems of Today*, in collaboration with Edgar B. Wesley (New York: Thomas Y. Crowell Company, 1925).

37. Just after Wesley joined Krey at Minnesota, he published *Bibliographies for Teachers of the Social Studies* (Philadelphia: McKinley Publishing Company, 1932). This was followed in five years by Wesley's popular *Teaching the Social Studies* (New York: D. C. Heath and Company, 1937); later editions were entitled *Teaching Social Studies in High School* and *Teaching Secondary Social Studies in a World Society*. A sixth edition of the latter titles, with Stanley Wronski as co-author, was marketed in 1973.

38. Heiss, "Edgar Bruce Wesley," p. 177.

39. Ibid., p. 207.

40. Ibid., p. 233.

41. Ibid., p. 237.

42. Ibid.

43. Wesley, *NEA: The First Hundred Years*.

CHAPTER 7: *Vision and Research:*
The College Becomes a Community of Values

1. Wesley, *NEA: The First Hundred Years*, p. 110.

2. Theodore Brameld, *Design for America* (New York: Hinds, Hayden and Eldredge, Inc., 1945).

3. Craig Kridel, "Theodore Brameld's Floodwood Project: A Design for America," a paper presented to a meeting of the American Educational Studies Association, November 4, 1977, p. 12.

4. See George Seldes, *Lords of the Press* (New York: J. Messner, Inc., 1938).

5. Theodore Brameld, "A Plea for Propaganda in Defense of Public Education," *School and Society* 56 (December 1942), pp. 609-10.

6. For a detailed discussion of this concept, together with a closer look at the controversy which it sparked in Floodwood, see Craig Kridel, "The Theory and Practice of Theodore Brameld's 'Defensible Partiality': A Mid-Century 'Resolution' to the Imposition Controversy," *Journal of the Midwest History of Education Society* 5 (1977), pp. 120-34.

7. See especially the chapter entitled "Shall the Schools Indoctrinate?" in Theodore Brameld, *Ends and Means in Education: A Mid-Century Appraisal* (New York: Harper and Brothers, 1950), pp. 86-94.

8. Ibid., pp. 92-93.

9. See Mary Ann Raywid, *The Axe-Grinders* (New York: Macmillan Company, 1962).

10. See, for example, Theodore Brameld, "Can We Prepare Now for the Post-War Period?" *Education* 63 (February 1943), pp. 340-45; and Theodore Brameld, "The Need for an American Plan," *Frontiers of Democracy* 6 (January 1940), pp. 111-12.

11. Theodore Brameld, "High School Students Work on a Design for America," *Teachers College Record* 46 (January 1945), p. 250.

12. See Theodore Brameld, "We Look at the Future," *Educational Leadership* 3 (May 1946), pp. 374-76.

13. Kridel, "Theory and Practice." See also Lewis E. Harris, "A Study of Certain Factors in the Evolution and Development of the Floodwood Community School" (Ph.D. dissertation, New York University, 1952), p. 212.

14. Kridel, "Theodore Brameld's Floodwood Project," p. 14.

15. The exchange of articles between Bode, Childs, and Brameld is reviewed in Kridel, "Theory and Practice." See also Kridel, "Theodore Brameld's Floodwood Project," p. 15.

16. See Henry C. Johnson, Jr., "Reflective Thought and Practical Action: The Origins of the John Dewey Society," *Educational Theory* 27 (Winter 1977), pp. 65-75.

17. To follow this thought further: Kridel, in "Theodore Brameld's Floodwood Project" (p. 4), has written that "Brameld, whose writing followed a 'successful' world war and rapidly improving technology in the fields of transportation and communication, acknowledged the 'ever-shrinking planet' and saw the community for reconstruction as encompassing the whole world. Man was caught in a 'planetary transformation': post-war planning and reconstruction must be aimed 'toward the desperate plight, growing power, and emerging goals of the underdeveloped areas of the world, inhabited by the bulk of the world's population.' " All this is true, of course, but Brameld's thought should not be perceived as standing alone. There were others before him who voiced reconstructionist sentiments, although they may not have had this description at their disposal; others after him would devote their careers to similar concerns while calling them by different names. Brameld not only fit into a continuum of thought, but his own career was also a sort of continuum. For example, his earlier social reconstructionist thought and his later study and fieldwork in anthropology during the 1960's and 1970's would lead to his all-encompassing concept "anthrotherapy."

18. "Putting Over Communism in Floodwood, Minnesota," *Friends of the Public Schools Bulletin*, Volume 12, Number 8, Serial 137, pp. 5-6.

19. The strike extended from November 25 to December 28, 1946. While Minneapolis Mayor Hubert Humphrey's efforts to get the Federation of Teachers and the School Board to resolve their differences bore fruit and averted a strike, St.

Paul teachers set up picket lines on November 25, 1946 (*Minneapolis Morning Tribune*, November 25, 1946). The St. Paul teachers wanted a $50.00 a month increase for the last four months of 1946 and revision of the salary schedule to reach a goal of $2,400 minimum and $5,000 maximum annually for classroom teachers. They also demanded a $1,000 a year increase per teacher for 1947 and budgetary increases to allow for the hiring of more teachers to help end overcrowding in classrooms. In addition, they wanted increased appropriations to modernize equipment and facilities. Finally, they insisted that the city recognize the Teachers Joint Council as the bargaining agent for St. Paul teachers. The St. Paul City Council maintained that under present legal limits it could not grant retroactive pay raises. The city also refused to recognize the Teachers Joint Council as the negotiating unit for the teachers. For five days (November 25-30), teachers were off the picket lines while negotiations continued. The talks broke down on November 30 and the teachers resumed their positions on the picket line (*Minneapolis Morning Tribune*, November 30, 1946). The St. Paul teachers' strike lasted five weeks, ending on December 28, 1946. Virtually all of the teachers' demands were met. The St. Paul Charter Commission called for the separation of school and other municipal funding in order to meet certain of the teachers' fiscal demands (*Minneapolis Morning Tribune*, December 28, 1946). The strike ended when the demands of the teachers were met.

20. See, for example, Theodore Brameld, ed., *Workers' Education in the United States* (New York: Harper and Brothers, 1941) and Theodore Brameld, "Workers' Education — A Neglected Opportunity," *Educational Forum* 4 (May 1940), pp. 401-8.

21. Theodore Brameld, "Informal Remarks." Stenotype record of informal remarks by Chairman of Adult Education Committee, American Federation of Teachers, Conference on Workers' Education, sponsored by the Department of Labor, Washington, D.C., September 28-29, 1945 (College of Education Papers: Theodore Brameld File).

22. See, for example, Theodore Brameld, *Minority Problems in the Public Schools* (New York: Harper and Brothers, 1946).

23. Theodore Brameld to Robert Beck, July 1977 (Robert Beck Papers).

24. Ibid.

25. Theodore Brameld to John Tate, January 26, 1940 (College of Education Papers: Theodore Brameld File).

26. Theodore Brameld to Robert Beck, July 1977 (Robert Beck Papers).

27. Ray E. Clough to an unnamed person, July 1, 1940 (College of Education Papers: Theodore Brameld File).

28. Ibid.

29. Wesley Peik, "Reactions" (College of Education Papers: Theodore Brameld File).

30. Theodore Brameld to Wesley Peik, March 26, 1946 (College of Education Papers: Theodore Brameld File).

31. Theodore Brameld to Wesley Peik, September 20, 1944 (College of Education Papers: Theodore Brameld File).

32. Ibid.

33. Haggerty, *Children of the Depression*, p. 16.

34. Ibid.

35. Walter Cook, "Tax Slashing Balks Education," *Eastern Illinois State Teachers College Bulletin*, February 20, 1934.

36. Ibid.

37. Ibid.

38. University of Minnesota, *President's Report, 1934-1936*, p. 7.

39. Ibid., pp. 5-6. Also involved in this battle, Coffman notes, were the American Youth Council and the Educational Policies Commission, the latter of which was created by both the National Education Association and the Department of Superintendence.

40. Ibid., p. 7.

41. Theodore Brameld to Robert Beck, July 1977 (Robert Beck Papers).

42. See, for example, testimony by the U.S. Department of Indian Affairs as reported by the *St. Paul Pioneer Press* (March 24, 1941).

43. *St. Paul Pioneer Press*, especially from December 1, 1940, to November 9, 1942, the days after the Minnesota Supreme Court upheld Rockwell's discharge. See also College of Education Papers: John G. Rockwell File.

44. Wesley Peik to Deane W. Malott, January 11, 1941 (College of Education Papers: John G. Rockwell File).

45. Ibid.

46. Ibid.

47. Harl Douglass, "Does the Future of Secondary Education Depend upon Statistical Research in Foundational Thinking?" *Education* 53 (January 1933), pp. 284-89.

48. Lotus Coffman to Wesley Peik, July 13, 1938 (College of Education Papers: President's Office Correspondence, 1938).

49. Ibid.

50. See, for example, Nelson L. Bossing, "Teacher Education for the Core Curriculum," *Minnesota Journal of Education* 30 (January 1950), pp. 17-19; Nelson L. Bossing, "Core and Common Learnings Curriculum," in Robert H. Beck, ed., *The Three R's Plus* (Minneapolis: University of Minnesota Press, 1956); and Nelson L. Bossing and R. C. Faunce, *Developing the Core Curriculum* (Englewood Cliffs, N.J.: Prentice-Hall, 1958).

51. Wesley, *NEA: The First Hundred Years*, pp. 116-17.

52. Palmer O. Johnson, *An Evaluation of the Courses in Elementary Botany as Projected into Sequent Courses in the College of Agriculture and Forestry* (Minneapolis: University of Minnesota Press, 1934).

53. "This work began August 1, 1928. The Survey of Land-Grant Colleges and Universities of the United States was authorized by Congress in 1927 and was carried out by the U.S. Office of Education over a three-year period." Palmer O. Johnson, "Some Enumerative Statistics," p. 1 (MEG qJ636s). In speaking of the Land-Grant College Survey, a report entitled "Collegiate Educational Research: 1928-30" states:

During the past several years the Federal Government has been conducting a study of land grant colleges and universities. In connection with this study it called upon the University of Minnesota to provide a very large amount of data concerning the University's activities, its faculty, its finances, its alumni, its curriculum, its organization, its administration, etc. A local committee headed by Dean Coffey appointed for the purpose of cooperating with the Federal Government for the land grant survey has been affiliated with the Committee on Educational Research during this period. The active agent for the survey was Dr. Palmer Johnson . . . . Dr. Johnson, after about a year and a half spent at the University in the collection of data, devoted approximately three months to an analysis of these data at the Office of Education in Washington. The obligations of the University to the Federal Government for this data are now complete, or practically so. Much material, however, has been gathered concerning the University of Minnesota which is in need of further analysis and evaluation. Dr. Johnson has already gone far in such investigation and will continue during the current year during which time a number of his studies should reach the point of publication. (College of Education Papers: Committee on Educational Research).

54. Palmer O. Johnson, "Some Enumerative Statistics," p. 1.

55. Palmer O. Johnson, *Aspects of Land-Grant College Education* (Minneapolis: University of Minnesota Press, 1934).

56. Kenneth E. Anderson and Clarence M. Pruitt, "Palmer Oliver Johnson: Statistician and Science Educator," *Science Education* 44 (April 1960), p. 168.

57. Palmer O. Johnson, "Some Enumerative Statistics," pp. 9-10.

58. Ibid., p. 10.

59. Ibid.

60. Palmer O. Johnson and J. Neyman, "Tests of Certain Linear Hypotheses and Their Applications to Some Educational Problems," *Statistical Research Memoirs* 1 (June 1936) pp. 57-93.

61. According to Johnson, the essential feature of the Johnson-Neyman technique was the development of a new concept resulting in the determination of a "region of significance." "By its use," he explained, "it is possible to specify in terms of background variables the limits of the generalizability of the experimental evidence. One illustration of its use in educational experimentation is the specification in terms of student characteristics, where one method of treatment would be superior for students' certain abilities, while a second method would be superior for students of other ranges in abilities." Palmer O. Johnson, "Some Enumerative Statistics," p. 14.

62. For example, Palmer O. Johnson and Cyril Hoyt jointly published *The Theory of Linear Hypotheses with Applications to Educational Problems* (Bureau of Educational Research, College of Education, University of Minnesota, 1952).

63. Cyril Hoyt, "Test Reliability Obtained by Analysis of Variance," *Psychometrika* 6 (June 1941), pp. 153-60.

64. Interview with Raymond O. Collier, June 14, 1977 (Robert Beck Papers).

65. Although the "Working Statement of the Place of Research in the College of Education" does not carry the names of Ruth Eckert and Gerald Erickson as authors, it was prepared by them and circulated in the College of Education in May 1958.

CHAPTER 8: *A New Focus on Higher Education*

1. Ruth E. Eckert and Gerald Erickson, "A Half-Century of Progress in Higher Education: The College of Education's Contributions to Study and Research in this Field," ([Minneapolis], 1955) p. 1 (Robert Beck Papers).

2. *Bulletin of the University of Minnesota, 1908-1909*, p. 24.

3. In a letter written on February 23, 1927, Johnston proposed to Guy Stanton Ford, dean of the Graduate School, that Ph.D. students be trained specifically in the area of college teaching. He supported his proposal with a five-page rationale; at one point, he wrote: "My proposal succinctly is not that the Graduate School set up a doctor's degree in *education* for college teachers but that it provide the training for college teaching in each student's subject in order that the requirements of his degree and the atmosphere in which he does his work shall induce in the prospective teacher a recognition of the fact that both scholarship and teaching ability are necessary in his profession. The object of such a system would be to produce teaching scholars" (President's Papers: College of Education, 1927-1928).

4. Lotus Coffman to Marion Burton, February 8, 1918 (College of Education Papers: President's Office Correspondence, 1916-1927).

5. Ibid.

6. Ibid.

7. University of Minnesota, *President's Report, 1918-1919*, p. 174.

8. Cyril Hoyt, "Historical Sketch of the Bureau of Educational Research," January 1956 (Robert Beck Papers).

9. Of the $7,825, $1,500 was allotted for a statistician, $1,200 for a full-time assistant, $1,250 for miscellaneous help, $1,000 for supplies, and $1,000 and $1,875 to support a portion of the salaries of two professors who were devoting an unusual portion of their time to research.

10. Hoyt, "Historical Sketch," p. 3.

11. Melvin E. Haggerty, "The Relations of Departments of Education to Other Departments of the College," *Educational Monographs* 11 (1922), pp. 65-82.

12. Dorolese H. Wardwell, "Resources of the University of Minnesota Office of Educational Research for the Study of Education in Minnesota." A paper given as part of the program of the Minnesota Society for the Study of Education during Schoolmen's Week, 1961, under the auspices of the College of Education, March 27, 1961, p. 1 (Robert Beck Papers).

13. University of Minnesota, *President's Report, 1921-1922*, p. 181.

14. University of Minnesota, *President's Report, 1927-1928*, p. 215.

15. Ibid.

16. Melvin Haggerty, "The Training of the Superintendent of Schools," *Bulletin of the University of Minnesota* 28 (April 6, 1925), pp. 3-29.

17. Dean Schweickhard, "A Guide to the Supervision of General Industrial Education," *Bulletin of the University of Minnesota* 28 (October 1, 1925), pp. 3-12.

18. The Schoolmen's Week program for February 1928 indicates that earlier College of Education programs were then being distributed by the University Press.

19. John E. Stecklein, "The History and Development of the Bureau of Institutional Research at the University of Minnesota." A paper presented to the Conference on Institutional Research, Stanford University, July 19-25, 1959, p. 1.

20. Cook, "Organization for Research," p. 19.

21. *Bulletin of the University of Minnesota* 26 (August 4, 1923), p. 26.

22. Ibid.

23. Ruth E. Eckert and Robert J. Keller, "Origin and Background of the Institutional Research Program," in Ruth E. Eckert and Robert J. Keller, eds., *A University Looks at Its Program* (Minneapolis: University of Minnesota Press, 1954), pp. 3-4.

24. Ibid., p. 4.

25. Ibid.

26. Stecklein, "History and Development," p. 4.

27. Eckert and Keller, "Origin and Background," pp. 4-5.

28. University of Minnesota, *President's Biennial Message, 1928-1930*, p. 526.

29. Raymond A. Kent, ed., *Higher Education in America* (Boston: Ginn and Company, 1930).

30. Lotus D. Coffman, "Introduction," in Kent, ed., *Higher Education*, p. ix.

31. Ibid., pp. ix-x.

32. Melvin Haggerty, "The Improvement of University Instruction through Educational Research," in Kent, ed., *Higher Education*, p. 505.

33. Ibid.

34. Melvin Haggerty, *The Faculty*, vol. 2 of *The Evaluation of Higher Institutions* (Chicago: University of Chicago Press, 1937). Haggerty also authored volume 3 of the series, *The Educational Program* (1937).

35. Haggerty obviously held his son in high regard; this is exemplified by further remarks: "He assisted in the preparation of the inquiry schedules relating to the faculty, curriculum, instruction, institutional purposes and institutional study, and assumed major responsibility for the tabulation and statistical analysis of the

data derived from them . . . . It was he who first suggested the device of the pattern map, and more than any other person he developed the idea into its final form" (*The Faculty*, p. xi).

36. Haggerty, *The Educational Program*, p. xi.

37. Charles Boardman also acted as president of the North Central Association from 1949 to 1950 and as secretary from 1951 until his death in November 1959.

38. Eckert and Erickson, "Half-Century of Progess," p. 9.

39. Ibid

40. Ibid.

41. Wesley Peik to Malcolm Willey, January 28, 1948 (President's Papers: College of Education, 1946-1951).

42. Wesley Peik to James Morrill, February 1, 1951 (President's Papers: College of Education: Bureau of Field Studies and Surveys).

43. Ibid.

44. Ibid.

45. "Two New College Units Stress Cooperative Research and Development," *Lyceum* 2 (June 1979), p. 15.

46. Ibid.

47. Interview with Mary Corcoran, Ruth Eckert, and Robert Keller conducted by Robert Beck, 1977 (Robert Beck Papers).

48. Eckert and Erickson, "Half-Century of Progress," p. 11.

49. University of Minnesota, *President's Report, 1948-1950*, p. 117.

50. Eckert and Keller, eds., *A University Looks at Its Program*.

51. Stecklein, "History and Development," pp. 6-7.

CHAPTER 9: *Years of Growth, Years of Opportunity*

1. Interview with Marcia Edwards, March 25, 1977 (Robert Beck Papers).

2. Lotus Coffman to Melvin Haggerty, May 31, 1929 (College of Education Papers: President's Office Correspondence, 1928-1931).

3. Melvin Haggerty to Lotus Coffman, October 26, 1928 (College of Education Papers: President's Office Correspondence, 1928-1931).

4. Lotus Coffman to Melvin Haggerty, August 27, 1934 (College of Education Papers: President's Office Correspondence, 1934-1935).

5. Ibid.

6. University of Minnesota, *President's Report, 1937-1938*, p. 261.

7. Wesley Peik to Guy Ford, November 24, 1937 (College of Education Papers: President's Office Correspondence, 1937).

8. Guy Ford to Wesley Peik, November 27, 1937 (College of Education Papers: President's Office Correspondence, 1937).

9. University of Minnesota, *President's Report, 1948-1950*, p. 117.

10. Wesley E. Peik, *The Professional Education of High School Teachers* (Minneapolis: University of Minnesota Press, 1930).

11. Wesley Peik to Guy Ford, February 3, 1938 (College of Education Papers: President's Office Correspondence, 1938).

12. Ibid.

13. Ibid.

14. Peik's persistent interest in the idea of a curriculum laboratory is evident from correspondence between the dean, President Coffman, and President Ford during the years 1937 to 1939 (President's Papers: College of Education, 1934-1941).

15. "Notes on the Laboratory of Physiological Hygiene, University of Minnesota," (February 1945), p. 1. (MSDP L11 qA3n).

16. Ibid.

17. Ibid., p. 2.

18. Emma Birkmaier, ed., *Illustrative Learning Experiences: University High School in Action* (Minneapolis: University of Minnesota Press, 1952).

19. Interview with Emma Birkmaier, March 31, 1977 (Robert Beck Papers).

20. Interview with Dale Lange, May 19, 1977 (Robert Beck Papers).

21. Guy Bond to Robert Beck, August 8, 1977 (Robert Beck Papers).

22. Ibid.

23. Ibid.

24. Ibid.

25. Brueckner and Bond, *The Diagnosis and Treatment of Learning Difficulties.*

26. Interview with Robert Jackson, June 16, 1977 (Robert Beck Papers).

27. Donovan A. Johnson and William H. Glenn, *Exploring Mathematics on Your Own* (St. Louis: Webster Publishing Company, 1960). The first six pamphlets were also published under the same title by Doubleday in 1961.

28. "University High School, 1958," p. 3 (President's Papers: College of Education: University High School).

29. For a further discussion of this controversy, see Merle Borrowman, *The Liberal and Technical in Teacher Education* (New York: Teachers College, Columbia University, 1956).

30. The writer is indebted to Arnold Woestehoff, a former assistant of Wesley Peik's who worked to further the accreditation issue, for furnishing the documents which are crucial to understanding what Peik accomplished in this area.

31. Wesley Peik to Malcolm Willey, October 11, 1939 (College of Education Papers: President's Office Correspondence, 1939).

32. Ibid.

33. Wesley Peik to James Morrill, February 13, 1948 (College of Education Papers: President's Office Correspondence, 1947-1948).

34. James Morrill to Wesley Peik, March 3, 1948 (College of Education Papers: President's Office Correspondence, 1947-1948).

35. Willard Givens, "The Imprint of a Man on Education," *Minnesota Journal of Education* 32 (January 1952), p. 9.

CHAPTER 10: *The Expanding Educational Horizon*

1. Marcia Edwards to James Morrill, March 19, 1952 (President's Papers: College of Education, 1952-1955).

2. Ibid., p. 1.

3. Ibid.

4. Ibid.

5. Ibid., p. 2.

6. Ibid.

7. Ibid., p. 3. Edwards went on to say: "According to the recent faculty load study, we have a median advisory load of 47 undergraduates and 20 graduates, as compared with medians of 13 and 5 in another division whose undergraduate enrollment is similar to ours."

8. Ibid., p. 5.

9. Ibid.

10. Ibid., p. 6.

11. Ibid., p. 7.

12. Ibid., pp. 12-13, 14.

13. Ibid., p. 16.

14. Ibid.

15. From telephone conversations between James Morrill and Robert Beck.

16. Ibid.

17. Walter W. Cook, *The Measurement of General Spelling Ability Involving Controlled Comparisons between Techniques*, University of Iowa Studies in Education, NS 221 (Iowa City: University of Iowa, 1932).

18. Walter W. Cook, "Individual Differences and Curriculum Practice," *Journal of Educational Psychology* 39 (March 1948), p. 141.

19. Ibid.

20. Walter W. Cook, *Grouping and Promotion in the Elementary Schools*, number 2 in the *Individualization of Instruction* series (Minneapolis: University of Minnesota Press, 1941).

21. Walter W. Cook, "The Gifted and the Retarded in Historical Perspective," *Phi Delta Kappan* 39 (March 1958), pp. 249-55.

22. Ibid., p. 251.

23. Cook, "Individual Differences and Curriculum Practice," p. 146.

24. Ibid.

25. Walter W. Cook, C. H. Leeds, and R. Callis, *Minnesota Teacher Attitude Inventory* (New York: The Psychological Corporation, 1951).

26. See Walter W. Cook and Donald M. Medley, "Proposed Hostility and Pharisaic-Virtue Scales for the MMPI," *Journal of Applied Psychology* 38 (December 1954), pp. 414-18.

27. Ibid., p. 414.

28. *Minneapolis Morning Tribune*, January 1, 1950.

29. College of Education faculty meeting minutes, June 2, 1953.

30. Minnesota, Office of State Demographer, *Faces of the Future* (St. Paul: State Planning Agency, 1977).

31. "The Impact of the Educational Crisis in Minnesota," typescript (Robert Beck Papers).

32. University of Minnesota, *Alumni Reports*, January 1962.

33. See, for example, Walter W. Cook, "Curriculum Research," *Review of Educational Research* 26 (June 1956), pp. 224-40.

34. See, for example, Nolan C. Kearney, *Elementary School Objectives* (New York: Russell Sage Foundation, 1953).

35. Walter Cook to Ed Haislet, March 5, 1963 (Robert Beck Papers). Cook's ranking placed Minnesota first, followed by Illinois (graduate school), Wisconsin (graduate school), Michigan State, Ohio State, Michigan, Stanford University, Indiana, the University of California at Berkeley, Harvard (graduate administration), and the University of Chicago (graduate administration).

36. Ibid.

37. Ibid.

38. Walter Cook to James Morrill, April 1, 1954 (President's Papers: College of Education, 1952-1955).

39. Ibid.

40. An important source of information on the Psychoeducational Clinic is Richard Ugland, "The Psycho-Educational Center: An Historical Review" (University of Minnesota: College of Education, n.d. [1974]).

41. Maynard Reynolds to Robert Beck. Transcript of undated audiotape (Robert Beck Papers).

42. From notes compiled by Evelyn Deno, April 19, 1977 (Robert Beck Papers).

43. Interview with Bruce Balow, May 12, 1977 (Robert Beck Papers).

44. Mildred Thomson, *Prologue: A Minnesota Story of Mental Retardation, Showing Changing Attitudes and Philosophies Prior to September 1, 1959* (Minneapolis: Gilbert Publishing Company, 1963).

45. The extent of externally sponsored research and training grants for the academic year 1974-75 alone is given in *Externally Sponsored Research and Training*

Programs, 1974-1975, ed. by Nancy Mosier (Minneapolis: College of Education, Education Planning and Development Office, 1975).

46. Maynard Reynolds to Robert Beck. Transcript of undated audiotape (Robert Beck Papers).

47. Ibid.

48. Interview with Marian Hall, May 23, 1977 (Robert Beck Papers).

49. From a November 29, 1957, application for a college training grant under the National Mental Health Act.

50. Interview with Willard Hartup, June 16, 1977 (Robert Beck Papers).

51. Maynard Reynolds to Robert Beck. Transcript of undated audiotape (Robert Beck Papers).

52. Melvin Haggerty to Lotus Coffman, December 14, 1915 (College of Education Papers: Miscellaneous Correspondence, 1915-1950).

53. Melvin Haggerty to Lotus Coffman, November 11, 1915 (College of Education Papers: Miscellaneous Correspondence, 1915-1950).

54. College of Education faculty meeting minutes, February 2, 1955.

55. *University of Minnesota Self-Survey Report on Physics, Mathematics, and Child Welfare, 1956,* p. 9 (MAG qSe48r).

56. Ibid.

57. The faculty minutes for the February 2, 1955, meeting provide the following information on the faculty:

Full members of graduate faculty with major teaching responsibility in educational psychology:

1. Johnson, Palmer O.	Professor	Advanced Statistics, Methods of Research, Science.
2. Wrenn, C. Gilbert	Professor	Student personnel work, counseling psychology, higher education, psychology of personality and mental hygiene.
3. Dugan, Willis E.	Professor and Chairman, Educational Psychology	Student personnel work, group guidance, school counselor preparation, occupational information laboratory, undergraduate teacher education.
4. Mork, Gordon	Assoc. Professor	Learning, and coordinator undergraduate teacher education sequence (secondary).
5. Reynolds, Maynard	Assoc. Professor	Individual mental tests, special education, diagnosis and remedial teaching, director psychoeducational clinic.
6. Flanders, Ned	Assoc. Professor	Group dynamics, individual differences, undergraduate teacher education, social service research laboratory.

58. *University of Minnesota Self-Survey Report,* p. 10.

59. Ibid.

60. Ibid., p. 12.

61. "Memorandum Concerning the Administration Relocation of the Institute of Child Welfare," May 15, 1957 (President's Papers: College of Education: Institute of Child Welfare).

62. Nancy Mosier, unpublished manuscript on the history of the College of Education, chapter 3, p. 9 (College of Education: Education Planning and Development Office).

63. Institute of Child Development, *Annual Report, 1974-1975*, p. 5.

64. Ibid.

65. Ibid., pp. 44-45.

66. From notes compiled by Evelyn Deno, April 19, 1977 (Robert Beck Papers).

67. Interview with Willard Hartup, June 16, 1977 (Robert Beck Papers).

68. The Institute of Child Development's annual report for 1974-75 details the progression of the Institute's funding over the previous half century.

CHAPTER 11: *The College and the Counseling Tradition*

1. *Student Counseling in the College of Education* (College of Education, University of Minnesota, 1929).

2. William H. Edson, "The Ecology of a Student Personnel Office in a College of Education" in *Changes in Teacher Education: An Appraisal*. Report of the National Commission on Teacher Education and Professional Standards (Washington, D.C.: National Education Association, 1964), p. 301.

3. Interview with William Edson, May 3, 1977 (Robert Beck Papers).

4. Marcia Edwards to James Morrill, March 19, 1952, pp. 14-15 (President's Papers: College of Education, 1952-1955).

5. Ibid., p. 15.

6. Edson, "The Ecology of a Student Personnel Office," p. 305.

7. Ibid.

8. *Minnesotan* 12 (May 1959), p. 11.

9. Dale Wachowiak and Roger F. Aubrey, "The Changing World of Gilbert Wrenn," *Personnel and Guidance Journal* 55 (October 1976), p. 78.

10. Ibid.

11. Ibid.

12. Ibid.

13. The author is indebted to E. G. Williamson for his insights into the General College's background. Williamson was interviewed on March 29, 1977 (Robert Beck Papers). For a summary of Williamson's earlier role in counseling at the University, see Gray, *The University of Minnesota*, pp. 353-59.

14. Donald Paterson, "Reminiscences Concerning the Development of Student Personnel Work at the University of Minnesota," *Journal of College Student Personnel* 17 (September 1976), pp. 380-85.

15. Dorlesa Ewing, "E. G. Williamson: Direct from Minnesota," *Personnel and Guidance Journal* 54 (October 1975), p. 82.

16. E. G. Williamson, "Preface" to Donald G. Paterson, "Reminiscences," p. 380.

17. Ewing, "Direct from Minnesota," p. 82.

18. Williamson, "Preface," p. 380.

19. Gray, *The University of Minnesota*, p. 350. (Gray writes extensively of Johnston; see, for example, pp. 194-99).

20. Ibid., p. 350.

21. Paterson, "Reminiscences," pp. 382-83.

22. Ibid., p. 383.

23. Gray, *The University of Minnesota*, p. 351.

24. Lotus Coffman, "Educational Trends in a University," in Eurich, ed., *The Changing Educational World*, pp. 145-55.

25. Ibid., p. 148.

26. Harl Douglass, "Some Dangers of the Testing Movement," *Journal of the National Education Association* 23 (January 1934), pp. 17-18.

27. E. G. Williamson, "The Co-operative Guidance Movement," *School Review* 43 (April 1935), pp. 273-80. Douglass also cautioned against state and nationwide testing programs in his article "The Effects of State and National Testing on the Secondary School," *School Review* 42 (September 1934), pp. 497-509. In turn, Superintendent J. A. Hughes defended the University Testing Bureau in "The Pros and Cons of Co-operative Testing," *School Review* 43 (April 1935), pp. 248-51.

28. Harl Douglass, "Co-operative Testing and Straw Men," *School Review* 43 (June 1935), pp. 410-11.

29. Ibid., p. 410.

30. Ibid.

31. Ibid., p. 411.

32. Wachowiak and Aubrey, "The Changing World of Gilbert Wrenn," p. 78.

33. Ibid., p. 80.

34. Ibid.

35. Ibid.

36. Ibid.

37. Ibid., p. 84.

38. Ibid.

39. A flyer describing the project writes of BORN FREE as "a training and development grant from the Women's Educational Equity Act Program, U.S. Office of Education [that] is designed to broaden the range of career opportunities for both women and men. It provided for the creation of career development training materials for educators and parents, that will help to reduce sex biases and stereotyping at all educational levels, K-higher education. The shortened title of the project, BORN FREE, is an acronym that expresses exactly what the project is about: to 'Build Options, Reassess Norms, Free Roles through Educational Equity.' "

CHAPTER 12: *Reaching Out to State and Nation*

1. Emily Veblen, "Fifty-three Years: A Record of Growth," p. 6.

2. Stanley Wenberg to Robert Keller, September 28, 1966 (President's Papers: College of Education: Dean's Office).

3. Ibid.

4. Ibid.

5. *Minnesota Education* 2 (Spring 1975).

6. University of Minnesota, *Sixteenth Biennial Report of the Board of Regents*, p. 38.

7. Ibid.

8. University of Minnesota, *Fourteenth Biennial Report of the Board of Regents for the Fiscal Years 1905, 1906, Ending July 31*, p. 26.

9. Ibid.

10. University of Minnesota, *Sixteenth Biennial Report of the Board of Regents*, p. 38.

11. Ibid.

12. University of Minnesota, *President's Report, 1911-1912*, p. 148.

13. University of Minnesota, *President's Report, 1912-1913*, p. 87.

Notes

14. Gray, *The University of Minnesota*, pp. 206-17.

15. Coffman, "Educational Trends in a University," in Eurich, ed., *The Changing Educational World*, pp. 153-54.

16. In the words of Harold Benjamin, the center's first director, "the establishment of the Center has come largely from President Coffman's own analysis of adult educational needs in the fields in which the University is best suited to work" (*Minnesota Alumni Weekly* 36 [September 26, 1936], p. 46). See also the folder on the Center for Continuation Study in the University Archives.

17. College of Education faculty meeting minutes, March 11, 1935.

18. University of Minnesota, *Biennial Report of the President to the Board of Regents, 1934-1936*, p. 23.

19. Ibid.

20. Ibid.

21. Ibid.

22. Walter Cook to James Morrill, April 1, 1954 (President's Papers: College of Education, 1952-1955).

23. Ibid.

24. Ibid.

25. Ibid.

26. Ibid.

27. Ibid.

28. Ibid.

29. Education Planning and Development Office memorandum (Robert Beck Papers).

30. Willard R. Lane, "Service Activities of College of Education Staff Members," 1959 (Robert Beck Papers).

31. Ibid., p. 5.

32. Ibid., p. 6.

33. Ibid., p. 8.

34. Ibid., p. 10.

35. Ibid., p. 15.

36. Mosier, unpublished manuscript (Robert Beck Papers). See also Mosier, ed., *Externally Sponsored Research and Training Programs*, p. 48.

37. The author is grateful for a memorandum on this subject prepared by Warren Meyer and for an interview with Jerome Moss on July 6, 1977 (Robert Beck Papers).

38. Robert Keller, "The College of Education," p. 15 (AB 1.5 Box 2).

39. George M. Robb, *A Survey of Cooperative Programs of Educational Research, Curriculum Development, and Preparation of School Personnel between the University of Minnesota College of Education and the Elementary and Secondary Schools, 1967-1968*. Office of the Dean, College of Education.

40. Ibid., p. 3.

41. Ibid.

42. Ibid., p. 7.

43. For example, the University of Colorado was host to the Earth Science Curriculum Projects, which coordinated the interdisciplinary work of astronomers, geologists, geophysicists, meteorologists, oceanographers, physical geographers, and soil scientists. The Secondary School Science Project at Princeton worked out a curriculum entitled Time, Space, and Matter: Investigating the Physical World. Other campuses provided homes for the American Biological Sciences Curriculum, the Chemical Education Material Project, and the Physical Science Study Committee. See Joseph J. Schwab, "Recent Curricular Developments," in Hans O. Ander-

sen, ed., *Readings in Science Education for the Secondary School* (New York: Macmillan Company, 1969), p. 349.

44. Minnesota Social Studies Curriculum Center, *Preparation and Evaluation of Social Studies Curriculum Guides and Materials for Grades K to 14*. Final Report, Project No. HS-045, U.S. Office of Education (University of Minnesota, College of Education, August 1968). The summary of the final report lists nine specific objectives for the center:

(1) Identification of major concepts and generalizations which comprise possible structures for the various social science disciplines and identification of the methodology and important techniques used to advance knowledge in each field.

(2) An attempt to assess the possibilities of developing an integrating framework or structure for the social sciences as a whole. This attempt would involve a study of the points of divergence and convergence among the social sciences.

(3) Identification of those concepts, skills and attitudes most appropriate for inclusion in the social studies curriculum.

(4) Establishment of a curricular framework for grades K-12, with a few suggestions for grades 13-14.

(5) Development of teacher guides and resource units for grades K-12, illustrating the content to be taught and the ways in which the material can be presented. These guides might suggest the use of or modification of existing resource units and materials developed elsewhere where such materials seemed appropriate.

(6) Development of sample pupil materials at various grade levels where such material was not available but was needed to field test the courses suggested in the curricular framework.

(7) Preparation of explanatory materials for use by teachers to aid in their understanding of the point of view of the Curriculum Center as well as their use of resource units and pupil materials.

(8) Training of a selected group of teachers for the use and evaluation of the resource units and pupil materials in their schools.

(9) Development of evaluation instruments where needed. Field tests and evaluation of the resource units and pupil materials, including controlled research at some levels.

45. Interview with Darrell Lewis, May 3, 1977 (Robert Beck Papers).

46. Robb, *Survey of Cooperative Programs*, p. 3.

47. See Jack C. Merwin, "State of the College," p. 4. Office of the Dean, College of Education.

CHAPTER 13: *Putting the House in Order*

1. Marcia Edwards to James Morrill, March 19, 1952, p. 13 (President's Papers: College of Education, 1952-1955).

2. Ibid., p. 15.

3. Willis Dugan to Walter Cook, December 4, 1954 (Robert Beck Papers).

4. Ibid.

5. Marcia Edwards to James Morrill, March 19, 1952, p. 14 (President's Papers: College of Education, 1952-1955).

6. College of Education faculty meeting minutes, February 2, 1955.

7. College of Education faculty meeting minutes, November 16, 1955.

8. College of Education, Miscellaneous Minutes and Reports, 1914-1923.

9. Melvin E. Haggerty, "The College of Education as Related to Other Divisions of the University," in Eurich, ed., *The Changing Educational World*, pp. 90-118.

10. Ibid., pp. 102, 103.

11. Ibid., p. 103.

12. At that time, the word "athletics" was dropped from the department's title, although the department continued to sponsor women's athletics (without funding specifically designated for that purpose).

13. *Minneapolis Morning Tribune*, November 14, 1958.

14. *Minneapolis Morning Tribune*, December 6, 1958.

15. *SLA Faculty Bulletin*, February 19, 1959 (President's Papers: College of Education, 1945-1960: Joint Registration in SLA and the College of Education).

16. College of Education faculty meeting minutes, December 10, 1963. Five reports were included. Report I, "Proposals Relating to the Central Administration of the College of Education," was initially prepared for the faculty meeting of November 5, 1963; it was revised for the December 10 meeting. Report II, "Proposals Relating to the Administrative Organization of the College of Education at Divisional and Departmental Levels," was made at the November 5 meeting. Report III, "Proposals Relating to the Establishment of a Policy and Planning Committee," was initially prepared for the faculty meeting of November 5 and was revised for the December 10 meeting. The same held true for Report IV, "Proposals Relating to the Organization and Functioning of College Committees." Report V was entitled "Proposals Concerning the Scholarly Functions of the College of Education, University of Minnesota."

17. Ibid.

18. Keller, "College of Education," pp. 2-3 (AS 1.5 Box 2).

19. Ibid., p. 3.

20. College of Education faculty meeting minutes, June 9, 1965.

21. From a conversation with O. Meredith Wilson, June 22, 1977.

22. Stanley Kegler to Robert Keller, February 5, 1965 (President's Papers: College of Education, 1960-1969: University Elementary School Closing).

23. College of Education faculty meeting minutes, March 12, 1965.

24. Keller, "College of Education," p. 3.

25. College of Education faculty meeting minutes, December 14, 1965.

26. Ibid.

27. Information on additional years is available from the Education Planning and Development Office, College of Education.

28. See Jack C. Merwin, "Priority Setting and Resource Allocation over Four Years of Retrenchment in the College of Education at the University of Minnesota." This essay is an adaptation of a presentation made to the Association of Colleges and Schools of Education in State Universities and Land Grant Colleges and Affiliated Private Universities, Las Vegas, Nevada, October 14, 1975. Education Planning and Development Office, College of Education.

29. T. E. Kellogg, "Education Planning and Development Office: Report of Activity July 1, 1975 to June 30, 1977," p. 1. Education Planning and Development Office, College of Education.

30. Merwin, "Priority Setting," pp. 1, 9.

31. Another associate dean's position was provided for in the budget, but it was not filled between 1970 and 1973.

32. See Mosier, ed., *Externally Sponsored Research and Training Programs*.

33. College of Education, *Constitution (1965)*, Article III, Section 2. Office of the Dean, College of Education.

34. The recommendations could not go beyond principle only because constitutional changes have to be submitted to the faculty thirty days prior to any official action.

35. College of Education faculty meeting minutes, December 1, 1970.

36. College of Education faculty meeting minutes, March 15, 1971.

37. Ibid.

38. Interview with Clare Gravon, January 18, 1978.

39. J. Victor Baldrige, Myron Atkins, and Robert Howsam, *A Program for Increased Organizational Effectiveness for the University of Minnesota College of Education* University of Minnesota, College of Education, 1972) (MSG qA3p).

40. Malcolm Willey to Marcia Edwards, March 13, 1963 (President's Papers: College of Education, 1960-1969: Dean).

41. College of Education, *Regular Faculty Policy and Procedure Manual* (University of Minnesota, College of Education, 1975).

42. College of Education, "Contexts and Priorities for College of Education Planning" (University of Minnesota, College of Education, 1974).

43. University of Minnesota, Consulting Group on Instructional Design, *Biennial Report,* July 1, 1976.

Selected Bibliography

Andersen, Hans O. *Readings in Science Education for the Secondary School.* New York: Macmillan Company, 1969.

Beck, Robert H. "American Progressive Education: 1975-1930." Ph.D. dissertation, Yale University, 1942.

———. *The Three R's Plus.* Minneapolis: University of Minnesota Press, 1956.

Bennett, Charles A. *History of Manual and Industrial Education: 1970 to 1917.* Peoria: Chas. A. Bennett Co., Inc., 1926, 1937.

Bond, Guy L., and Dykstra, Robert. "The Cooperative Research Programs in First Grade Reading Instruction." *Reading Research Quarterly* 2: 5-141.

Bond, Guy L., and Wagner, Eva Bond. *Teaching the Child to Read.* New York: Macmillan Company, 1943.

Bossing, Nelson L. "Experimental Programs of Curriculum Development." *Minnesota Journal of Education* 20: 253-55.

———. *Principles of Secondary Education,* 2nd ed. Englewood Cliffs, N.J.: Prentice-Hall, 1955.

———. *Progressive Methods of Teaching in Secondary Schools.* Boston: Houghton Mifflin, 1935.

———. "Readjustments in the School Program for the Adolescent." *Education Digest* 7: 48-49.

———. "Some Major Trends Relating to the Curriculum and Their Implications for Teaching." *High School Journal* 22: 313-20.

———. "Teacher Education for the Core Curriculum." *Minnesota Journal of Education* 30: 17-18.

———. "Wanted: A New Leadership for the Secondary School." *National Association of Secondary School Principals Bulletin* 30: 92-100.

Bossing, Nelson, and Cramer, R.S. *The Junior High School.* Boston: Houghton Mifflin, 1965.

Bossing, Nelson, and Faunce, R.C. *Developing the Core Curriculum.* 2nd ed. Englewood Cliffs, N.J.: Prentice-Hall, 1958.

Brameld, Theodore. "Can We Prepare Now for the Post-War Period?" *Education* 63: 340-45.

———. *Design for America.* [With collaboration of Kenneth Hovet, Superintendent, and Dorothy O'Shaughnessy and Donna Traphagan of Floodwood High School.] New York: Hinds, Hayden and Eldredge, Inc., 1945.

———. *Ends and Means in Education: A Mid-Century Appraisal.* New York: Harper and Brothers, 1950.

———. "Labor's Stake in the Peace — A Proposed Agenda." *Frontiers of Democracy* 9: 140-42.

———. "Metaphysics and Social Attitudes — A Concluding Perspective." *The Social Frontier* 4: 256-58.

———. *Minority Problems in the Public Schools.* New York: Harper and Brothers, 1946.

———. "The Need for an American Plan." *Frontiers of Democracy* 6: 111-12.

———. "A Plea for Propaganda in Defense of Public Education." *School and Society* 56: 609-10.

———. "We Look at the Future." *Educational Leadership* 2-3: 374-76.

———. "Workers' Education — A Neglected Opportunity." *Educational Forum* 4: 401-8.

———., ed. *Workers' Education in the United States.* New York: Harper and Brothers, 1941.

Brueckner, Leo J. *Adapting Instruction in Arithmetic to Individual Differences.* Minneapolis: University of Minnesota Press, 1941.

———. *The Changing Elementary School. Report of the Regents Inquiry into the Character and Cost of Public Education in New York.* New York: Inor Publishing Co., 1939.

———. *A Curriculum Study of Teacher Training in Arithmetic.* Minneapolis: University of Minnesota Press, 1932.

———. *Improving the Arithmetic Program.* New York: Appleton-Century-Crofts, Inc., 1957.

———. *Scales for the Rating of Teaching Skill.* Minneapolis: University of Minnesota Press, 1929.

———. *The Sixtieth Mental Measurements Yearbook.* Highland Park, N.J., 1965.

Brueckner, Leo J., and Bond, Guy. *The Diagnosis and Treatment of Learning Difficulties.* New York: Appleton-Century-Crofts, Inc., 1955.

Brueckner, Leo J., and Grossnickle, Foster E. *Discovering Meanings in Arithmetic.* Philadelphia: The John C. Winston Co., 1959.

Brueckner, Leo J., and Melby, E. O. *Diagnostic and Remedial Teaching.* Boston: Houghton Mifflin, 1931.

Coffman, Lotus D. *The Social Composition of the Teaching Population.* Contributions to Education, No. 41. New York: Teachers College, Columbia University, 1911.

———. *Teacher Training Departments in Minnesota High Schools.* New York: General Education Board, 1920.

Cook, Walter W. "The Gifted and Retarded in Historical Perspective." *The National Elementary School Principal* 38: 14-21.

———. *Grouping and Promotion in the Elementary Schools.* Minneapolis: University of Minnesota Press, 1941.

———. "Individual Differences and Curriculum Practice." *Journal of Educational Psychology* 39: 141-48.

———. *The Measurement of General Spelling Ability Involving Controlled Comparisons between Techniques.* University of Iowa Studies in Education, No. 221. Iowa City: University of Iowa, 1932.

———. "Organization for Research of the College of Education at the University of Minnesota." *Scientia Paedagogica* 9: 7-43.

Cook, Walter W., and Clymer, Theodore. "Acceleration and Retardation."

In *Individualizing Instruction: Sixty-first Yearbook of the National Society for the Study of Education,* part 1. Chicago: The National Society for the Study of Education, 1962.

Cook, Walter W.; Hovet, Kenneth O; and Kearney, Nolan C. "Curriculum Research." *Review of Educational Research* 26: 224-40.

Cook, Walter W.; Leeds, C. H.; and Callis, R. *Minnesota Teacher Attitude Inventory.* New York: The Psychological Corporation, 1951.

Cook, Walter W., and Medley, Donald M. "Proposed Hostility and Pharisaic-Virtue Scales for the MMPI." *Journal of Applied Psychology* 38: 414-18.

Cook, Walter W., and Medley, Donald M. "The Relationship between Minnesota Teacher Attitude Inventory Scores and Scores on Certain Scales of the Minnesota Multiphasic Personality Inventory." *Journal of Applied Psychology* 39: 123-29.

Cook, Walter W., and Torrence, E. Paul. *Abstracts of Current Educational Research Studies.* Minneapolis: University of Minnesota, College of Education, 1961.

Coon, Horace. *Columbia: Colossus on the Hudson.* New York: E.P. Dutton and Company, Inc., 1947.

Counts, George S. *A Call to the Teachers of the Nation.* New York: American Education Fellowship Committee on Social and Economic Problems, 1933.

———. *Dare the Schools Build a New Social Order?* New York: The John Day Company, 1932.

———. *The Selective Character of American Secondary Education.* Supplementary Educational Monographs. Chicago: University of Chicago Press, 1922.

———. *The Social Composition of Boards of Education: A Study in the Social Control of Public Education.* Supplementary Educational Monographs. Chicago: University of Chicago Press, 1927.

Douglass, Harl R. *Organization and Administration of Secondary Schools.* Boston: Ginn and Company, 1932.

———. *Secondary Education for Youth in Modern America.* Washington, D.C.: American Council on Education, 1937.

Douglass, Harl R., and Boardman, Charles W. *Supervision in Secondary Schools.* Boston: Houghton Mifflin Co., 1934.

Eckert, Ruth E., and Keller, Robert J. *A University Looks at Its Program.* Minneapolis: University of Minnesota Press, 1954.

Edson, William H. "The Ecology of a Student Personnel Office in a College of Education." In *Changes in Teacher Education: An Appraisal.* Report of the National Commission on Teacher Education and Professional Standards. Washington, D.C.: National Education Association, 1964.

Eurich, Alvin C., ed. *The Changing Educational World.* Minneapolis: University of Minnesota Press, 1931.

Ewing, Dorlesa B. "E.G. Williamson: Direct from Minnesota." *The Personnel and Guidance Journal.* 54: 78-87.

Finney, Ross L. *Personal Religion and the Social Awakening.* New York: Eaton and Mains, 1913.

Gabriel, Ralph H. *The Course of American Democratic Thought.* New York: The Ronald Press, 1940.

Gray, James. *The University of Minnesota, 1851-1951.* Minneapolis: University of Minnesota Press, 1951.

Greer, John N. *The History of Education in Minnesota.* United States Bureau of Education. Circular of Information No. 2. Contributions to American Educational History No. 31. Washington: Government Printing Office, 1902.

Griffin, Clifford S. *The University of Kansas: A History.* Lawrence: University of Kansas Press, 1974.

Haggerty, Melvin E. "The Ability to Read: Its Measurement and Some Factors Conditioning It." *Indiana University Studies* 4: 2-63.

————. "Arithmetic: A Cooperative Study in Educational Measurements." *Indiana University Studies* 2: 385-507.

————. *Art, A Way of Life.* Minneapolis: University of Minnesota Press, 1935.

————. *Children of the Depression.* Minneapolis: University of Minnesota Press, 1933.

————. *The Educational Program.* The Evaluation of Higher Institutions, vol. 3. Chicago: University of Chicago Press, 1937.

————. *Enrichment of the Common Life.* Minneapolis: University of Minnesota Press, 1938.

————. *The Faculty.* The Evaluation of Higher Institutions, vol. 2. Chicago: University of Chicago Press, 1937.

————. "Imitation in Monkeys." *Journal of Comparative Neurology and Psychology* 19: 337-455.

————. "The Low Visibility of Educational Issues." *School and Society* 41: 273-83.

————. *Rural School Survey of New York State.* Ithaca, N.Y.: Joint Committee on Rural Schools, 1922.

————. "Studies in Arithmetic." *Indiana University Studies* 3: 2-110.

Haggerty, Melvin E., and Smith, Dora V. *Reading and Literature.* 3 vols. Yonkers-on-Hudson: World Book Company, 1927-1928.

Harris, Albert J. *How to Increase Reading Ability.* 4th rev. ed. New York: David McKay Company, 1963.

Heiss, George D. "Edgar Bruce Wesley and the Social Studies." Ed.D. thesis, Rutgers University, 1967.

Hoyt, Cyril J. "Test Reliability Obtained by Analysis of Variance." *Psychometrika* 6: 153-60.

Hutson, Percival W. *Training of the High School Teachers of Minnesota.* Educational Monograph No. 3., vol. 26 (no. 46), Minneapolis: University of Minnesota, College of Education, 1923.

James, George F. "The Basic Philosophy of Froebel." National Education Association, *Journal of Proceedings and Addresses* (1912): 621-24.

————. "The Relation of the State University to Other Parts of the System of Public Instruction." National Education Association, *Journal of Proceedings and Addresses* (1912): 780-81.

————, ed. *Handbook of University Extension.* Philadelphia: American Society for the Extension of University Teaching, 1893.

————, ed. *The Proceedings of the First Annual Meeting of the National Conference on University Extension.* Philadelphia: J.B. Lippincott Company, 1892.

————, ed. *University Extension.* Philadelphia: American Society for the Extension of University Teaching, 1892-1894.

Johnson, E. Bird, ed. *Forty Years of the University of Minnesota.* Minneapolis: The General Alumni Association, 1910.

Johnson, Henry C., Jr., and Johanningmeier, Erwin V. *Teachers for the Prairie: The University of Illinois and the Schools, 1868-1945.* Urbana: University of Illinois Press, 1972.

Johnson, Palmer O., and Neyman, J. "Tests of Certain Linear Hypotheses and Their Applications to Some Educational Problems." *Statistical Research Memoirs* 1: 57-93.

Kent, Raymond A., ed. *Higher Education in America.* Boston: Ginn and Company, 1930.

Kiehle, David L. *Education in Minnesota.* Part I. Minneapolis: H. W. Wilson Company, 1903.

————. *Education in Minnesota.* Part II. Minneapolis: H. W. Wilson Company, 1902.

Koos, Leonard V. *The Adjustment of the Teaching Load in a University.* Washington, D.C.: Government Printing Office, 1919.

————. *The Administration of Secondary-School Units.* Chicago: University of Chicago Press, 1917.

————. *The American Secondary School.* Boston: Ginn and Company, 1927.

————. *The Community College Student.* Gainsville: University of Florida Press, 1970.

————. *The High School Principal.* Boston: Houghton Mifflin, 1924.

————. *The Junior College.* 2 vols. Minneapolis: University of Minnesota Press, 1924.

————. *The Junior College Movement.* Boston: Ginn and Company, 1925.

————. *The Questionnaire in Education: A Critique and Manual.* New York: Macmillan Company, 1928.

————. *Trends in American Secondary Education.* Cambridge, Mass.: Harvard University Press, 1926.

Koos, Leonard V., and Kefauver, G.N. *Guidance in Secondary Schools.* New York: Macmillan Company, 1932.

Koos, Leonard V., and Woody, Clifford. *The Training of Teachers in the Accredited High School of the State of Washington.* Eighteenth Yearbook of the National Society for the Study of Education, 1919.

Kridel, Craig. "Theodore Brameld's Floodwood Project: A Design for America." Paper delivered at the annual meeting of the American Educational Research Association, Philadelphia, November 4, 1977.

————. "The Theory and Practice of Theodore Brameld's 'Defensible Partiality': A Mid-Century 'Resolution' to the Imposition Controversy." *Journal of Midwest History of Education Society* 5: 120-34.

Minnesota Commission on Higher Education. *Higher Education in Minnesota.* Minneapolis: University of Minnesota Press, 1950.

Morison, Samuel E. *The Development of Harvard University Since the Inauguration of President Eliot, 1869-1929.* Cambridge, Mass.: Harvard University Press, 1930.

Myers, Burton D. *History of Indiana University*, vol. 2. Bloomington: Indiana University Press, 1952.

Osman, Charles H. *History of The Ohio State University*, vol. 2. Columbus: The Ohio State University Press, 1926.

PaDelford, Harold E. "A Historical Study of Vocational Education in Minnesota with Special Reference to the Minnesota Vocational Association." Master's paper, University of Minnesota, 1967.

Paterson, Donald G. "Reminiscences Concerning the Development of Student Personnel Work at the University of Minnesota." *Journal of College Student Personnel* 17: 380-85.

Peik, Wesley E. *The Professional Education of High School Teachers.* Minneapolis: University of Minnesota Press, 1930.

Pollard, James E. *History of The Ohio State University: The Story of Its First Seventy-five Years, 1873-1948* Columbus: The Ohio State University Press, 1952.

Raywid, Mary Ann. *The Axe-Grinders.* New York: Macmillan Company, 1962.

Report of the Committee of Seventeen. Washington, D.C.: Department of Secondary Education of the National Education Association, n.d. [The report was presented at the Los Angeles meeting of the National Education Association in 1907.]

Rudy, S. Willis. *The College of the City of New York: A History, 1847-1947.* New York: City College Press, 1949.

Smith, Dora V. *Basic Aims for English Instruction.* Chicago: National Council of Teachers of English, 1942.

———. *Class Size in High School English.* Minneapolis: University of Minnesota Press, 1931.

———. *Evaluating Instruction in Secondary School English.* Chicago: National Council of Teachers of English, 1941.

———. *Fifty Years of Children's Books.* Champaign, Ill.: National Council of Teachers of English, 1963.

———. *Selected Essays.* New York: Macmillan Company, 1964.

Ugland, Richard. "The Psycho-Educational Center." Duplicated and undated. University of Minnesota Archives.

Umstattd, James G. *The Odyssey of Jim Umstattd.* Privately printed by the Whitley Company, Austin, Texas, 1977.

University of Minnesota, College of Education. *Training for Elementary School Teaching.* Minneapolis: May 1934.

Van Wagenen, Marvin J. *Comparative Pupil Achievement in Rural, Town and City Schools.* Minneapolis: University of Minnesota Press, 1929.

———. *Educational Diagnosis and the Measurement of School Achievement.* New York: Macmillan Company, 1926.

———. *Historical Information and Judgment in Pupils of Elementary Schools.* New York: Teachers College, Columbia University, 1919.

———. *A Teachers' Manual in the Use of the Educational Scales.* Bloomington, Ill.: Public School Publishing Co., 1928.

Veblen, Evelyn. "Fifty-three Years: A Record of Growth." Unpublished manuscript, December 17, 1938. University of Minnesota Archives.

Wachowiak, Dale, and Aubrey, Roger F. "The Changing World of Gilbert Wrenn." *Personnel and Guidance Journal* 55: 75-85.

Wattenbarger, James L. "Leonard V. Koos: Leader of Pioneers." *Community and Junior College Journal* 47: 50-51.

Wesley, Edgar B. *NEA: The First Hundred Years.* New York: Harper and Brothers, 1957.

———. *Teaching the Social Studies.* New York: D.C. Heath and Company, 1937.

Index

Brueckner, Leo, 69, 104; and individual differences, 107, 108; and remedial mathematics, 58; and testing and measurement, 93. Works: *Adapting Instruction in Arithmetic to Individual Differences*, 107, 108; *The Changing Elementary School*, 109; *The Diagnosis and Treatment of Learning Difficulties* (with Guy Bond), 107, 108; *Diagnostic and Remedial Teaching* (with E. O. Melby), 104, 106-7, 108, 124; *Scales for the Rating of Teaching Skill*, 104, 108

Bruininks, Robert, 242

Buchman, Roland, 137

Bureau of Cooperative Research, 62, 69-70, 141-42; as federal research station, 69, 142. *See also* Bureau of Educational Research

Bureau of Educational Investigations, 142, 144

Bureau of Educational Research (BER), 62, 70, 142-55; faculty research in, 143-44; and graduate training, 137-38, 153-54

Bureau of Field Studies and Surveys, 151-52. *See also* Center for Educational Policy Studies

Bureau of Institutional Research (BIR), 140, 143-55; and graduate training, 137; past apprentices of, 154

Bureau of Recommendations, 197

Burris, Russell, 244

Burton Hall, 53

Burton, Marion, 57; and registration policy, 76-77

Butler, Nicholas Murray, 21, 29

Career development. *See* guidance counseling

Carlson, William, 94, 106

Carr, Edwin, 118

Cary, Miles E., 127

Cattell, James M., 164

Center for Continuation Study, 38, 92, 212-13; purpose of, 213. *See also* education, adult; education, continuing; extension, university

Center for Early Education and Development, 191, 244

Center for Economic Education, 223

Center for Educational Policy Studies, 152, 243

Center for Research on Human Learning, 244

Certification, teacher. *See* teacher certification

Chase, Naomi, 184

Chautauqua Literary and Scientific Circle, 41

Chautauqua movement, 36-40; and Methodism, 36, 40; ideals of, 40; and university extension, 36, 37, 39, 40, 46. *See also* extension, university

Child Development Clinic, 181

Child Development. *See* Institute of

Child development, research on, 191-92

Child Study Center, 181

Child Welfare. *See* Institute of

Childs, John, 123-24

Christmas Carol Sing, 91-92

Civil War: effects of, on education, 2-3

Clark, Shirley, 235-36

Clinical Experiences. *See* Department of

Clymer, Ted, 165

Coffman, Lotus D., 57, 58-59, 71, 77; and applied research, 63-65; and Bureau of Cooperative Research, 62, 69-70, 141-42; and continuing education, 211-12; and esthetics, 100-101; and faculty reorganization, 72-73; and Haggerty–Van Wagenen dispute, 88-89; and higher education, 140-41, 144-45; personality of, 71; and registration policy, 73-77; *The Social Composition of the Teaching Population*, 63

College of Continuing Education and Extension, 214

College of Education: and affirmative action, 226, 238; authorized by regents, 13, 35, 47; budget problems of, 34, 55; constitution and by-laws, 232, 239-40; and "controlled growth," 233; current organization of, 242-44; departmentalization of, 173-74, 225-45; divided aims of, 105-6; "divisions" of, 233, 235; early courses in, 10, 11, 50, 127, 140, 153, 213; early departments of, 28, 70-71, 73, 92, 142, 168-69, 173, 182, 184, 188-89, 229-30; early organization of, 13; executive and general faculties in, 73, 229; mission statement of, 232; new building for, 51; organizational report on, 232; and out-

Index

Index

Kroenenberger, Henry, 95

Laboratory of Physiological Hygiene, 161
Land Grant Act of 1862. *See* Morrill Act
Land-Grant College Survey, 134
Lane, Willard, 216
Lange, Dale, 164
Leadership Training Institute, 219-20
Learning disabilities. *See* special education
Lewis, Darrell R., 155; duties of, as associate dean, 238; and economic education, 223
Lloyd, David, 47
Lord, Livingston, 18

Marshall Junior-Senior High School, 234
McClure, Dorothy, 118
McConnell, T. R., 94-95, 147-48, 150; *Studies in Higher Education,* 150
McMurray, Frank, 44
Measurement. *See* testing and measurement
Measurement Services Center, 155, 244
Melby, Ernest O., 95, 104, 106-7; *Diagnostic and Remedial Teaching* (with Leo Brueckner), 104, 106-7, 108, 124; *Supervisory Organizations and Instructional Programs in Albert Lea* (with Fred Englehardt), 144
Mental retardation. *See* special education
Merrill, Elijah, 4-5
Merwin, Jack: and collegiate planning, 236-37; as dean, 234; and reorganization, 231
Metropolitan School Study Council, 217. *See also* Educational Research and Development Council
Meyer, Warren, 162, 168
Michaels, William, 106
Miller, W. S., 70-71, 92-93, 106; Miller Analogies Test, 93, 199
Minneapolis Handicraft Guild, 70, 98, 229
Minnesota Alumni Association, 180
Minnesota Center for Curriculum Studies (MCCS), 220-21
Minnesota College Teachers of Education and Psychology, 208
Minnesota Council of School Executives, 160, 207-8
Minnesota Council for Special Education, 183
Minnesota Daily, 168
Minnesota Deans of Women, 208
Minnesota Education, 209
Minnesota Education Association, 15, 19, 160, 207
Minnesota Grange, 25-26
Minnesota Pre-School Scale, 110
Minnesota Pre-School Test, 109
Minnesota Research Coordinating Unit for Vocational Education, 218
Minnesota Research and Development Center, 244
Minnesota School Districts Data Processing Joint Board, 220
Minnesota School Mathematics Center (Minnemast), 221-22
Minnesota Social Studies Curriculum Center, 222
Minnesota Society for the Study of Education, 208
Minnesota State Board for Vocational Education, 218
Minnesota State Council on Economic Education, 223
Minnesota State Department of Education, 160, 207, 209
Mississippi Valley Historical Association, 113, 117
Mitchell, Dorothy, 240
Model school, 47; and argument for new building, 51-52. *See also* University Elementary School, University High School
Modern School Practices, 163
Modisett, Ellen, 118
Moore, Marjorie, 154
Moore, Shirley G., 244
Mork, Gordon, 162, 166
Morrill Act, 8; and educational philosophy, 7, 23; and later legislation, 9; and Minnesota land grant, 24; quoted, 23
Morrill, James, 152, 170
Morse, Horace T., 114
Moss, Jerome, Jr., 218, 242
Mott, Alice, 47, 65
Mueller, Van, 242
Murra, Wilber, 118

National Association of Colleges and Departments of Education, 170

293

Index

Index